THE BUSINESS OF ABOLISHING THE BRITISH SLAVE TRADE

1783–1807

THE BUSINESS OF ABOLISHING THE BRITISH SLAVE TRADE
1783–1807

Judith Jennings
The Women's Center, University of Louisville

FRANK CASS
LONDON • PORTLAND, OR

First published in 1997 in Great Britain by
FRANK CASS & CO. LTD.
Newbury House, 900 Eastern Avenue
London IG2 7HH, England

and in the United States of America by
FRANK CASS & CO. LTD
c/o ISBS 5804 N.E. Hassalo Street
Portland, Oregon, 97213-3644

British Library Cataloguing in Publication Data
The business of abolishing the British slave trade,
1783–1807
1. Slavery - Great Britain - History 2. Slavery – Law and legislation - Great Britain - History
I. Jennings, Judith
306.3'62'0941

ISBN 0-7146-4697-0 (cloth)
ISBN 0-7146-4235-5 (paper)

Library of Congress Cataloging-in-Publication Data
The business of abolishing the British slave trade, 1783–1807 / by Judith Jennings.
p. cm.
Includes bibliographical references (p.) and index.
ISBN 0-7146-4679-0 (cloth). -- ISBN 0-7146-4235-5 (paper)
1. Woods, Joseph--Views on slavery. 2. Hoare, Samuel--Views on slavery. 3. Harrison, George, 1747?–1827--Views on slavery. 4. Phillips, James, bookseller--Views on slavery. 5. London Abolition Committee--History--Sources. 6. Antislavery movements --Great Britain--History--Sources. 7. Quaker abolitionists--Great Britain--History--Sources. 8. Slave-trade--Great Britain--History--Sources. I. Jennings, Judi, 1947–
HT1162.B87 1997
380.1'44'09042--dc20 96-27425
CIP

Printed in Great Britain by
Bookcraft (Bath) Ltd, Midsomer Norton, Avon

Contents

Acknowledgements

I wish to acknowledge the support and encouragement of Professors David Brion Davis and Seymour Drescher. Both of these outstanding scholars found time to answer my inquiries and provide valuable advice. Professor James Walvin read the manuscript twice and provided excellent editorial suggestions.

The mosaic of manuscript materials presented here is a tribute to the patience of many librarians and archivists. Special thanks go to Malcolm Thomas, Librarian at Friends House, for his friendship and assistance. The staff of the Public Record Office and the British Library in London, the Library Company and American Philosophical Society in Philadelphia and the Benjamin Franklin Papers at Yale were always pleasant, professional, and helpful.

Professor Carl Cone of the University of Kentucky, a true gentleman and scholar, directed my dissertation, my first study of abolition. I received early advice and encouragement from Professor Ian Christie and especially from Professor John Dinwiddy in the Eighteenth Century Seminar at the Institute of Historical Research.

I want also to acknowledge the life-long support of my mother, Dorothy Hornsby Jennings Hornbeck, who always firmly believed that I could do anything, including writing something new about the British slave trade. This book is dedicated to her.

Introduction

The British slave trade was abolished by Act of Parliament on 25 March 1807, and historians have been trying to explain why ever since. In 1808, Thomas Clarkson, an abolitionist, published his *History of the Rise, Progress and Accomplishment of the Abolition of the African Slave Trade*. Clarkson identified scores of early opponents of slavery and the slave trade beginning in 1516 and continuing until the founding of the London Abolition Committee in 1787. He then focused on the role of the London Abolition Committee, giving special emphasis to his own activities and the interaction of the Committee with William Wilberforce and other Parliamentary leaders including Charles James Fox and Wilberforce's evangelical allies.[1]

Wilberforce's sons, Robert and Samuel, later wrote a biography of their father stressing the key role of his leadership and that of other evangelical Members of Parliament in the success of abolition. Since then, many historians have focused their attention almost exclusively on Wilberforce and the evangelicals of the Clapham Sect.[2] 'Explaining abolition's passage', according to the Evangelical interpretation, 'entails a careful and imaginative analysis of the well-documented motives and behaviour of a handful of leading actors.'[3]

In 1944, Eric Williams 'challenged the entire frame of reference' of abolition historiography by writing *Capitalism and Slavery* 'linking the rise and fall of slavery with two consecutive phases of capitalism, mercantile and industrial.'[4] Some historians have since sought to refute Williams's interpretation, while others are closely examining just how socio-economic developments across the globe may have influenced abolition.[5]

The publication of the two-volume study by David Brion Davis, *The Problem of Slavery in Western Culture* and *The Problem of Slavery in the Age of Revolution*, in 1966 and 1975, opened the doors of abolition historiography even wider and inaugurated a remarkably rich era of new scholarship. Drawing on both Marx and Freud, Davis argues that Anglo-American Quakers 'pioneered the development of abolition into a broader social movement' and 'simultaneously forged an ideological defense, albeit unconsciously, of the emergent capitalist industrial order'.[6]

Today, established historians are working fruitfully in many fields of abolition historiography. Some, like Seymour Drescher and David Eltis, analyse the profitability of slavery and the slave trade. Their work proves that abolition occurred at a time when profits from the slave trade were increasing and sales of slave products were on the rise. Professor Drescher has also become the leading historiographer of abolition, tracking the myriad new work on the subject while producing research of his own.[7]

Roger Anstey synthesized the politics of abolition in *The Atlantic Slave Trade and British Abolition, 1769-1810.* In *England, Slaves and Freedom* and other essays and books, James Walvin continues the process of political analysis and shows how abolition related to other reform movements of the late eighteenth and early nineteenth centuries.[8]

Scholars are now adding fresh insights and new fields of enquiry to the already rich historiographical mix of abolition. In *Britons: Forging the Nation, 1707–1837*, Linda Colley looks at the connections between anti-slavery and the development of British national identity. In her path-breaking study, Colley shows how abolition is situated within the context of 'the invention of Britishness' and the 'evolution of British nationalism'.[9]

In *The Culture of English Antislavery, 1780–1860*, David Turley carefully delineates the complex components of anti-slavery that made it a multi-layered and dynamic culture shaping and shaped by all those participating in abolition. As Turley shows, anti-slavery was not a simple linear development but a series of complex attitudes in an uneven process of change.[10]

From this wealth of research, it is becoming clear that abolition was part of complex and global political, economic, social and intellectual currents. Abolition both represented and stimulated what Seymour Drescher calls 'profound changes in historical and moral frames of reference as well as in political and economic institutions'.[11]

Given this global view and the breadth and depth of recent research, it is not surprising to find, as Seymour Drescher says, many anti-slaveries. 'There were anti-slave trade, anti-black, humanitarian, egalitarian, religious and secular variants', as Drescher shows, 'sometimes operating separately and sometimes in tandem or tension'.[12]

What is still missing in the historiography of abolition is, as David Brion Davis first pointed out in 1975, information about the day-to-day writings and activities of the individual abolitionists who formed local committees and organized grassroots support.[13] The current study selects four Quaker founders of organized abolitionism in Great Britain and examines their writings and activities throughout their lifetimes, spanning the period from the mid-1700s to the early 1800s.

Three of these four men, Joseph Woods, Samuel Hoare and George Harrison, were founding members of the first association formed in Britain in 1783 to work for abolition of slavery and the slave trade. The fourth man, James Phillips, was not a member of the association but worked closely with the group. All four were founding members of the London Abolition Committee in 1787. All four maintained connections with abolition throughout their lifetimes. Three of the four lived to see the British Parliament declare the slave trade illegal in 1807.

Archival research at the Library of the Society of Friends and the British Library in London and at the Philadelphia Library Company has produced new empirical evidence about the abolitionist writings and activities of these four men. This study pieces together a mosaic of previously unused primary source materials to present a collective portrait of Joseph Woods, woollen-draper, Samuel Hoare, banker, James Phillips, bookseller and printer, and George Harrison, warehouseman and banker.

The study traces the close personal, business, professional, social and religious ties that drew these four men together as abolitionist activists. The new information presented here provides the kind of empirical social markers at the local or micro level that Seymour Drescher calls for in the current historiographical debate about abolition on the global or macro level.[14]

Tracing the activities of these four abolitionists from their participation in the first association in 1783 and over the course of their lifetimes addresses the problem of which activists, what actions and what period of time best represent the British anti-slave trade movement. At the same time, the abolitionist activities of these four men must be seen in the broader context of the changing social and economic systems of their day. 'The key questions' about abolition, as D.B. Davis says, 'concern the relationship between anti-slavery and the social system as a whole.' In Seymour Drescher's words: 'One must look closely at social position and group dynamics in analyzing antislavery texts.'[15]

Since these four men were merchants and bankers actively engaging in the eighteenth-century market economy, this study draws on the ground-breaking work of John Brewer, Neil McKendrick, J.H. Plumb, Roy Porter and a host of other scholars researching the development of consumer societies in western Europe, the United States and other parts of the world. In *The Birth of a Consumer Society*, John Brewer and others suggest how 'the broadening of the market ... transformed relationships' in every sphere of human activity in late eighteenth-century Britain.[16] More recently, in *Consumption and the World of Goods*, Brewer, Roy Porter and a cadre of international scholars develop new methodologies and vocabularies to explore the links between material culture and political and social systems world-wide.[17]

By examining the lives of these four men, this study seeks to address larger questions in the historiography of abolition. Because there were many anti-slaveries, to understand the significance of abolition in the largest sense, it is necessary to articulate the differences among its various forms and to understand each one. Was there a distinct movement aimed solely at abolishing the British slave trade as well as the larger and better documented movement against slavery? If so, how was the anti-slave trade movement defined and differentiated from abolitionism in general?

Another key question is that posed by James Walvin in *England, Slaves and Freedom*: how does the historian describe and explain 'the transformation of abolition from a minority … sentiment into an organized and public debate'?[18] This book does not attempt the difficult task of measuring public opinion and its impact on Parliamentary legislation, although, as Seymour Drescher shows, public opinion certainly played an important role in the campaign to abolish the British slave trade.[19] It focuses, instead, on the documented activities of these four men and other members of the London Abolition Committee in educating and mobilizing public opinion. The impact of their efforts is not measured quantitatively but is assessed through the letters and petitions received by the London Abolition Committee and by the observations and comments of contemporaries.

London is the geographical focus here because all four men lived in London and participated in the London Abolition Committee. The study does not purport to be an exhaustive survey of all abolition efforts throughout Great Britain, in the emerging American nation, or elsewhere. The four men presented here did have contacts with fellow abolitionists in Manchester, Bristol, Edinburgh, Paris, Philadelphia and other parts of the world, but abolitionist activities in those and other places outside London are examined only in so far as they relate to the activities of the four individuals who are the subject of this book.

A final key issue concerns the way in which abolitionism was transformed from a small group activity to a mass movement. How do the lives and actions of these four abolitionists relate to the larger transformations simultaneously taking place in British politics, economy, society and culture? At the heart of this question is the problem of how individuals make history.

The approach used here is to reject any notion that history is somehow determined by either material or subconscious forces. Instead, history is seen as a dynamic process of uneven change over time. The abolition of the British slave trade was the result of a dialectical process whereby history was shaped by individuals making choices and taking action, and, at the same time, those same individuals were being shaped by the history they were helping to create.

The goal here is to write history in the active voice. Writing history as it is lived means allowing for individual human agency while at the same time recognizing larger cultural forces that, at any given time, are beyond individual human control. It is this constant process of interaction between the individual and larger cultural forces that links the activities of these four men at the micro or grass-roots level with the international or macro level of abolition.

The challenge is to show how these four anti-slave trade activists acted and interacted over the course of their lifetimes in multiple contexts as fathers, sons, husbands, Quakers, men who sought to influence national policy, abolitionists, and businessmen deeply engaged in the daily economic life of an evolving commercial order. The challenge is to recapture history as it is lived, as a process of change over time, and as individuals making choices, acting, and reacting within social, cultural and economic settings.

NOTES

1. Thomas Clarkson, *The History of the Rise, Progress, and Accomplishment of the Abolition of the African Slave-Trade By the British Parliament*, 2 vols., new impression (London: Frank Cass, 1968).
2. R.I. and Samuel Wilberforce, *Life of William Wilberforce* (Philadelphia, PA: Henry Perkins, 1839). Frank Klingberg, *The Anti-Slavery Movement in England* (New Haven, CT: Yale University Press, 1926). Reginald Coupland, *Wilberforce* (Oxford: Clarendon Press, 1926). E. M. Howse, *Saints in Politics* (Toronto: University of Toronto Press, 1952).
3. Seymour Drescher, 'Whose Abolition? Popular Pressure and the Ending of the British Slave Trade', *Past and Present* (1994), p. 139.
4. Eric Williams, *Capitalism and Slavery* (Chapel Hill: University of North Carolina Press, 1994). Seymour Drescher, 'Review Essay of *The Antislavery Debate*', *History and Theory*, (October 1993), p. 311.
5. See, for example, Seymour Drescher, *Capitalism and Anti-Slavery: British Abolition in Comparative Perspective* (Oxford: Oxford University Press, 1987). Seymour Drescher, *Econocide: British Slavery in the Era of Abolition* (Pittsburgh, PA: University of Pittsburgh Press, 1977). David Eltis, *Economic Growth and the Ending of the Transatlantic Slave Trade*, (Oxford: Oxford University Press, 1987). David Eltis and James Walvin (eds), *The Abolition of the Atlantic Slave Trade: Origins and Effects in Europe, Africa, and the Americas* (Madison: University of Wisconsin Press, 1981).
6. David Brion Davis, *The Problem of Slavery in Western Culture* (Ithaca, NY: Cornell University Press, 1966). David Brion Davis, *The Problem of Slavery in the Age of Revolution 1770–1823* (Ithaca, NY: Cornell University Press, 1975). Drescher, 'Review Essay', *History and Theory* (October, 1993), pp. 311–29.
7. Seymour Drescher, *Capitalism and Anti-Slavery: British Abolition in Comparative Perspective*. Drescher, *Econocide: British Slavery in the Era of Abolition*. David Eltis, *Economic Growth and the Ending of the Transatlantic Slave Trade*. Drescher, 'Review Essay', *History and Theory*. Drescher, 'Whose Abolition?', *Past and Present*.
8. Roger Anstey, *The Atlantic Slave Trade and British Abolition 1769–1810* (Atlantic Highlands, NJ: Humanities Press, 1975). James Walvin, *England, Slaves and Freedom* (Jackson, University Press of Mississippi, 1986). David Eltis and James Walvin (eds), *The Abolition of the Atlantic Slave Trade: Origins and Effects in Europe, Africa, and the Americas* (Madison: University of Wisconsin Press, 1981). Edward Royle and James Walvin, *English Radicals and Reformers* (Lexington: University Press of Kentucky, 1982).
9. Linda Colley, *Britons: Forging the Nation, 1707–1837* (New Haven, CT: Yale University Press, 1992), p. 3.
10. David Turley, *The Culture of English Antislavery, 1780–1860* (New York: Routledge, 1991).
11. Seymour Drescher, 'British Way, French Way: Opinion Building and Revolution in the Second French Slave Emancipation', *American Historical Review*, 96, 3 (June 1991), p. 709.
12. Seymour Drescher, 'The Long Goodbye: Dutch Capitalism and Antislavery in Comparative Perspective', *American Historical Review*, 99, 1 (Feb. 1994), p. 69.
13. D.B. Davis, *The Problem of Slavery in the Age of Revolution*, pp. 238–9.

14. Seymour Drescher calls for more 'precise markers from social history' in his review of *The Antislavery Debate* in *History and Theory*, p. 329.
15. Ibid., p. 324. D.B. Davis, *The Problem of Slavery in the Age of Revolution*, p. 348.
16. John Brewer, Neil McKendrick, and J.H. Plumb, *The Birth of a Consumer Society: The Commercialization of Eighteenth-Century England* (Bloomington: Indiana University Press, 1982).
17. John Brewer and Roy Porter (eds), *Consumption and the World of Goods* (London: Routledge, 1993) p. 65.
18. J. Walvin, *England, Slaves and Freedom*, p. 104.
19. Seymour Drescher, 'Whose Abolition?', *Past and Present*. Also by Seymour Drescher, 'Public Opinion and the Destruction of British Colonial Slavery', in James Walvin (ed.), *Slavery and British Society, 1776–1846* (Baton Rouge: Louisiana State University Press, 1982).

1

Four Merchants and Philosophers in 1783

Joseph Woods was born on 19 September 1738 in Bartholomew Lane by the Exchange in the City of London. He was the first son of Edward Woods and his second wife, Sarah Neale. Edward Woods kept a pastry shop on the corner of Bartholomew Lane and was a freeman member of the company of vintners. Edward also owned two houses at Winchmore Hill, a London suburb. Joseph Woods later recalled spending 'a considerable part' of his 'early days' at his parents' home in Winchmore Hill.[1]

Joseph Woods and his parents were Quakers, like their parents before them.[2] Quakerism began, as religious historian William Braithwaite shows, in 1647 when George Fox felt called 'to declare the truth' that the inner light of salvation is present in every woman and man. Fox named those who shared his view 'Friends', and by 1652 meetings of Friends were being held in Yorkshire. In the next few years, meetings of Friends, called Quakers by detractors, were established in Lancashire, Cumberland, Devon, Cornwall, Hertfordshire, London, Bristol, Norwich, and as far away as Barbados, France, and Holland.

When the Church of England was restored along with the Monarchy in 1660, Friends were persecuted for their refusal to pay tithes and for their 'testimonies' against paid priesthood and prescribed forms of worship. In 1675, Friends established the Meeting for Sufferings in London to record and redress their persecutions. The next year, Robert Barclay defended the Friends' beliefs and practices in an *Apology for the True Christian Divinity Professed and Preached by Those Who Are in Derision Called Quakers*.

The worst of the Quaker persecutions came to an end with the Toleration Act of 1689 as, according to Braithwaite, did the heroic age of Quakerism. When George Fox died in 1691, Quakers had no official creed but they did have an organizational structure that covered Great Britain, included pockets of western Europe, and stretched across the Atlantic to the North American colonies.[3]

Historians estimate that the number of Friends peaked at about 60,000 in 1680 and then dropped to between 20,000 and 32,000 by the end of the eighteenth century.[4] By the mid-1700s, British Friends were coming together regularly at the Yearly Meeting in London to set policies. The

Meeting for Sufferings was becoming an experienced political association, calling on Members of Parliament and petitioning Parliament and the Monarch on behalf of Friends.[5]

Like British Quakerism, the British economy and society were changing and evolving in the last quarter of the eighteenth century. In *The Birth of a Consumer Society* Neil McKendrick, John Brewer and J.H. Plumb show how rising real income, rising population, rising production, better transportation, and increasing economic centralization in London were rapidly transforming Britain into a consumer society. Focusing on the demand side of the developing market economy, they argue that while a desire to consume was not new to the late eighteenth century, the potential of an ever-increasing segment of society was being raised to new levels.[6]

More recently, in *Consumption and the World of Goods*, John Brewer, Roy Porter and a cadre of international scholars have begun measuring the scope and plumbing the depths of consumer societies world-wide. Roy Porter concludes that whether or not there was a 'consumer revolution' in late eighteenth-century Britain, as Neil McKendrick had argued earlier, 'no one doubts that aggregate consumption of services and material goods – necessities, decencies and luxuries – was rising among an impressive social cross-section'.[7]

Edward Woods, Joseph's father, like many Friends in the late eighteenth century, was engaging in trade and doing quite well. 'The most conspicuous characteristic' of many late eighteenth-century Friends, according to D.B. Davis, was 'quite simply, their incredible economic success'. Economist David Landes shows how such Quaker practices as selling high quality goods at fixed, marked prices helped Friends move ahead in the developing consumer economy. John Brewer says credit and debt were two of the biggest problems facing late-eighteenth-century tradesmen, but Quaker entrepreneurs were able to command significant amounts of capital and credit through intermarriages and by combining business and religious ties.[8]

Financially prosperous second-generation Friends like Edward and Sarah Woods were faced with the problem of reconciling money and morals. Edward Woods was a ministering Friend, and he advised the London Quaker organization on financial matters. He served on a committee which was responsible for paying common expenses and for the administrative oversight of Quaker property.[9] Poor Friends in good standing had traditionally received informal financial assistance from Quaker meetings but, in the eighteenth century, the central organization began defining membership rights more tightly.[10]

Birth and education were becoming important criteria for membership in what was coming to be considered the Society of Friends. Joseph Woods, like the sons of other rising Quaker families, was sent away to school.[11]

When Joseph Woods was growing up, William Massey's school for boys at Wandsworth was 'much patronized by the Society of Friends' and combined the study of religion and the classics with good business practices.

Massey recommended beginning 'lower Scholars with reading in the Bible and Spelling' and then moving on to arithmetic. Advanced students learned merchant's accounts, bookkeeping, geography, history, the Latin Testament, and Aesop's *Fables*. Massey believed in 'evening tasks' and advocated seating students according to scholarly achievement as 'This raises an Emulation in them to gain Places'.[12] Joseph Woods later wrote, 'Boys go first to school to learn to spell and read, and afterwards rise in progression ... in order to discipline them into learning proper and useful for their intended station.'[13]

In 1753 when Joseph was 15, the last of his father's sons by a previous marriage died. Joseph thus became the eldest child and the only surviving son. At Michaelmas in 1755 when Joseph was 17, Edward advanced him £2,000 to establish a woollen drapery business. A few years later, Joseph was described as a woollen draper in Blackfriars.[14]

Edward Woods died in June 1756. By Edward's will, the advance to Joseph became 'so much of his fortune'. Joseph also inherited the copyroll rights (after the death of his mother Sarah) on a farm costing £1,400 at Revel End near Redbourne in Hertfordshire. The two houses at Winchmore Hill went to Sarah Woods during her lifetime and afterwards to Rachael, the only other child of Edward and Sarah.[15]

In 1769, Joseph Woods, now 31, married Margaret Hoare, age 21. Margaret's marriage portion was £2,500.[16] Like Joseph's family, Margaret's family were second-generation Quakers engaged in trade. One of her grandmothers was a Quaker minister in Ireland, and Quaker leader William Penn attended the wedding of another.[17]

Margaret's father Samuel Hoare was born in Ireland and 'engaged young in the Irish provision trade'. He moved to London and married Grizell Gurnell in 1744. He thus became a partner in his wife's family firm which was known first as Gurnell and Hoare, and later Gurnell, Hoare, Harman and Company located at Frederick Place in the Old Jewry.[18]

Between 1745 and 1761, Samuel and Grizell Hoare had 10 children, seven of whom survived. Margaret was born second but was the eldest surviving child of the seven. Margaret and two siblings were born at Dyer's Court in the City of London but, by 1750, the family had moved to Paradise Row in Stoke Newington. A granddaughter later remembered Samuel Hoare setting off to work in the City in 'a green coach with red wheels'. The same granddaughter described Margaret as 'the great favourite' of her mother Grizell.[19]

In 1771, two years after her marriage, Margaret Hoare Woods began keeping a journal as a means of 'more frequent reflection and self-examination'. As the journal indicates, her main concerns over the next ten years, in addition to her spiritual development, were raising children and establishing patterns of family life. By 1772, her husband's woollen drapery shop was located in White Hart Court, just off Lombard Street, in the heart of the City. There, she gave birth to their first child, a boy named Samuel, on 30 August 1772.[20]

In August 1773 Margaret was pregnant again, but she was stricken with measles and lost the child. After that, Margaret moved to Paradise Row, Stoke Newington, where her mother and father had their home. Joseph kept a sleeping room at his shop in the City and travelled to Stoke Newington at weekends.

A third child born to Margaret and Joseph Woods in October 1774 lived only a few days. After that, between 1776 and 1781, the couple had two healthy sons and one daughter. During that time, they took a family holiday to Margate and began spending three weeks to a month every summer with Joseph's mother at Winchmore Hill.[21]

In 1774, Joseph Woods began what was to become a life-long friendship and correspondence with fellow Quaker William Matthews. Matthews, the son of an Oxfordshire shoemaker, taught at a highly regarded Quaker school in Burford. After 1768, he became a teacher at Coggeshall in Essex.

In 1777 Matthews gave up teaching and moved to Bath, where he opened first a brewery and then a coal yard. In 1777, evincing the Quaker trait of combining religious, social, and economic ties, the more well-established Woods loaned Matthews £100 for two and a half years at £12 interest. In 1781 Woods advanced Matthews another £50 to help further his new career in Bath.[22]

In the course of commenting on various issues of their day, Joseph Woods made it clear, to Matthews at least, that he believed women's abilities were limited by nature. 'Their province, I humbly conceive', he wrote to Matthews in September 1774, 'lies in Matters of Imagination and Taste.' Woods was a man who measured his words carefully even in private. 'Nature has assigned certain boundaries between the minds of the Sexes. I mean has established a distinction, I do not say a superiority ....'[23]

Margaret Woods, meanwhile, was struggling with the idea of submission to her husband and family. 'I have often felt the hard struggles between inclination and duty', Margaret wrote in her journal in October 1774. 'O Lord God!' she prayed in July 1775, 'Keep me from thinking more highly of myself than I ought to think ... grant that I may walk in that humility which holds self in no esteem.' In 1776, in a letter to a woman friend, she wrote: 'I hardly know what to think of thy opinion concerning the equality of the sexes,... The word obey sounds harsh but I believe is a duty on our part.'[24]

While Margaret Woods stayed in Stoke Newington with the children, Joseph Woods kept shop in White Hart Court and led the active life of a London merchant. According to a contemporary, Joseph could often be found 'in the Quaker corner at the Carolina Coffee House, Burchin Lane' talking to Friends who were interested in North America. The contemporary describes Woods as 'slow, silent, thoughtful, and of melancholic appearance especially when seen walking in the streets'. But Woods liked good talk and 'in company he brightened up, and his conversation was cheerful, and very sensible'.[25]

Woods' companions and interests were in no way limited to Quakers. He wrote essays which were published anonymously in the widely read *Gentleman's Magazine*.[26] He belonged to a club that met regularly at the London Tavern to talk and drink. He corresponded with men of learning like Baron Thomas von Dimsdale, a pioneer in the practice of inoculation and physician to the Empress of Russia.[27] In March 1775, Woods met Philip Sansom, an Anglican who had been a woollen card manufacturer but was becoming a successful American merchant, and the two became close friends.[28]

At the same time, Woods was developing strong trans-Atlantic connections despite the increasing tensions between Britain and her North American colonies. In April 1774, he sent wool cloth to Dr Thomas Parke of Philadelphia and advised him about the actions of the British government in response to the dumping of tea in Boston harbour.[29]

That same year, William Dillwyn, a Quaker businessman from Pennsylvania, arrived in England. Dillwyn visited factories and canals, saw the sights, and called on Quaker friends and relatives. In London, Dillwyn 'supped ... very agreeably' with friends at the home of Joseph Woods.[30]

For Woods, the political questions then being raised by the American colonists centred more on preserving the existing rights of British subjects than on expanding the franchise or redefining ideas about equality. 'We are arrived at an important Period of the English History', he wrote to Matthews in October 1775, 'which must forever determine whether the Rights of Englishmen may be carried with them across the Atlantic or whether they are prohibited from Exportation ....'[31] Once fighting broke out, Woods wrote little more to Matthews about the subject of American rights, perhaps because of Quaker pacifism.

During the war years, Woods became well acquainted with several American Loyalists in London. In 1777, William Dillwyn, who had dined with Woods on his earlier trip, relocated to London, remarried, re-established himself in business, and resumed his former acquaintances.

Dillwyn married Sarah Weston of London and began building a new home, Higham Lodge, in Walthamstow, Essex.[32]

In 1779, Woods became friends with the Reverend Thomas Coombe of Philadelphia, whom he described as 'liberal, friendly and poetical'. Woods considered Coombe 'a sincere, honest-hearted Christian, tho' a parson'. Woods also met Jacob Duche, who had served on the board of directors of the Library Company of Philadelphia and 'offered up the first prayer in the Continental Congress'. When fighting broke out, Duche came to London and became Chaplain to the Foundling Hospital.[33]

By the time the American Revolution was ending, Woods had friends and customers on both sides of the Atlantic. In May 1783, the directors of the Library Company of Philadelphia, which now included Woods' correspondent, Dr Thomas Parke, asked Woods and William Dillwyn to be their purchasing agents in London. In September 1783, Woods shipped two trunks of current books and journals to Philadelphia, including the writings of Joseph Priestley, Baron Thomas von Dimsdale's defence of inoculation, and philosophical works by Berkeley and Hume.[34]

Adam Smith's *Inquiry into the Nature and Causes of the Wealth of Nations* published in 1776 was among the titles in this first shipment of books to the Philadelphia Library Company. Smith's book was a thorough-going critique of the economic system of mercantilism. 'Consumption', Smith argued, 'is the sole end and purpose of all production.' Smith considered this 'a maxim ... so perfectly self-evident, that it would be absurd to attempt to prove it'.[35]

The Directors of the Library Company were pleased with the selections. Woods and Dillwyn began sending books and articles twice a year by spring and autumn ships. The directors assigned the amount of money to be spent and specifically requested some titles. The agents could use their discretion in choosing the rest. Woods invariably signed the correspondence and the shipping orders, although he often mentioned making his choices in conjunction with Dillwyn.[36] Woods placed the semi-annual book orders, amounting to about £100, with another friend and colleague, the bookseller James Phillips.[37]

James Phillips was born at Trewirgn near Redruth in Cornwall in 1745. His father, William Phillips, like the fathers of Joseph and Margaret Woods, was a Quaker engaged in trade. William Phillips 'from his youth engaged in the copper trade' and had an interest in a Welsh-owned iron foundry in Bristol at a time when copper was becoming the major extractive industry in Cornwall and Bristol was replacing Swansea as the centre for smelting.[38]

James Phillips' mother died giving birth to him. In 1749, when James was four, his father William met Catherine Payton, a Quaker minister. William Phillips was, by all accounts, devoted to Catherine from the first but she felt called to minister abroad. She travelled to Ireland and Scotland and then to South Carolina and Holland before eventually returning to Cornwall and marrying William.[39]

Young James, meanwhile, was sent to Quaker school at Boley Hill in Rochester, Kent.[40] Upon completing his education, James went to London, while his older brother stayed in Cornwall to work in the family mining business. In 1768, James Phillips, aged 23, a freeman and woolman of London, married Mary Whiting, aged 21, daughter of Judith and John Whiting, a linen draper. The next year, the first of the couple's 12 children was born.[41]

James Phillips was related to Mary Phillips of Tottenham, who had married Luke Hinde, a stationer with a shop in George Yard, near the popular George and Vulture Inn, just off Lombard Street. When Luke died, the Widow Hinde took over her husband's business which included printing and selling books for the British Quaker organization. Printing and bookselling were especially important to Friends who, as Quaker historian Russell Mortimer points out, often referred to their early religious leaders as the 'first publishers of the Truth'.[42]

In April 1775, Mary Hinde resigned 'her house and trade' to James Phillips and recommended 'him to succeed me' in the bookselling and publishing business. In May 1775, the Quaker organization 'agreed to accept of James Phillips to transact the Business of the Society in Mary Hinde's stead'.[43] James Phillips' print shop and bookstore in George Yard was not far from White Hart Court where Joseph Woods had his woollen drapery business.

As Russell Mortimer explains, by printing manuscripts authorized by the Friends organization and selling them to Quakers in London and the country, printers like Phillips

> could be assured of a certain minimum market to cover his costs; a certain circulation to the meetings in the provinces was secure, and casual sales at the bookshop could confidently be expected.[44]

James Phillips was in no way limited to publishing Quaker works or selling exclusively to Quaker customers. In 1778, for example, Phillips was directed by the Quaker organization to send '*suitable* Books' to selected booksellers who were not Friends so that others might learn of Quaker beliefs and practices.[45] Like the Widow Hinde, Phillips was free to publish works at his 'own risque'.[46] Before the American Revolution, for example, Phillips printed and sold the 'celebrated Letters of TAMOC CASPIPINA', supporting American independence, written secretly by Woods' acquaintance, the Reverend Jabob Duche, *T*he *A*ssistant *M*inister *O*f *C*hrist *C*hurch *A*nd *S*aint *P*eter *I*n *P*hiladelphia *I*n *N*orth *A*merica.[47]

Phillips bought wool from Joseph Woods[48] and drank coffee 'almost every morning' with Woods and other Quakers in the Carolina Coffee House.[49] Phillips was, according to a contemporary,

> the most undaunted man I ever knew, talking, joking, and laughing with the utmost freedom, and with equal boldness to all description of people, often using phrases to persons in higher stations which others dare not utter.[50]

Another contemporary remembered the home of James Phillips as 'the resort of many eminent men, Friends and others.'[51]

By the end of the American Revolution, James Phillips was conducting a national and international business as a bookseller. In 1783 Dr George Logan, the grandson of James Logan, wrote to Phillips from Philadelphia asking him to select 'the most valuable publications' declaring he was 'willing to allow … a Commission on the purchases'.[52] In England, Phillips purchased and distributed books for Richard Reynolds, a Quaker entrepreneur who married the daughter of Abraham Darby and became the manager of Darby's booming iron works at Coalbrook Dale.[53]

James Phillips served as 'the active agent' in 'distributing thousands [of pounds] entrusted to his charge by the munificent R. Reynolds'.[54] Reynolds was a large-scale philanthropist. His granddaughter estimated Reynolds gave away £10,000 annually and as much as £200,000 over the course of his lifetime. 'Unwilling to be known as the giver of large sums … it was … his habit to employ others to act for him in London and elsewhere in dispensing such sums as he wished to devote to charitable purposes', Reynolds' granddaughter later wrote.[55] As a financial agent for Reynolds, Phillips not only advised him about charitable giving but managed investments for him, including giving financial assistance to other entrepreneurs.[56]

Another friend of James Phillips who shared his close connection with Richard Reynolds was George Harrison. Harrison was born in Kendal, Westmorland, in 1747, the son of a shoemaker. Like Woods and Phillips, Harrison was born into a Quaker family and was sent away to school. Harrison attended Gilbert Thompson's School for Boys at Penketh in Lancashire.[57]

Gilbert Thompson was 'celebrated' as an educator, and his well-known school, housing 60 students, was described in idyllic terms as a place where boys went 'bird-nesting, nutting, and sliding'.[58] Years later, Harrison's son described '"An Agreement Signed By Most of the Penketh Scholars" with my father's name at the head' promising to 'pay bond to the Master as often as any of them … mark their names or initials on the meeting house, school, the Master's Dwelling house etc'.[59]

At Penketh, the young Harrison met Samuel Fothergill, an internationally known Quaker minister who lived nearby on the country estate of his brother, Dr John Fothergill. John Fothergill was a London physician whose wealth at the time of his death was publicly estimated at property worth £80,000, a botanic garden valued at £10,000, and a practice 'calculated at near £7,000 p.a.'.[60] Family memoirs imply the Fothergill brothers saw outstanding abilities in the shoemaker's son and agreed to pay for Harrison to have an advanced education. Years later, Harrison publicly and privately described Samuel Fothergill as 'my revered patron in early life'.[61]

After finishing at Penketh, Harrison 'was removed for the completion of his classical education to the public Grammar School at Sedbergh in Yorkshire', an Anglican school which the Fothergill brothers had attended.[62] At Sedbergh, Harrison studied under Doctor Bateman 'reputed the profoundest Greek scholar of his time'. Harrison's well-connected classmates included the future Bishop of Rochester, the Vice Chancellor of the Duchy of Lancaster, and an Undersecretary of State.

Harrison completed his studies at Sedbergh by the age of 19 and returned home to Kendal, 'preparing to go forth in the world with his fortune of £5.7.1'. Samuel Fothergill, however, 'again wrote' to Harrison, this time 'inviting him to spend six months at Warrington Academy at the expense of John Fothergill'.[63] So Harrison rounded out his education at the Dissenter's academy that was already becoming well known for science and scholarship.

In 1766, Harrison, having completed his education, was employed by Richard Reynolds to serve as a private tutor to his son William, aged 8. Reynolds, ever-conscious of his own lack of classical learning, paid Harrison £30 p.a. to teach his son Latin and science. Harrison stayed in the Reynolds' home for three years. According to Reynolds' granddaughter, Harrison 'proved a valuable acquisition to ... [the] family and to [Reynolds] personally, as he was a man of exemplary integrity, of refined manners, and possessed of considerable literary and scientific attainments'.[64]

In 1769, Harrison left Reynolds to work for David Barclay in London.[65] David Barclay 'was the head of a most extensive House in Cheapside, chiefly engaged in the American trade'. Like Reynolds, Barclay was a philanthropist who 'helped his relations set up their own businesses'. Barclay assisted not only his relatives, but 'young men whom he ... bred in his mercantile house, and of whose virtuous dispositions he approved'. Years later, after Barclay's death, it was said

> Some of the most eminent merchants of the City of London are prompt to acknowledge the gratitude they owe to David Barclay, for means of their first introduction into life, and for the benefits of his counsel and continuance in their early stages of it.[66]

From London, George Harrison continued his friendship and correspondence with Richard Reynolds. The two exchanged respectful and affectionate letters. Harrison sent Reynolds books, maps, and a biographical chart by Dr Priestley. In 1771, Harrison and Reynolds arranged to meet 'at the Star at Hockcliff'. In 1772, Reynolds visited Harrison's father during a trip to Kendal.[67]

In 1777, George Harrison, aged 30, married Susanna Cookworthy, aged 34, the youngest daughter of William Cookworthy of Plymouth. Cookworthy had discovered 'China-earth' and started a china factory in Plymouth. Financed by 14 shareholders, including Richard Champion, the factory employed 50 to 60 skilled workers, most notably Henry Bone. After the factory moved from Plymouth to Bristol, Cookworthy turned the patent over to Richard Champion for an annual fee and retired from china-making.[68]

Cookworthy had religious and literary links to James Phillips and other Quaker families, and he was acquainted with men of science and learning who were known throughout the country. Cookworthy was a Quaker minister, and he and Catherine Payton Phillips, step-mother of James Phillips, had ministered together in Devon.[69] Cookworthy wrote an essay on the divining rod which was published by James Phillips and illustrated by Richard, James's older brother.[70] As a lively intellectual and wealthy entrepreneur, Cookworthy entertained the likes of Captain Cook and Joseph Banks at his family home in Plymouth. Cookworthy was well known for his intellectual pursuits but also for his absent-mindedness.[71]

After the early death of his beloved wife, Cookworthy became attracted to the work of Swedish born mystic and scientist, Emmanuel Swedenborg, an interest shared to some extent by his future son-in-law George Harrison and other Quakers. In 1772 George Harrison recorded meeting the Reverend Thomas Hartley, Rector of Winwick in Northamptonshire and a disciple of Swedenborg's, at the home of James Phillips. Harrison discussed Swedenborg's ideas with Hartley.

Hartley and Cookworthy later agreed to collaborate on a translation of Swedenborg's *Heaven and Hell* which was eventually published in 1778 in 'a handsome quarto volume' by James Phillips, paid for by Cookworthy.[72] George Harrison's son later recalled Cookworthy 'could not forbear being diverted with the translation of such a work having been made and published by a Public Friend'.[73]

Relatives report that Cookworthy was 'much pleased' with the marriage of his youngest daughter, Susanna, to 'George Harrison of London a man of very respectable character'. Quaker records list Harrison's occupation as 'warehouseman' at the time of his marriage.[74] Immediately after the marriage, Cookworthy made Harrison banker for his personal funds in

London and schemed how 'to make George my banker for the Sick and Hurt money'. Cookworthy supplied drugs from his warehouses to the Commissioners of the Sick and Hurt, a contract that in 1777 amounted to nearly £700. Cookworthy also engaged Harrison to purchase tin shreds and do other London business on his behalf.[75]

Like the families of Joseph Woods and James Phillips, the Harrison family was growing and changing during the years of the American Revolution. Between 1779 and 1790, three daughters and a son were born to George and Susanna. The family moved from Addle Street to Fish Street Hill to Bullhead Passage, Wood Street, in the City.[76]

During the War, Susanna Harrison was visiting her father in Plymouth when 'the combined fleets of the French and Spanish appeared off Plymouth Sound'. Suzannah wrote in 'full detail' to George. Harrison 'carried the Letter to the Royal Exchange' where it was 'pronounced by all the merchants who heard it read, to be the most circumstantial account which had been received'.[77]

When William Cookworthy died in 1780, he provided generously for his family, especially his daughter Suzannah and her husband George. After remembering his brothers, nieces, nephews and servants, Cookworthy divided his property, including revenue from his drug business, interest in an estate in Cornwall and personal property, among his three daughters. He appointed George and Suzannah Harrison joint executor and executrix.[78]

Living, working and worshipping in London, Harrison became close friends with Joseph Woods and James Phillips. Harrison visited the home of James Phillips and shared the friendship of American expatriot William Dillwyn. Harrison's father-in-law William Cookworthy discussed Swedenborg's ideas with Joseph Woods. Woods and Harrison later took a long walking trip together.[79] By the time the American Revolution was ending, George Harrison, like Joseph Woods and James Phillips, was well established in business and well acquainted with men of wealth and learning from a wide variety of religious backgrounds.

Samuel Hoare attended school with George Harrison and was the younger brother of Joseph Woods' wife, Margaret. Hoare was born in 1751 at his parents' home in Paradise Row, Stoke Newington, the second son in the family.[80] At the age of five, Samuel went to Gilbert Thompson's school at Penketh where George Harrison was also a student. Harrison was four years older than Hoare, so the two would have spent a few years together at school.

After completing Penketh, Hoare briefly attended a seminary kept by John Riveaux in the Grange Road, Highbury. Then, at the age of 14, he was 'bound apprentice to Henry Gurney, a Norwich woolen manufacturer'. Gurney, like Hoare, was a Quaker and the son of a banker. A family member later wrote that in Norwich Samuel had a deep religious experience while reading *Paradise Lost*. He became closely associated with a ministering Friend and travelled with him through the north of England, although Hoare himself did not become a minister.[81]

The Hoare family memoirs contain an earnest letter written from young Samuel, aged 20, to a friend. The letter begins by referring to 'We who, I gratefully acknowledge, have had an education superior to the great part of mankind'. Hoare was developing a sense of duty commensurate with his sense of place in society. 'Except our righteousness exceed those who have not had these advantages', he went on, 'how can we expect to be accepted of him who rewards every man according to his works, justly proportionate to the talent afforded?'[82]

In 1772, when Hoare was 21, he completed his apprenticeship and returned to London. He lived with his parents in Stoke Newington and became a partner in Bland and Barnett Bank, 62 Lombard Street. In 1776, Samuel's older brother Joseph died of consumption, making Samuel the eldest son in the family. That same year, Samuel married Sarah Gurney of Keswick, a woman of 'some fortune'. The two took up residence at 36 Old Broad Street in the City of London. Between 1777 and 1783, Samuel and Sarah Hoare had four children, three daughters and a son.[83]

In summer of 1780, the Gordon Riots raged around the Hoare family home in Old Broad Street. 'The cry of "No Popery" is heard from every corner ...', wrote Sarah Hoare on 4 June to her mother in Norwich. The next day, Horse Guards and armed volunteers arrived and 'halted exactly opposite our house. Three times the commanding officer exhorted the people to disperse.' When the crowd 'obstinately refused', the soldiers 'fired near a hundred pieces' leaving '4 unhappy men dead on the spot and 15 wounded'.

Sarah and Samuel sent their children to his parents' house in Stoke Newington. The 'Nurse had hysterics', but they stayed in the City, going out only twice in five days, both times to attend Quaker meetings. When the riots were over and peace was restored, Samuel himself wrote to his in-laws. Hoare blamed neither Catholics nor Protestants but believed, as did many at the time and since, that the crisis could have been averted if City officials had acted more decisively. 'We are now restored to peace through the assistance of Military Aid', he wrote on 10 June, 'but I think this would have been totally unnecessary had the Civil Magistrates done their duty at first.'[84]

Samuel Hoare soon developed close connections in London and in the American colonies. His daughter, Sarah, later remembered that her father was 'zealous for American independence'.[85] During the war years, his friends included James Phillips and George Harrison as well as his brother-in-law Joseph Woods. All four shared the friendship of William Dillwyn.[86] When Dillwyn and Woods began purchasing books for the Library Company of Philadelphia, they used the banking services of Samuel Hoare at Bland and Barnett, just as they placed their book orders with James Phillips.[87]

By 1783, Joseph Woods, James Phillips, George Harrison, and Samuel Hoare were developing close personal relations with each other through ties of religion, business, friendship, and kinship. In 1783, for example, when Samuel Hoare's young wife Sarah died suddenly following the birth of a healthy son, Samuel took his four children to live in Stoke Newington. There, as his oldest daughter later recalled, they were 'constantly associated with the children of my Aunt Woods'. In later years, Samuel's daughter Sarah remembered being 'instructed by an indulgent Aunt'.[88]

As merchants and bankers in the heart of the City, all four men were deeply engaged in the daily economic transactions of the rapidly evolving commercial order. As Roy Porter shows in *London*, trade, banking and population were quickly increasing in the late eighteenth century. '[O]f all the many developments in eighteenth century-marketing', writes John Styles in *Consumption and the World of Goods*, 'it was the increase in the number of shops that probably had the biggest direct impact'.

A contemporary essay in *The Gentleman's Magazine* complains that 'now merchants are as numerous as clerks ...'.[89] Another contemporary source indicates that London merchants were not only becoming more numerous, but they were more likely to be consumers themselves. 'A tradesman of the present day is as seldom found in his shop as at Church', complained 'The Grumbler' in *The Lady's Magazine*. Instead, the tradesman went to the coffee-house to read the news, dressed his daughters in silk, and served two meats at dinner. 'During 2 or 3 of the summer months, he and his family take a *tower* ... to Margate, Brighton, or some other of the watering places.'[90]

Like the merchants lampooned in *The Lady's Magazine*, these four Quaker businessmen were consumers as well as sellers of goods and services. Joseph Woods summarized his day-to-day activities in London 'in a few words' as 'Buying, selling, dining, reading, sleeping, and smoking'.[91] All four men at one time or another took their families on holiday to Margate, Brighton, Bath, or Dover.

Joseph Woods, with a dry sense of humour, described his shipments to the Philadelphia Library Company as a 'kind of Commerce' in books and ideas. He wryly mocked the contrast between the quiet life conducive to reading and reflection and the busy life of the London merchant. Writing to a Library Company Director, Woods wondered whether 'Philosophy which, Milton assures us, "seeks sweet retired Solitude" can ever condescend to inhabit such situations' as the City of London. Exaggerating his own proximity to the fish market in order to underscore the contrast with Milton, Woods went on to say, 'My habitation is not far distant from that School of Inurbanity and Clamour, commonly known by the name of Billingsgate'. Woods closed for himself and William Dillwyn by saying, 'however low we may rank as Merchants or Philosophers, we are desirous to be esteemed'.[92]

As well-educated men of religion, all four Quakers were grappling with moral concerns at the same time as they were engaged in buying and selling. Quietism was one of the knotty philosophical issues confronting Joseph Woods. In his correspondence with Matthews, Joseph Woods proclaimed himself a quietist. 'I become more and more a quietist', Woods wrote Matthews.[93]

Quaker theologian Rufus Jones defines quietism as the belief that 'every act that has to do with religion and salvation ... must be done in man by some Divine Power beyond him'. Simply put, quietism posed the age-old dilemma between reason and revelation. As Rufus Jones explains, 'Quietism, having eliminated reason, has never told its adherents how to discriminate between the false light and the true.'[94]

Classically educated and fond of philosophizing, Woods solved the quietist dilemma to his own satisfaction by concluding that faith and reason should not be incompatible. 'That the evidence of Faith is superior to that of Reason, Tertullian (I think) is a notable example, who ... declares he believes because it is impossible', Woods explained to Matthews. But 'The faith of your correspondent is ... unable to reach those heroic efforts', he continued. 'If the guide posts ... contradict what is laid down on the maps, or differ from other credible intelligence, he, poor man, is subject to doubts.' Woods later stated, 'I am obliged to content myself with poring through the darkened glass of Reason.'[95]

Woods had little patience for Quaker 'enthusiasts', or Friends who tried to persuade by 'artificial refinement of Expression, the Pride and Pomp of Words, and the affected Ornaments of Rhetoric ...'. He privately criticized 'that Zeal which blusters, terrifies, scorches, blasts, burns, and lays waste'. He was particularly critical of some American ministers 'who speak like Oracles without doubt or hesitation ...', adding, 'they are continually reminding us of the Practice in Philadelphia, as of the example of a Superior Court'.[96]

The theological tensions inherent between quietism and evangelicalism extended to questions of leadership and discipline within the Quaker organization. According to James Jenkins, a contemporary observer with definite opinions, '... an Aristocracy of Elders ruled with an almost exclusive sway' in the late eighteenth century. Jenkins was the illegitimate son of a Bristol Quaker and a family servant. He became an ironmonger in

Ireland but returned to London in 1779 where he kept notes on prominent Friends. Jenkins characterized the London Quaker organization as being dominated by 'feudal chiefs, who always expected, and often obtained, the obsequious obedience of their humbler brethren ...'.[97]

The case of William Matthews, the correspondent of Joseph Woods, seems to confirm Jenkins' assessment. In the early 1780s, Matthews questioned the Quaker practice of 'disowning' (that is, expelling from membership) Friends who paid tithes or married non-Quakers. Matthews believed disownment on these grounds to be an undue stress on form 'which exercizes the zeal of our members in small unimportant things...'.[98]

Watching from afar, Joseph Woods likened the struggle of Matthews against the Quaker organization to that of David against Goliath. 'The Meeting for Sufferings is the Giant, and you are the Dwarf', Woods wrote in a letter to Matthews, 'you will doubtless consider the length and strength of the Giant's arm before you rebelliously refuse to register his Edict....' Matthews did not take Woods' advice. He was disowned in 1783 despite his strenuous objections.[99]

Joseph Woods was not inclined to speak in Quaker meetings and 'always kept at a proper and humble distance from Church Discipline'. From a safe distance, Woods hoped that 'friends of a liberal turn ... might acquire strength ... so as to repress, if not extinguish the flaming Zeal' of the enthusiasts.[100]

James Phillips, George Harrison, and Samuel Hoare, all in their mid-thirties, were, however, among 'a host of new speakers'. 'Young men whose naturally good abilities had been greatly improved by liberal education', according to James Jenkins, they 'now expressed themselves with a warmth of feeling and weight of argument, which the hitherto all powerful chieftains, could neither suppress nor controvert'.[101] James Phillips served as a representative to the London Yearly Meeting in 1773 and in 1784 was named a correspondent to Cornwall. Samuel Hoare was chosen as a London representative to the Yearly Meeting in 1781. George Harrison was appointed cashier of the Yearly Meeting in 1784.[102]

While Woods did not take a leadership role within the national organization, he was part of what he called 'a little flock' of like-minded Quaker merchants and philosophers who shared literary interests and an ecumenical outlook. Thomas Letchworth was one important member of the flock respected by Woods for his 'liberality of sentiment'. Between 1773 and 1775, Letchworth edited *The Monthly Ledger,* which, as the name suggests was more concerned with secular than with religious matters. As editor of *The Monthly Ledger*, Letchworth welcomed correspondence from 'men ... of every denomination'. Woods, his friend Matthews, and other liberal-minded Friends contributed anonymous essays.[103]

Quaker writer Edmund Rack was another of the little flock. Rack moved to Bath in 1775 where he wrote the highly successful *Mentor's Letters Addressed to Youth* and found a patron in Mrs Macaulay. In 1778, Rack established, with William Matthews, the Bath and West of England Agricultural Society. The next year the two started the Bath Philosophical Society. Woods assisted them by procuring books and distributing publications in London, while Rack contributed essays to *The Monthly Ledger.*[104] 'The principles and precepts which I have endeavoured to enforce are such as wise and good men of all denominations agree in admitting', wrote Rack shortly before his death.[105]

As a publisher and bookseller, James Phillips was important to the writers of the little flock. He published the third and final volume of Letchworth's *Monthly Ledger* in 1775. According to Matthews, the *Ledger* 'met with a very considerable sale' but was not thought to be a suitable publication for a minister. Jenkins says 'the subscriptions [were] gradually decreasing ... it died a natural death'.[106] More successfully, Phillips sold *Mentor's Letters* written by Edmund Rack and Rack's essays, letters, and poems. Duche's PAPERS OF TAMOC CASPIPINA published by Phillips was edited by Edmund Rack. Phillips also sold the papers presented at the Bath Society for Agricultural, Arts, Manufacturers and Commerce and at the Bath Philosophical Society.[107]

By 1783, Joseph Woods, James Phillips, George Harrison and Samuel Hoare were 'merchants and philosophers' deeply engaged in the rapidly developing market economy of London. At the same time, they were participating in the 'Anglo-American Empire of Goods', described by Timothy Breen as 'a shared material culture' straddling the Atlantic, 'constantly nourished by flows of commodities'.[108] The four had a wide range of friends and contacts in England and North America and were willing to work with men of all denominations.

NOTES

1. London, Library of Society of Friends, London and Middlesex Quarterly Meeting Digest of Marriages, 1732, Marriage of Edward Woods and Sarah Neale. London and Middlesex Quarterly Meeting Digest of Births, 1738, Birth of Joseph Woods. J. William Frost (ed.), *The Records and Recollections of James Jenkins Respecting Himself and Others from 1761 to 1821* (New York: Edwin Mellen Press, 1984), pp. 284–5. London, Public Record Office, Will of Edward Woods, Prob 11/823, folio 185. London, Library of Society of Friends, Matthews MSS, 107 letters from Joseph Woods to William Matthews written between 1774 and 1812, 4 July 1787.
2. This is indicated by their listings in their certificates of marriage since 'Up to 1861, both parties to a Quaker marriage had to be in membership', E.H. Milligan and M.J. Thomas, *My Ancestors were Quakers* (London: Society of Genealogists, 1983).
3. William Braithwaite, *The Beginnings of Quakerism* (Cambridge: Cambridge University

Press, 1955). William Braithwaite, *Second Period of Quakerism* (Cambridge: Cambridge University Press, 1961).

4. Richard Vann estimates the peak at 60,000, declining to 32,000 by the end of the century, but adds that it is hard to calculate definite numbers after Toleration. Richard T. Vann, *The Social Development of English Quakerism, 1655–1755* (Cambridge, MA: Harvard University Press, 1969), pp. 159–60. David Turley quotes the 60,000 figure for 1680 but puts the number at 'perhaps 20,000 by 1800'. David Turley, *The Culture of English Antislavery* (London: Routledge, 1993), p. 9.
5. N.C. Hunt, *Two Early Political Associations: The Quakers and the Dissenting Deputies in the Age of Sir Robert Walpole* (Oxford: Clarendon Press, 1961). London, Library of Society of Friends MSS, Minute Books of the Yearly Meeting and Minute Books of the Meeting for Sufferings.
6. Neil McKendrick, John Brewer, and J.H. Plumb, *The Birth of a Consumer Society*.
7. John Brewer and Roy Porter (eds), *Consumption and the World of Goods* (London: Routledge, 1993), p. 65.
8. D.B. Davis, *The Problem of Slavery in the Age of Revolution, op. cit.*, p. 233. David S. Landes, *The Unbound Prometheus: Technological Change and Industrial Development in Western Europe from 1750 to the Present* (Cambridge: Cambridge University Press, 1969). J. Brewer, *et al.*, *Consumer Society*, p. 198.
9. Edward Woods was a member of the Six Weeks Meeting in London. See, for example, Library of Society of Friends MSS, *Minutes of the Six Weeks Meeting*, Vol. 10 (1745–47).
10. See R. Vann, *The Social Development of English Quakerism* on the idea of membership.
11. Matthews MSS, 28 January 1809, Joseph Woods recalled 'my old school-fellow Samuel Waring of Benson'. Samuel Waring later became correspondent for the London Yearly Meeting, Yearly Meeting Minute Books, 9 June 1795. Joseph also recalled 'another of my old school-fellows was William Crowley', who had a brother named Thomas. Thomas Crowley also became a correspondent to the London Yearly Meeting, Yearly Meeting Minute Books, 19 May 1777.
12. London, Library of Society of Friends MSS, Wandsworth MSS, Vol. I, p. 96, Obituary for William Massey. John Thompson MSS, No. 353, 19 April 1758, Copy of a Letter from William Massey to Thomas Jones on his School at Wandsworth.
13. Matthews MSS, 17 June 1807.
14. London and Middlesex Quarterly Meeting Digest of Burials, 1753, Edward Woods, age 31. Will of Edward Woods, Prob 11/823, folio 185. London, Library of Society of Friends, Tracts, Vol. 00/174.
15. Public Record Office, Will of Edward Woods, Prob 11/823, folio 185.
16. London and Middlesex Quarterly Meeting Digest of Marriages, 1769. Public Record Office, Will of Joseph Woods, Prob. 11/1535. folio 356 records Margaret's marriage portion.
17. Joseph Joshua Green, 'Biographical and Historical Notices of Jonathan Gurnell', typescript copy in Library of Society of Friends (1914), pp. 30–6.
18. London, Library of Society of Friends, Dictionary of Quaker Biography, 'Samuel Hoare, (1716–1796)'. Joseph Joshua Green, 'Biographical and Historical Notices of Jonathan Gurnell', pp. 30–6. Sarah and Hannah Hoare, *Memoirs of Samuel Hoare* (London: Headley Brothers, 1911), pp. 2–5, 45. The firm continued in business as Harman and Co. till 1846.
19. London and Middlesex Quarterly Meeting Digest of Births, London and Middlesex Quarterly Meeting Digest of Burials. S. and H. Hoare, *Memoirs*, p. 5.
20. London, Library of Society of Friends MSS, The Journal of Margaret Hoare Woods, 7 volumes (1771–1821). See Vol. I (1771–75). London and Middlesex Quarterly Meeting Digest of Births, 1772, Birth of Samuel Woods lists parents' residence as White Hart Court.
21. Journal of Margaret Hoare Woods, Vol. I (1771–75) and Vol. II (1775–81). London and Middlesex Quarterly Meeting Digest of Births, 1776, Joseph Woods; 1778, Margaret Woods; 1781, George Woods. London and Middlesex Quarterly Meeting Digest of Burials, 1774, son who lived one week.
22. See Matthews MSS. For William Matthews (1747–1816), see A.J. Turner, *Science and Music in Eighteenth-Century Bath* (Bath: University of Bath, 1977), p. 90. Woods returned

to Matthews the '1777 Feb 5 Bond-£100/2 1/2 yrs interest £12', Matthews MSS, 10 August 1779. Woods later wrote 'Thou mayst draw on me for the £50 or I will send it down in Bank Notes by Post ....', Matthews MSS, 16 August 1781.

23. Matthews MSS, 22 September 1774.
24. Journals of Margaret Hoare Woods, Vol. I (1771–75), October 1774, 27 July 1775. Vol. II (1776–81), 8 July 1776.
25. Frost (ed.), *The Records and Recollections of James Jenkins*, p. 404, 507.
26. Woods' obituary mentions his contributions to *The Gentleman's Magazine* (*The Gentleman's Magazine*, 81 (Jan.–June 1812), p. 669).
27. Woods recalled his participation in the London Tavern Club in Matthews MSS, 18 April 1807. Matthews MSS, 4 July 1787, indicates Woods had by then known Baron Dimsdale many years. Dimsdale was at one time a Quaker but left the organization. For more information about Dimsdale, see Peter Razzell, *The Conquest of Smallpox* (Sussex: Calliban Books, 1977).
28. Woods first met Philip Sansom in March 1775 and mentioned him frequently in subsequent letters to Matthews. Matthews MSS, 25 March 1775, 12 July 1775, 23 December 1775, 26 January 1776, 25 August 1777, 30 November 1778, 31 May 1779, 9 February 1780 and 1 October 1791.
29. Woods' letter to Parke is printed in 'An Englishman's Opinion of the Bostonians in 1774', *Pennsylvania Magazine of History and Biography*, 10, 3 (1886), pp. 265–6.
30. William Dillwyn (1743–1824) was born into a third generation Pennsylvania Quaker family. In 1768, he married Sarah Logan Smith of Burlington, New Jersey. She died in 1769 giving birth to their daughter Susannah. Dillwyn visited Britain for the first time in 1774 and permanently relocated there in 1777. He deserves a full-scale biography, and there are ample primary and secondary source materials documenting his life. For example, Philadelphia, Historical Society of Pennsylvania, Dillwyn–Emlen Correspondence, 5 vols, (1770–1824), contain his letters to his daughter, Susannah. Secondary sources include T. Mardy Rees, *A History of Quakers in Wales and their Emigration to North America* (Carmarthen: W. Spurrell and Son, 1925), pp. 248–9, and D.B. Davis, *Slavery in the Age of Revolution*, pp. 233–5. Dillwyn's manuscript diaries number nine volumes and cover the period 1774–90. The originals are in the National Library of Wales in Aberystwyth. Cited here are London, Library of Society of Friends, microfilms, 'Diaries of William Dillwyn', 9 vols. Vols 1–7 cover his travels through England in 1774–75. For his dinner with Woods see Notebook 3, 1 December 1774.
31. Matthews MSS, 28 October 1775.
32. Dictionary of Quaker Biography, 'William Dillwyn'.
33. For Coombe, see Matthews MSS, 31 May 1779, 9 February 1780 and 13 July 1780. For Duche, see: Matthews MSS, 31 May 1779; Austin Gray, *Benjamin Franklin's Library* (New York: Macmillan, 1936), p. 19; and Theodore Compton, *Recollections of Tottenham Friends and the Forster Family* (London: Edward Hicks, 1893), pp. 78–9.
34. Philadelphia, Library Company of Philadelphia Records, Box I #7438, folio 32, 6 September 1783, 'Invoice of Books Shipped by Joseph Woods'.
35. Adam Smith, *An Inquiry into the Nature and Causes of the Wealth of Nations*, R.H. Campbell, A.S. Skinnner and W.B. Todd (eds) (Oxford: Clarendon Press, 1976), p. 625.
36. Library Company of Philadelphia Records, Box I #7438 (1732–84), 16 December 1783, 25 September 1784, Box II #7439 (1785–89), 29 October 1785.
37. Library Company of Philadelphia Records, Box II # 7439, folio 11, 8 September 1785. Invoice of books bought from James Phillips.
38. Dictionary of Quaker Biography, 'William Phillips', *Victoria County History of Cornwall*, p. 293.
39. For Catherine Phillips, see *Memoirs of the Life of Catherine Payton Phillips* (London: James Phillips, 1795). Frost (ed.), *Records and Recollections of James Jenkins*, p. 261.
40. Library of Society of Friends MSS, Norman Penney Notebooks, Number 2.
41. London and Middlesex Quarterly Meeting Digest of Marriages, 1768, James Phillips and Mary Whiting. London Middlesex Quarterly Meeting Digest of Births, 1769, Judith Phillips; 1773, William Phillips; 1774, John Phillips; 1775, infant daughter; 1777, Frances;

1778, Richard; 1780, James; 1780, infant; 1782, twins John and Joseph; 1785, Catherine; 1789, Edwin. Three of the children died in infancy or childhood. London and Middlesex Quarterly Meeting Digest of Burials, 1775, infant daughter; 1777, John, age 3; 1780, infant.

42. London, Library of Society of Friends, 'Minutes of the Enfield Monthly Meeting, 1756–78', marriage certificate for Luke Hinde and Mary Phillips. Russell Mortimer, 'Quaker Printers 1750–1850', *Journal of the Friends Historical Society*, 50, 3 (1962–64), pp. 100–14.
43. Minutes of the Meeting for Sufferings, Vol. 33, 1771–75, 7 April and 5 May 1775.
44. Russell Mortimer, 'Quaker Printers 1750–1850', *Journal of the Friends Historical Society*, op. cit.
45. Minutes Books of the Yearly Meeting, Vol. 16 (1778–81), 27 March 1778.
46. London, Friends House MSS, Minute Books of the Morning Meeting, Vol. 6, 9 November 1772. Mary Hinde given permission to publish the works of John Woolman 'at her own risque'.
47. Theodore Compton, *Recollections of Tottenham Friends and the Forster Family* (London: Edward Hicks, 1893), pp. 78–9, identifies Duche as the author and Phillips as the printer.
48. London, Library of Society of Friends, Gibson MSS, 6 vol. autograph collection of Thomas Thompson (who married Frances, daughter of James Phillips), Vol. II, p. 175, Receipt for £6 17s. received from James Phillips signed by Joseph Woods, 7 April 1779.
49. Frost (ed.), *The Records and Recollections of James Jenkins*, p. 404.
50. Frost (ed.), *Records and Recollections*, p. 315.
51. Compton, *Recollections of Tottenham Friends*, pp. 56–78.
52. Gibson MSS, Vol. IV, p. 119, Dr George Logan to James Phillips, 17 June 1783.
53. Dictionary of Quaker Biography, 'Richard Reynolds' (1735–1816). Reynolds was born in Bristol and attended boarding school at Pickwick in Wiltshire. In 1757, he married Hannah, daughter of Abraham Darby, and became a partner, with Thomas Goldney, in Darby's iron and coal works. Richard and Hannah Reynolds had a son and a daughter, but Hannah died in 1762. When Abraham Darby died in 1763, Richard Reynolds moved to Coalbrook Dale and managed the business during the minority of Darby's son. Hannah Mary Rathbone, *Letters of Richard Reynolds, With A Memoir of His Life* (London: Charles Gilpin, 1852). Mrs Eustace Gregg (ed.), *Reynolds and Rathbone Diaries and Letters, 1753–1839* (privately printed, 1905).
54. Christiana Phillips, *A Short Memoir of William Phillips, The Eminent Geologist and Mineralogist* (London: James Wade, 1891), p. 7.
55. Rathbone, *Letters*, p. 73.
56. Library of the Society of Friends, Temporary MSS 508, folio 36 #3, Richard Reynolds to James Phillips, 23 October 1793, discusses a sum of £2,000 entrusted to Phillips.
57. London and Middlesex Quarterly Meeting Digest of Marriages for 1777 describes George Harrison as the son of Edward and Sarah Kendall of Westmorland [George Harrison, Jr], *Memoir of William Cookworthy. By his Grandson* (London: William and Frederick Cash, 1854), p. 133.
58. Thomas Joseph Pettigrew, *Memoirs of the Life and Writing of the late John Coakley Lettsom*, 3 vols (London: Nichols, Son, and Betley, 1817), Vol. 1, pp. 7–8.
59. [George Harrison], *Memoir*, p. 134.
60. John Fothergill's obituary in *The Gentleman's Magazine*, 51 (April 1781), pp. 165–7.
61. [George Harrison], *Memoir*, pp. 134–8. For George Harrison's gratitude to Samuel Fothergill, see Library of Society of Friends MSS, Portfolio 22, folio 144, George Harrison to Alice Chorley, 26 November 1821. George Harrison, *Adversaria* (London: Sold by Dalton, Harvey, and Dalton; William Phillips, J., and A. Arch, 1818), p. vi.
62. Betsy Croner and Christopher Booth, *Chain of Friendship: Selected Letters of Dr. John Fothergill of London, 1735–1780* (Cambridge, MA: Belknap Press, 1971).
63. [George Harrison], *Memoir*, pp. 134–8.
64. Rathbone, *Letters*, pp. 32–3.
65. Gregg, *Reynolds–Rathbone Diaries and Letters*, p. 172. Rathbone, *Letters*, p. 33.
66. London, Library of Society of Friends MSS, Vol. S 462, pp. 103–10, copy of obituary for

David Barclay in *Morning Chronicle*, 5 June 1809. Dictionary of Quaker Biography, 'David Barclay' (1729–1809).

67. Rathbone, *Letters*, pp. 91–125.
68. London and Middlesex Quarterly Meeting Digest of Marriages, 1777, George Harrison of London, son of Edward and Sarah Kendall of Westmorland, married Susanna Cookworthy of Plymouth. Dictionary of Quaker Biography, 'William Cookworthy' (1705–80). [G. Harrison], *Memoir*, pp. 22–3. John Penderill-Church, *William Cookworthy 1705–1780* (Truro: Bradford and Barton, 1972), p. 69. William Tallack, 'William Cookworthy', *Friends Quarterly Examiner*, 27 (1893), pp. 219–30. A. Douglas Selleck, *Cookworthy, 1705–80, and His Circle* (Plymouth: Baron Jay Ltd, 1978). Theodore Compton, *William Cookworthy* (London: Edward Hicks, Jr, 1895).
69. *Memoirs of Catherine Phillips*, pp. 211–41.
70. A.D. Selleck, *Cookworthy*, op, cit. [G. Harrison], *Memoir*, p. 206.
71. J. Penderill-Church, *Cookworthy*. W. Tallack, 'William Cookworthy', *Friends Quarterly Examiner*, pp. 219–30.
72. Theodore Compton, 'Thomas Hartley', *The New Church Magazine*, 10, 3 (March 1891), pp. 132–5. In 1763, Cookworthy had also paid for the publication in Plymouth of *The Doctrine of Life*, the first of Swedenborg's works to be published in England.
73. [George Harrison], *Memoir*, p. 118.
74. Theodore Compton, *Tottenham Friends*, p. 100. London, Library of Society of Friends MSS, Minutes of the Two Weeks Meeting, Vol. 9, p. 420. Harrison described his occupation as warehouseman when he asked for a certificate of marriage. See also, London and Middlesex Digest of Births, 1782, Mary Harrison, lists George Harrison's occupation as warehouseman.
75. [George Harrison], *Memoir*, pp. 107–8, 146.
76. London and Middlesex Quarterly Meeting Digest of Births, 1779, Lydia Harrison; 1780, Susanna Harrison; 1782, Mary Harrison; 1790, George Harrison. Mary died at age six. London and Middlesex Quarterly Meeting Digest of Burials, 1788, Mary Harrison.
77. [George Harrison], *Memoirs*, pp. 146–7.
78. London, Public Record Office, Will of William Cookworthy, Prob 11/1075, folio 125.
79. William Dillwyn's Journals, Notebook 3, 29 November, 2, 3 December 1774. George Harrison, like Woods, met Dillwyn on his first visit to London. Matthews MSS, 30 November 1778, 30 September 1788.
80. London and Middlesex Quarterly Meeting Digests of Births, 1751, Samuel Hoare.
81. S. and H. Hoare, *Memoirs*, p. 8. Henry Gurney's father, John, was the founder of Gurney and Company of Norwich.
82. Ibid., p. 63.
83. Ibid., p. 12. Norfolk and Norwich Quarterly Meeting Digest of Marriages, 1776, Sarah Gurney, daughter of Samuel and Sarah Gurney, marriage to Samuel Hoare of London. London and Middlesex Quarterly Meetings Digest of Births, 1777, Sarah Hoare; 1779, Hannah Hoare; 1781, Grizell Hoare; 1783, Samuel Hoare.
84. S. and H. Hoare, *Memoirs*, pp. 52–61. Roy Porter, *London: A Social History* (Cambridge, MA: Harvard University Press, 1995), pp. 158–9.
85. Ibid., pp. 12–13.
86. William Dillwyn Journals, Notebook 3, 29 November, 2, 3 December 1774. Hoare was among those who dined with Dillwyn at the home of Joseph Woods, on Dillwyn's first visit to London. Hoare and George Harrison visited Dillwyn the next day; and Hoare accompanied Dillwyn to a public lecture that evening.
87. Library Company of Philadelphia Records, Box III #7440, folio 12, Draft from James Pemberton on Hoare to pay for books, 1 November 1790.
88. London and Middlesex Quarterly Meeting Digest of Burials, 1783, Sarah Hoare, aged 26. S. and H. Hoare, *Memoirs*, p. 19.
89. R. Porter, *London*, pp. 131–59. J. Brewer and R. Porter (eds), *Consumption and the World of Goods*, p. 542. *The Gentleman's Magazine*, 54 (January–June 1784), pp. 92–3.
90. *The Lady's Magazine*, 23 (April 1792), pp. 201–3.
91. Matthews MSS, 10 November 1786.

92. Library Company of Philadelphia Records, Box II #7439, Joseph Woods to Mr Mordecai Lewis/Merchant, 17 September 1785. Austin Gray missed the joke and described Woods as 'the "honest and diligent bookseller" of Billingsgate, London'. Austin Gray, *Benjamin Franklin's Library* (New York: Macmillan, 1936), p. 49.
93. Matthews MSS, 4 July 1787.
94. W.C. Braithwaite, *The Second Period of Quakerism*, Introduction by Rufus Jones.
95. Matthews MSS, 6 December 1774, 19 October 1780.
96. Matthews MSS, 14 May 1777, 7 June 1777, 22 June 1778, 23 September 1782, 14 June 1784.
97. Jenkins (1753–1831) eventually became a member of the London Stock Exchange and retired a wealthy man. His 'records and recollections respecting himself and others from 1761 to 1821' is an invaluable, although decidedly not dispassionate, source for contemporary Quakerism. Frost (ed.), *Records and Recollections*, p. 128.
98. William Matthews, *An Explanatory Appeal to the Society in General and His Friends in Particular* (no publisher listed, 1783), pp. 12–13.
99. Matthews MSS, 9 February 1780. W. Matthews, *An Explanatory Appeal to the Society in General and His Friends in Particular*, op. cit.
100. Matthews MSS, 23 September 1782, 14 May 1777.
101. Frost (ed.), *Records and Recollections*, pp. 128–33. He mentions James Phillips and Samuel Hoare by name when describing the new leaders.
102. Minute Books of the London Yearly Meeting, Vol. 14 (1770–73), Vol. 15 (1774–77), Vol. 16 (1778–81), Vol. 17 (1782–85).
103. Dictionary of Quaker Biography, 'Thomas Letchworth' (1739–1784). [Joseph Woods], Preface to *Twelve Discourses, Delivered Chiefly at the Meeting House of the People Called Quakers, in the Park, Southwark, by the Late Thomas Letchworth* (London: Printed by J.W. Galtin for W. Richardson, 1787), p. x. Letchworth was also well respected by William Matthews. William Matthews, *The Life and Character of Thomas Letchworth* (Bath: R. Crutwell, 1786). Jenkins says 'Dr. Lettsom, John Scott, Joseph Woods, William Matthews, Edmund Rack, and James Phillips were all literary contributors' to *The Monthly Ledger*, Frost (ed.), *Records and Recollections*, p. 175. William Matthews began writing to Joseph Woods about their mutual interest in *The Ledger* and much of their early correspondence is taken up with a discussion of articles in it, Matthews MSS, 9 July 1774, 22 September 1774.
104. Dictionary of Quaker Biography, Dictionary of National Biography, 'Edmund Rack' (1735/6–87). Turner, *Science and Music in Eighteenth-Century Bath.* Kenneth Hudson, 'The Bath and West of England Society', (Bath, 1976). Reverend John Collinson, *The History and Antiquities of the County of Somerset,* 3 vols (Bath: R. Crutwell, 1791). Rack's 'writings first appeared in newspapers and magazines, especially *The Monthly Ledger* ... under the title Eusebius', according to Collinson. Matthews MSS, 9 February 1780, 10 August 1779, 27 November 1783.
105. Quoted in Turner, *Science and Music in Eighteenth-Century Bath*, p. 92.
106. Matthews, *Life and Character of Thomas Letchworth*, pp. 22–4. Frost (ed.), *Records and Recollections*, p. 175.
107. *The Monthly Ledger*, 3 (September 1775), contains a notice for *Poems* by Edmund Rack sold by James Phillips. In 1778 and 1785, Phillips sold the 3rd and 4th editions of Rack's popular *Mentor's Letters*. In 1781, Phillips was selling *Essays, Letters, and Poems* by Edmund Rack, Secretary to the Society for the Encouragement of Agriculture, Arts, Manufactures and Commerce and to the Philosophical Society lately Instituted at Bath. J. Collinson, *The History and Antiquities of the County of Somerset*, says Rack edited the TAMOC PASPIPINA papers, Vol. 1, pp. 77–82.
108. Brewer and Porter (eds), *Consumption and the World of Goods*, p. 527.

2

The First Abolition Association, 1783–87

During colonial times, some American Friends called on the British Quaker organization to take action against the slave trade. In 1763, for example, Anthony Benezet, an early abolitionist, appealed to George Harrison's future patron, Dr. John Fothergill. 'Though personally unknown' to Fothergill, Benezet wrote to 'request a little of thy attention' to a 'Matter of deep Concern to many well-minded People in these parts of the World which if it ever receives a proper check must come from amongst you; I mean the Negro Trade.' In 1773, Benezet again wrote to Fothergill urging him to join in 'using the best endeavours in our power to draw the notice of the government upon the grievous iniquity and great danger attendant on a farther prosecution of the Slave Trade'.[1]

Not all American Quakers opposed slavery or supported abolition of the slave trade. Jean Soderlund has detailed the course of abolition in Pennsylvania and the varied and conflicted responses of Quakers and others. Many American Friends who did oppose the slave trade looked to British Quakers for support, but the Quaker organization in London only reluctantly supported colonial petitions for abolition.[2]

Independence demanded new solutions on both sides of the Atlantic. In 1782, even before the peace treaty was signed, Philadelphia Friends began pressing the British organization to initiate action against the slave trade. In June 1783, the British Quakers appointed a 23-member committee to consider the slave trade. James Phillips, George Harrison and Samuel Hoare were among those appointed.

At almost the same time, James Pemberton was writing to James Phillips from Philadelphia requesting books. Referring to an American Friend then travelling in Britain, Pemberton added

> I expect he will find it in his place with our other American brethren to cooperate with you in deliberating on the most effectual mode of exerting your Endeavours with your Rulers, to remove the abomination of … the most infamous trade.

Pemberton closed with a request to 'present my respectful remembrance to thy mother-in-law [step-mother] Catherine Phillips whose Gospel labours in these parts … are not forgotten …'.[3] As a travelling minister before her marriage, Catherine Phillips visited Charleston, South Carolina. There she conversed with a slave who told her he was well cared for but that many slaves were not. She recorded the incident in her *Memoirs* later published by James Phillips.[4]

On 7 July 1783, a few weeks after the official Quaker committee was appointed, George Harrison, Samuel Hoare and Joseph Woods met informally with William Dillwyn, John Lloyd and Dr Thomas Knowles. The purpose of the six was

> to consider what steps could by them be taken for the Relief and Liberation of the Negro Slaves in the West Indies, and the Discouragement of the Slave Trade on the Coast of Africa.[5]

William Dillwyn was already a long-standing associate of at least four of the six Friends and a long-time opponent of slavery. Dillwyn had attended the school founded by abolitionist Anthony Benezet in Philadelphia. Benezet 'very early took pains to interest his feelings on the subject of slavery and the slave trade'. In 1773, Dillwyn and two Friends had written a pamphlet entitled 'Brief Considerations on Slavery and the Expediency of its Abolition'.[6] Like Harrison and Hoare, Dillwyn was a member of the official Quaker committee appointed to consider the slave trade.

John Lloyd was the third son of Sampson Lloyd II, a wealthy merchant and banker in Birmingham. Lloyd went into the tobacco business with his brother-in-law Osgood Hanbury in 1773. Lloyd travelled through the American Colonies on business between 1775 and 1777 where he witnessed and became opposed to slavery. Lloyd was also a member of the official Quaker committee on the slave trade appointed in June.[7]

Thomas Knowles was born in Yorkshire and became an apothecary. At age 35 he took up the study of medicine. Knowles first studied at Edinburgh and then went to the University of Leyden where he took a degree of Doctor of Medicine. Returning to London, he became a licentiate of the Royal College of Physicians. Mary Morris Knowles, his wife, was an artist whose needlework won her the friendship of the Royal Family. Thomas and Mary Knowles lived in Lombard Street not far from George Yard and White Hart Court.[8] Knowles was the landlord of James Jenkins and physician to Thomas Letchworth, the friend of Joseph Woods.

Like Harrison, Hoare, Dillwyn and Lloyd, Knowles was a member of the 23-member Quaker committee on the slave trade. According to Jenkins, Knowles, like Hoare, Harrison, Phillips and Woods, opposed zealous, exclusionary Friends. Again, according to Jenkins, Knowles often spoke out against what Jenkins called the dominance of the 'feudal lords' within the Quaker organization.[9]

Why did these six men come together in July 1783 to establish another abolition group, especially since all except Woods were already serving on the official Quaker slave trade committee? Probably because as an informal association operating outside the official Quaker structure, the group could act without submitting written materials to the central Quaker organization for review. Quakers in charge of reviewing publications were described colourfully if not dispassionately by James Jenkins as

> the heretofore licensors of the Quaker press – a phalanx of male and female critics, who hack, and hew, and alter at their pleasure … to shorten, and chop, and lop, and pare down what *they* deem too long, exuberant, or in the smallest degree of a heterodox tendency.[10]

The tensions between liberal Quakers like Phillips, Woods, Hoare, and Harrison and the more evangelical 'feudal lords' described by Jenkins were certainly real but may not have been as deep as Jenkins, sometimes prone to hyperbole, indicates or as clear cut to the members of the association of six. John Lloyd, for example, was married to Elizabeth Corbyn, daughter of Thomas Corbyn described by Jenkins as 'Pope Corbyn'. Jenkins describes George Dillwyn, a ministering Friend from America, as 'extremely tenacious of his opinion' and says that 'George Harrison [and] James Phillips … used often to come into contact with his extreme earnestness to gain his point'. Yet George was the brother of William Dillwyn and dearly beloved by many British Friends.[11]

Yet the six did meet quietly on their own, and 'It was not … known to the world that such an association existed'.[12] Joseph Woods had no qualms about such private discussions where 'If ... anything was hazarded which was not according to the mind and will of Friends, we were not offended with each other'. Yet even Woods, who was often critical of Quaker leaders, went on to explain, 'he did not wish to give offense by throwing it in the Teeth' of the Quaker organization.[13] Moreover, George Harrison later observed, 'The Quaker Society do not hold themselves amenable for the sentiments which come from the pen of anonymous writers …'.[14]

Although the group met privately, they immediately decided 'that the public mind should be enlightened'. They directed Joseph Woods and another member to apply to the printer of the *General Evening Post* for the 'regular admission of a short piece on the subject of the slave trade once a week'. William Dillwyn noted in a letter to an American Friend that some British Quakers had qualms about printing anti-slavery materials written by non-Friends.[15] This suggests another reason why the group may have decided to form a separate association.

Meeting every two weeks from July until November 1783, the group quickly expanded its scope by directing members to apply to the Norwich

Mercury and the Bath *Chronicle*, papers in York and Liverpool, *Lloyd's Evening Post* in London, and papers in Bristol, Cork, Dublin, Kent, Sherborne and Newcastle. The articles selected for publication drew from a wide range of sources, including a history by the Abbé Raynal, travel accounts of North America, the East Indies and Africa, and selections from Blackstone's *Commentaries* and the writings of Montesquieu. The group also excerpted articles from such periodicals as the *Annual Register* and the *Monthly Review.*

Joseph Woods prepared an anonymous essay on Hume's remarks respecting slavery. John Lloyd contributed a paper for publication which included extracts from *The Wealth of Nations.*[16] The essay and paper written by Woods and Lloyd have not come to light, but both Hume and Smith opposed slavery on the grounds of economic interest. 'The experience of all ages and nations' demonstrated to Smith that the labour of slaves 'although it appears to cost only their maintenance, is in the end the dearest of any. A person who can acquire no property can have no other interest but to eat as much and labour as little as possible.'[17]

The informal association of six met at the homes of members, frequently at the London residence of Joseph Woods. The surviving minute book is written in Woods' careful hand. Each article selected for publication is numbered so that it could be rotated to different publications in an orderly fashion. By the end of November 1783, ten groups of articles were circulating to 12 newspapers in London and the country.[18]

At the same time, James Phillips was working hard on the official Quaker committee. Quickly deciding 'a short address to the publick on this important subject' was needed, the committee directed William Dillwyn and John Lloyd to prepare one.[19] By October 1783, Dillwyn and Lloyd had completed a statement for the official committee entitled *The Case of our Fellow Creatures, the oppressed Africans, respectfully recommended to the serious Consideration of the Legislature of Great Britain by the people called Quakers.* As soon as the Quaker organization approved the 15-page pamphlet, James Phillips began printing 2,000 copies.[20] In *The Case,* which was published anonymously, Dillwyn and Lloyd argued that abolition of the slave trade was 'required by the calls of justice and humanity, but is also consistent with sound policy'.[21]

In December 1783, David Barclay instructed James Phillips on how to present *The Case* to the Royal Family. Barclay, the wealthy and influential merchant who was responsible for bringing George Harrison to London, was experienced in giving evidence before the Bar in Commons and had entertained George III. Now, in the uncertain political atmosphere following American independence, Barclay advised Phillips to 'postpone the delivery of any, until it is known who are to be Ministers and whether we are to have a new Parliament'.[22]

In May 1784 after elections were held, Quakers distributed *The Case* to all Members of the newly elected Parliament, key Cabinet leaders, and the Royal Family. Later, the Committee ordered Phillips to print 10,000 copies. The pamphlets were then to be distributed 'as generally as may be throughout the nation'.[23]

Joseph Woods, meanwhile, was completing a public statement of his own for the informal committee. His 32-page essay entitled *Thoughts on the Slavery of Negroes* also appeared anonymously in 1784. Woods began by saying he knew people would ask 'why a system, which has been established and encouraged for near a century, should *now* be attacked; or why *this*, of the many oppressions ... should be singled out'. His answer was simple, because of 'The humanity of the present age'.[24] By choosing this argument, Woods was framing public discourse about slavery and the slave trade within the developing concept of humanitarianism.

As some Quakers and other reformers had done before him, Woods insisted on the essential humanity of Africans, maintaining 'They cannot be denied to be men'. Yet, consistent with his earlier views on the political rights of Americans and the limited intellectual abilities of women, Woods' idea of African humanity had nothing to do with notions of equality. Even 'the oldest and wisest men' could not 'remedy all the defects of political government', he believed, so that was not his aim. Observing 'there is in every nation, a very considerable disparity between man and man', he was willing to grant the argument that Africans were inferior.[25]

As a successful businessman, Woods was well aware of the economic value of slavery and the slave trade. He realized the 'very sufferings' of the Africans 'are the source of public revenue and private wealth'. So he was quick to distinguish his idea of humanity from a 'romantic attempt of relieving every distress, in every quarter of the globe'.

Woods directed his economic arguments instead to the growing number of individual consumers, asking them to weigh considerations of humanity against the price of slave products. 'The objection' to ending slavery and the slave trade 'from motives of commercial policy, amounts to this', he asserted

> that the claims of religion and morality ought to be subservient to those of avarice and luxury, and that is better thousands of poor unoffending people should be degraded and destroyed ... than that the inhabitants of Europe should pay a higher price for their rum, rice, and sugar.[26]

Woods did not argue, as Dillwyn and Lloyd had done in *The Case*, that trade in African goods would be more profitable than the slave trade. He argued instead that the slave trade went beyond the humanitarian limits of what should be bought and sold. As with the American Revolution, Woods was less concerned with the inherent rights of people elsewhere than with defining British rights, in this case, to buy and sell. The slave trade was 'a disgraceful commerce,' he contended, which could not be considered legitimate because 'No right exists … to alienate from another his liberty … and therefore every purchase of a slave is in contradiction to the original inherent rights of mankind.'[27]

Although the practice of humanity ought to be the responsibility of individuals, Woods believed that, in the case of the slave trade the British Parliament should intervene. '[T]he revenue of the government, the profits of the merchants, and the luxury of the people, have involved the whole nation', he wrote, again insisting on the shared responsibility of consumers. He ended by calling for 'a candid inquiry into this subject' which he believed 'must surely terminate in a call … for the gradual indeed, but total abolition of slavery and, till that be accomplished, for some authoritative act … rigidly to prohibit the importation' of slaves.[28]

Woods' central argument is essentially that identified by Seymour Drescher in *Capitalism and Anti-Slavery*: 'trade itself was disgraced by the commerce in human beings'. Drescher identifies a long-standing duality in British attitudes, questioning the morality but accepting the economic imperative of the slave trade and colonial slavery. According to Drescher, British writers had long maintained that involvement in slavery and the slave trade might be necessary for colonials but was not acceptable for Englishmen.[29]

Woods was also addressing another major theme in the ethical discourse of the eighteenth century: the relationship between civic virtue and the rise of the commercial economy.[30] In *The Wealth of Nations*, Adam Smith specifically rejected benevolence and humanity as realistic expectations for economic conduct. 'It is vain to expect it [the help of brethren] from their benevolence only…', Smith wrote. 'We address ourselves not to humanity but to … self-love ….'[31]

In his *Thoughts on Slavery*, Joseph Woods argued, contrary to Adam Smith, that the slave trade was a disgrace to commerce and a violation of humanity. By so doing, Woods was developing his own solutions to the problem of how to create wealth while maintaining virtue. As D.B. Davis observes, 'One of the striking features of British intellectual history, in the decades following *The Wealth of Nations*, is the sharp divergence of the standards of utility and moral sentiment.'[32] By choosing not to accept the premises of Smith, Woods was contributing to that divergence.

By proposing to rid British commerce of the disgrace of the slave trade, Woods was appealing both to successful merchants like himself and to the rapidly increasing numbers of consumers. At a time when sugar consumption was rising by 80 per cent, appealing directly to British consumers of slave-produced commodities was a crucial step in creating public understanding of abolition issues. As David Eltis points out, the growing consumption of sugar and other slave products made abolition relevant to the British consuming public.[33]

Woods helped make the connection between abolition and the growing number of consumers by focusing on the commodities of slavery rather than on the issue of slavery itself. In his *Thoughts*, Woods repeatedly pointed out that sugar, rum, tobacco and other slave products were luxury goods. As David Eltis explains,

> … slave grown products such as sugar, coffee, tobacco, and even cotton generally did nothing to fill biological or subsistence needs …. Rather, they were quintessentially social and cultural products that formed part of the widened range of goods and services to which a significant sector of early industrializing society aspired.[34]

Joseph Woods, who was engaged in the market economy himself on a daily basis, was now appealing to the rapidly increasing numbers of British consumers to exercise their own economic responsibility and moral judgement. By insisting that considerations of humanity, and not calculations of profit, be the standard by which to judge the slave trade, Woods was proposing humanitarianism as a non-sectarian standard for merchants and consumers to judge what could properly be bought and sold in the expanding market economy.

Yet Woods used the language of paternalism in articulating his concept of humanitarianism. He focused on the duties of English*men* to treat African *men* according to the principles of humanity. 'To relieve the miserable and to do good to all men are the plain and practical precepts of humanity', said Woods, 'which fall within the line of every man's duty.' Throughout the essay he described Africans as powerless, referring to them as 'poor', 'unoffending' and 'helpless'.[35]

When Woods wrote *men*, it seems safe to conclude that he did not mean women. Woods himself distinguished between the intellectual abilities of men and women, as has been seen. Fellow abolitionist Thomas Clarkson later described Woods' essay as 'manly yet feeling'.[36] By *manly*, Clarkson may have meant rational, but he also may have meant it was especially appealing to well-educated British men like himself.

A brief comparison of Woods' *Thoughts* with the ideas of John Woolman, a more radical Quaker contemporary, shows how Woods' concept of humanitarianism was limited in other ways. Like Woods, John Woolman, an American Quaker, struggled with the meaning of virtue in a developing market economy. Woolman, for example, insisted on giving money to a Southern slave-master to pay for slave services, refused to use slave products, and was reluctant to accept travelling expenses from slave-owning Friends.

Woolman died in Yorkshire in 1772 while travelling through England on a religious visit. In 1775, Thomas Letchworth, the close friend of Woods, published an abridgement of Woolman's works. Letchworth's edition omitted the account of Woolman paying for slave services and refusing to accept money from slave-owning Friends. Yorkshire Friends objected to some of the omissions in Letchworth's edition but were rebuffed by the Meeting for Sufferings. Not long afterwards, Letchworth's edition was reprinted by James Phillips with the same omissions, and George Harrison was among those directed to correct the press.[37]

Like Letchworth, Phillips, Harrison, and the Meeting for Sufferings, Woods was more cautious than Woolman in reconciling the tensions between Quaker religious beliefs and economic practices. Woods was seeking, as John Woolman was not, a way of attacking slavery and the slave trade without challenging the social hierarchy and political inequality which created and sustained the trade.

By formulating a non-sectarian and non-threatening but moral and virtuous standard for economic conduct, Woods was able to resolve what Joyce Appleby sees as long-standing tensions between religion and consumption. She points out that 'In both Christian and classical thought the central unworthiness of human beings stemmed from their desiring things that were unnecessary, that is from their desire to consume.'[38] By choosing to oppose some forms of commerce as immoral, moderate Quakers like Woods could participate in other forms of buying and selling in good conscience. The distinction between moral and immoral commerce was a particularly important distinction for Friends, like Woods, Harrison, Hoare and Phillips, who were involved in trade daily.

The non-sectarian arguments put forth by Joseph Woods in his *Thoughts* were highly rational and carefully stated. Woods sought to appeal to the reason not to the emotions or religious views of readers. Yet the style of discourse employed by Woods in his *Thoughts*, carefully choosing words and arguing in a highly rational manner, had the perhaps unintended consequence of making his paternalism and ideas about the inequality of Africans also seem reasonable.

While *Thoughts on the Slavery of Negroes* helped to broaden Quaker abolitionism into non-sectarian humanitarianism, it also helped to establish the idea of inequality close to the heart of developing humanitarianism. Woods was aiming to reach a wide public of like-minded readers of all denominations by using non-sectarian language and highly rational arguments. Thomas Clarkson later described Woods' essay as 'a Sober and dispassionate appeal to the reason of all, without offending the prejudices of any'.[39]

On 6 July 1784, the informal association endorsed Woods' essay by ordering James Phillips to print 2,000 copies. The essay was printed anonymously, and the association directed widespread distribution to Friends and non-Friends. The group specified copies be sent to: Bristol and Liverpool, centers of the slave trade; Granville Sharp, a leader in the 1772 legal case limiting the right of a British master forcibly to dispatch his slave, James Somerset, back to the colonies; James Ramsay, an Anglican priest who had lived in and written about the West Indies; Quaker leaders Edward Stabler in Virginia and Moses Brown in Providence, Rhode Island; and Beilby Porteus, Bishop of Chester.[40]

By distributing Woods' pamphlet widely, the informal association began to connect with abolitionists of other denominations in Britain and North America. Before long, 'A communication having been made to the committee, that Dr. Porteus ... had preached a sermon before the S[ociety for the] P[ropogation of the] G[ospel] ... Samuel Hoare was deputed to obtain permission to publish it.' Porteus gave permission, and the group ordered Phillips to print 1,000 copies of the Bishop's sermon. Hoare's contact with Porteus then 'led him to a correspondence with Mr. Ramsay'. James Ramsay was a Scottish-born Anglican cleric who had served in the West Indies, returning to England in 1781.[41]

Meanwhile, Joseph Woods' *Thoughts* had 'been honoured with the remarks of an anonymous writer'. Mistakenly assuming James Ramsay was the author, the anonymous critic argued that slaves in St Kitts were better off than the poor in London. In a postscript to a second edition issued in 1785, Woods made it clear that Ramsay was not the author while maintaining his own anonymity. Woods side-stepped the domestic issue by saying if it were true that slaves were better off in St Kitts, poor people would be flocking to live there.[42]

The fragmentary record book of the informal committee ends in 1784, but a contemporary account indicates that most of the group continued to be active for the next three years.[43] One of the six founders, Dr Thomas Knowles, died of a fever, and Joseph Woods attended his funeral. Knowles left all his 'Goods, Books, ... and two shares in the navigation from Leeds to Liverpool' to his wife Molly, making her sole executrix. When Molly Knowles died years later, Woods reported she 'is said to have accumulated 50 or 60 thousand pounds'.[44]

Although not a member of the association of six, James Phillips continued to gather and publish anti-slavery materials after 1784. The second edition of Woods' *Thoughts* published in 1785 contained a notice for other abolitionist publications being sold by Phillips. By then, the list numbered six titles.[45]

By January 1785, Parliament had still taken no action on slavery or the slave trade. Yet the British Quaker organization believed

> that many sensible minds of various denominations have been impressed with the serious consideration [of slavery and the slave trade] who till lately had never contemplated this weighty subject.[46]

NOTES

1. London, Library of Society of Friends, Spriggs MSS, 156/56 Benezet to Joseph Phipps and John Fothergill, 28 May 1763. Gibson MSS, Vol. I, p. 27, Benezet to John Fothergill, 28 April 1773.
2. Jean Soderlund, *Quakers and Slavery: A Divided Society* (Princeton, NJ: Princeton University Press, 1985). Judith Jennings, 'The American Revolution and the Testimony of British Quakers Against the Slave Trade', *Quaker History*, 70, 2 (Fall 1981), pp. 99–103. D.B. Davis, *The Problem of Slavery in the Age of Revolution*, pp. 221–7.
3. London, Library of Society of Friends MSS, Portfolio Series, Portfolio 6, #152, James Pemberton to James Phillips, 22 July 1783.
4. Catherine Phillips, *Memoirs of the Life of Catherine Payton Phillips* (London: James Phillips, 1795).
5. London, Library of Society of Friends, Thompson-Clarkson MSS, 3 vols and index, Autograph Collection of Thomas Thompson who obtained autographs from everyone listed in Clarkson's *History*,Vol. II, p. 9., Minute Book, 7 July 1783.
6. George Brookes, *Friend Anthony Benezet* (Philadelphia: University of Pennsylvania Press, 1937). [William Dillwyn, Richard Smith, David Wills], *Brief Considerations on Slavery and The Expediency of Its Abolition. With Some Hints on the Means Whereby It May Be Gradually Effected* (Burlington: Isaac Collins, 1773).
7. Dictionary of Quaker Biography, 'John Lloyd' (1750/1–1811). After Hanbury's death in 1784, Lloyd moved to London and took over the tobacco business. In 1790, he closed the tobacco business and became a banker in Lombard Street (London, Library of Society of Friends MSS, John Lloyd's Diary 1776–1811). Little evidence has come to light about Lloyd and his views. The diary is the only entry relating to Lloyd in the Library of Society of Friends card catalogue. Lloyd is mentioned only in passing by Clarkson and James Jenkins. The main source is Humphrey Lloyd, *The Quaker Lloyds in the Industrial Revolution* (London: Hutchinson, 1975). He is also mentioned by Samuel Lloyd, *The Lloyds of Birmingham*, 3rd edition (Birmingham: Cornish Brothers Ltd, 1908). Neither of these secondary sources explain Lloyd's opposition to slavery.
8. Dictionary of Quaker Biography, 'Thomas Knowles' (1734–86), 'Mary Knowles' (1733–1807). Frost (ed.), *Records and Recollections of James Jenkins*, pp. 254–6. Matthews MSS, 27 November 1783.
9. Frost (ed.), *Records and Recollections*, p. 129.
10. Ibid., p. 178.
11. Ibid., pp. 192, 225.
12. T. Clarkson, *History of the Rise, Progress and Accomplishment of the Abolition of the Slave Trade*, Vol. 1, p. 125.
13. Matthews MSS, 24 November 1784. Woods was speaking of his conversations with Thomas Letchworth who had recently died.
14. George Harrison, *Some Remarks on A Letter Lately Published and Addressed to the Archbishops and Bishops of the Church of England on Joseph Lancaster's Plan for the Education of the Lower Orders of the Community* (London: J. Arch, Cornhill, 1806), p. 5.
15. D.B. Davis, *Slavery in the Age of Revolution*, p. 224.
16. Thompson-Clarkson MSS, Vol. II, p. 9, Minute Book, 7 July–17 November 1783.

17. D.B. Davis, *Problem of Slavery in Age of Revolution*, pp. 352–4. Smith, *Wealth of Nations*, p. 98.
18. Thompson-Clarkson MSS, Vol. II, p. 9, Minute Book, 7 July–17 November 1783. T. Clarkson, *History of the Rise, Progress and Accomplishment of the Abolition of the Slave Trade*, Vol. 1, p. 123.
19. London, Library of Society of Friends MSS, Letters Between London and Philadelphia Meetings for Sufferings, Philadelphia to London, August 1782. Meeting for Sufferings Minute Book, Vol. 36, 20 June 1783.
20. London, Library of Society of Friends MSS, Meeting for Sufferings Committee on the Slave Trade Minute Book, 3 October 1783, indicates that Dillwyn and Lloyd were the authors of the pamphlet. Meeting for Sufferings Minute Book, Vol. 36, 17 October 1783 authorized the pamphlet to be printed. Patrick Lipscomb and Edward Milligan present further evidence in favour of Dillwyn and Lloyd in 'A Note on the Authorship of *The Case of Our Fellow-Creatures*', *Quaker History*, 55 (Spring, 1966), pp. 47–51. Roger Anstey mistakenly identifies Anthony Benezet as the author of *The Case* in *The Atlantic Slave Trade and British Abolition*, p. 381. His error is repeated by Seymour Drescher in *Capitalism and Antislavery*, p. 63, and James Walvin in *England, Slaves and Freedom, 1776–1838*, p. 102.
21. [William Dillwyn and John Lloyd], *The Case of our Fellow-Creatures* (London: James Phillips, 1783).
22. Thompson-Clarkson MSS, Vol. III, p. 121, David Barclay to James Phillips, 19 December 1783. Thomas Clarkson says David Barclay 'assisted' at one of the meetings of the association of six. T. Clarkson, *History*, Vol. 1, p. 126. Dictionary of Quaker Biography, 'David Barclay'. King George III and his young bride Queen Charlotte watched the Lord Mayor's parade from Barclay's home near the Mansion House in 1761. Barclay was married to John Lloyd's sister Rachel (Thompson-Clarkson MSS, Vol. III, p. 117, Obituary for David Barclay printed in *The Morning Chronicle*, 15 June 1809). Barclay had given evidence before the Bar of Commons about American issues and won the praise of Lord North.
23. William Dillwyn and John Lloyd, *The Case of our Fellow-Creatures*. Library of Friends Society MSS, Meeting for Sufferings Minute Book, Vol. 37, 27 August 1784.
24. [Joseph Woods], *Thoughts on the Slavery of Negroes* (London: James Phillips, 1784).
25. Ibid., pp. 12, 15, 31.
26. Ibid., pp. 7, 18–19.
27. Ibid., p. 29.
28. Ibid., pp. 31–2.
29. Seymour Drescher, *Capitalism and Anti-Slavery: British Mobilization in Comparative Perspective* (Oxford: Oxford University Press, 1987), p. 19.
30. J.G.A. Pocock, *Virtue, Commerce and History: Essays on Political Thought and History, Chiefly in the Eighteenth Century* (Cambridge: Cambridge University Press, 1985).
31. Smith, *Wealth of Nations*, p. 14.
32. Davis, *Problem of Slavery in Age of Revolution*, p. 354.
33. David Eltis, *Economic Growth and the Ending of the Transatlantic Slave Trade* (Oxford: Oxford University Press, 1989), p. 38. Eltis says British sugar consumption rose 80 per cent between 1785 and 1805.
34. Ibid., p. 20.
35. [J. Woods], *Thoughts*, p. 31.
36. T. Clarkson, *History*, Vol. 1, pp. 125–6.
37. Compare *The Works of John Woolman* (London: Thomas Letchworth, 1775) and *The Works of John Woolman* (Philadelphia: Joseph Cruikshank, 1774). Letchworth was given permission to publish his abridgement by the Morning Meeting, London, Library of Society of Friends, Morning Meeting Book, Vol. 6, 27 February 1775. James Phillips was given permission to print a new edition 'at his own risque', Meeting for Sufferings Minute Book, Vol. 34, 1 September 1775. George Harrison was directed to correct the press, ibid., 8 September 1775.
38. Brewer and Porter (eds), *Consumption and the World of Goods*, p. 166.
39. Clarkson, *History*, Vol. I, p. 125.

40. Thompson-Clarkson MSS, Vol. II, p. 9, 6 July 1784. T. Clarkson, *History*, Vol. I, p. 125. James Walvin, *England, Slaves and Freedom, 1776–1838*, pp. 41, 81 and 82.
41. T. Clarkson, *History*, Vol. I, pp. 125–6.
42. [Joseph Woods], *Thoughts on the Slavery of Negroes*, 2nd edn (London: James Phillips, 1785), Postscript, pp. 33–9.
43. Thompson-Clarkson MSS, Vol. II, p. 9, 6 July 1784. T. Clarkson, *History*, Vol. I, pp. 125–200.
44. London and Middlesex Quarterly Meeting Digest of Burials, 16 November 1786, Thomas Knowles. Matthews MSS, 6 December 1786, Woods mentions attending Knowles' funeral. Public Record Office, Prob 11/1147, folio 573, Will of Thomas Knowles. Matthews MSS, 18 April 1807, on the death of Molly Knowles.
45. [Joseph Woods], *Thoughts on the Slavery of Negroes*, 2nd edn (London: James Phillips, 1785).
46. London, Library of Society of Friends, Friends House MSS, Letters between London and Philadelphia Meeting for Sufferings, January 1785.

3

The London Abolition Committee, 1787–91

By 1785 the Quaker members of the informal association of six were becoming acquainted with two young Anglicans who were showing an interest in the issue of the slave trade. William Wilberforce was one. Not yet 30, Wilberforce had recently become an Evangelical. According to his two sons, Wilberforce had been urged to take up the cause of abolition as early as 1785 and had promised to consider it.[1]

That same year, Thomas Clarkson, a student at Cambridge, was writing his prize-winning paper on the slave trade. In *An Essay on the Slavery and Commerce of the Human Species, Particularly the African*, Clarkson argued, like Woods, that the sale of slaves was an unacceptable form of trade. Clarkson brought his essay to London where he met James Phillips and William Dillwyn. The informal Quaker association agreed to finance the printing of the essay by Phillips.[2]

Clarkson began presenting copies of his publication to Members of Parliament. In the process, he met Wilberforce. By then Clarkson had, by his own account, determined to devote his life to abolition. Clarkson says that after talking with Wilberforce, he proposed a union to his Quaker allies at a gathering in the home of James Phillips. The Quakers agreed, according to Clarkson on condition that Wilberforce would promise his support.

As both Clarkson and Wilberforce's sons agree, Wilberforce publicly declared his intention to take up the cause of abolition at a dinner party in early 1787. Clarkson reported Wilberforce's commitment to James Phillips and the other Quaker abolitionists. According to Clarkson, 'All were unanimous for the formation of a Committee.'[3]

By May 1787 there were a growing number of individuals in London and elsewhere concerned about slavery and the slave trade, as Thomas Clarkson takes great pains to show in his detailed history. The Anglican Granville Sharp, for example, after orchestrating the Somerset case in 1772, had led the public outcry against the owners of the slave ship *Zong* who tossed dying slaves overboard to collect insurance. In 1786, Sharp formed the Committee for the Black Poor in London. Samuel Hoare and other members of that Committee raised funds and made plans to relocate free blacks from London to Africa. In April 1787, three Royal Navy ships carrying

411 blacks, financed by Sharp's Committee, left London for Sierra Leone.[4]

On 22 May 1787, 12 men, representing a range of religious and political beliefs, met together to form a committee. Joseph Woods, James Phillips, George Harrison and Samuel Hoare were there. William Dillwyn and John Lloyd also attended, meaning all five of the surviving founders of the informal association participated.

Of the six remaining members of the committee, three were Quakers: Joseph Hooper, John Barton and Richard Phillips, a cousin of James Phillips. Three were Anglicans: Granville Sharp, Thomas Clarkson and Philip Sansom, the friend of Joseph Woods. Wilberforce did not join the group but promised his co-operation.

The minute books of the London Abolition Committee, with emendations by Thomas Clarkson, are now in the British Library. According to the minutes, the 12 men formed themselves into a Committee

> for procuring such Information and Evidence, and for distributing Clarkson's *Essay* and such other Publications, as may tend to the Abolition of the Slave Trade, and for directing the application of such monies as are already, or may hereafter be collected, for the above Purposes.

At the first meeting 'it was resolved that the said Trade was both impolitick and unjust'.[5] By adopting this resolution, the group was joining moral arguments against the slave trade, such as those being developed by Joseph Woods, with the economic arguments put forth by Adam Smith.

Unlike the earlier association of 1783, this group was public from the beginning. At the first meeting, Samuel Hoare was appointed Treasurer. The committee decided to finance its activities by subscriptions and authorized members to begin collecting donations. As John Brewer points out, by pooling funds, small donors could exercise charity without depending on aristocratic patronage.[6]

The four Quaker merchant/philosophers on the Committee soon began combining their public abolition activities with their businesses, just as they had earlier combined book buying and business in their transactions with the Library Company of Philadelphia. Samuel Hoare became the Committee's banker at the first meeting. At the second meeting, two days later on 24 May, James Phillips was directed to print 2,000 copies of *A Summary View of the Slave Trade* prepared by Thomas Clarkson. Before long, the Committee set up headquarters in a room in the Old Jewry, not far from George Yard and White Hart Court, and hired a clerk.[7]

By early June 1787, Clarkson says

> The Committee [was] finding that their meetings began to be

> approved by many, and that the cause under their care was likely to spread, [and they began] forseeing also the necessity there would soon be of making themselves known as a public body throughout the Kingdom.

The Committee then 'thought it right', continues Clarkson, 'that they should assume some title, which should be a permanent one, and which should be expressive of their future views'.

So, says Clarkson, 'This gave occasion to them to reconsider the object, for which they had associated, and to fix and define it in such a manner, that there should be no misunderstanding about it in the public mind'. According to Clarkson, the 12 men debated whether to focus on the slave trade or on the larger issue of slavery. 'In looking into the subject, it appeared to them that there were two evils, quite distinct from each other, which it might become their duty to endeavour to remove.' One was 'the Evil of the Slave Trade', the other was 'the Evil of Slavery itself'.

According to Clarkson, 'It appeared soon to be the sense of the committee, that to aim at the removal of both would be to aim at too much, that by doing this we might lose all'. Clarkson says he began by believing it didn't matter 'where they began', but on further examination, he came to believe it did matter in terms of laws and the prospects for success. By focusing on the slave trade alone, they would not incur the objection of meddling with the property of the slave owners or 'letting loose an irritated race of beings' who were 'unfit for their freedom'. Moreover, the British government had the indisputable right to regulate commerce but it was doubtful whether it could legally or effectively manage the internal affairs of colonies.

'Impressed by these arguments, the Committee were clearly of opinion', says Clarkson, 'that they should define their object to be the abolition of the Slave-Trade, and not of the slavery which sprang from it ....' As Clarkson explains, by 'aiming at the abolition of the Slave Trade, they believed they were laying the axe at the very root' of the problem of slavery. He praised the decision, observing that the Committee 'took a ground which was forever tenable'.[8]

The minute books do not record the debates of the Committee, but there are indications that Committee members were not as unanimous as Clarkson indicates. Granville Sharp, for one, was never happy with the decision to focus on the slave trade alone. Ten years later, Sharp still felt strongly enough to write, 'I thought (and shall ever think) it my duty to expose the monstrous *impiety* and *cruelty* not only of the *Slave Trade*, but of Slavery itself ...'.[9] Samuel Hoare, on the other hand, even in later years did not support the emancipation of slaves in the West Indies. He questioned the possibility of emancipation and considered the honour of the country pledged to the slave owners.[10]

So, from the very beginning, the London Abolition Committee, as it came to be called, represented an amalgam of viewpoints and a spectrum of opinions. The decision to focus on the slave trade alone was both the defining moment for the London Abolition Committee and a means of finding common ground among its members.

Despite his misgivings about the focus of the Committee, Granville Sharp was named Chair, meaning his name would appear on all official correspondence. Roger Anstey says Sharp agreed to serve as Chair only if the Quaker members agreed to write letters of support 'in the ordinary style, laying aside every peculiarity of their sect'. Sharp hoped in this way the Abolition Society would appeal to all denominations of Christians.[11]

While the choice of Sharp underscored the non-sectarian nature of the group, the title of Chair seems to have had little to do with who actually conducted the meetings. Clarkson says Sharp was so modest he 'never was once seated as the chairman', often waiting to enter the meeting room last so as not to be called on to preside. Joseph Woods later privately questioned Sharp's efficacy, although never his sincerity. 'My pious, benevolent, Friend Granville Sharpe is a very well meaning man ...', Woods confided to Matthews years later, 'but his manner of writing is excessively prolix, and his Arguments seldom conclusive or satisfactory'.[12]

In his *Thoughts*, Woods, like Sharp, had first argued against both slavery and the slave trade, but Woods quickly accepted the Committee's decision to focus on the trade alone. He took pains to explain to Matthews in almost the same words used by Clarkson that

> The Trade is carried on by merchants in this Country for the interdiction of which this legislature is certainly competent. The Emancipation of Slaves already in the plantations must, if it ever takes place, be a work of gradual and slow consummation and possibly cannot originate here without interfering with the legislative Rights of the Colonies.[13]

Woods was a moderate abolitionist, not an emancipationist like Granville Sharp or a religious radical like John Woolman. As a man of business, Woods understood slavery and the slave trade in commercial and political terms as well as human terms. It made sense to him to separate slavery and the slave trade, and he was instrumental in defending that distinction.

As David Eltis, Seymour Drescher and other historians have made clear, the British slave trade was reaching its peak years in the 1780s.[14] It was not the profitability of the slave trade that was in question but, as Woods had argued earlier in his *Thoughts*, the moral limits of British commerce. By separating slavery and the slave trade, the slave trade could be viewed as a diseased branch of British commerce, and it was not necessary to deal with the issue of the rights of slaves, just as Granville Sharp feared.

Having defined its purpose, the London Abolition Committee directed James Phillips to draw up 'a circular letter to be forwarded to the Country giving some Account of the Proceedings of the Committee' and to print 250 copies. The members then began making a list of potential supporters throughout the country, 'qualified on account of their judgment and the weight of their character to take an useful part'. When the list was complete, Samuel Hoare, Joseph Woods and James Phillips were directed to revise the circular letter and distribute 5,000 copies of a summary view of evidence prepared by Clarkson. The initial list numbered 116 names; 43 can be positively identified as Quakers. Thomas Clarkson said that nine-tenths of them were Friends.[15]

While Quaker members distributed letters, Thomas Clarkson was dispatched to Bristol, Liverpool, and Lancaster to gather evidence and support. Clarkson's decision to devote his life to abolition meant that he, in effect, worked for the Committee. The Committee directed Clarkson 'to communicate an account of his Progress by Letter to Treasurer Samuel Hoare and draw on the treasurer for the money necessary for his expenses'.[16]

Hoare soon found it necessary to rein in what the Committee evidently saw as excess enthusiasm and spending on the part of young Clarkson. 'I hope the zeal and animation with which thou hast taken up the cause will be accompanied with temper and moderation', Hoare wrote in a letter to Clarkson in August 1787. 'Although we have hitherto procured a liberal support, it may not continue.'[17]

The Committee had indeed received liberal and wide-ranging support. When the group first announced that Hoare would accept subscriptions, he received more than £136 in the first two days. Money and words of support came from religious leaders as diverse as Methodist John Wesley, the Fellows of Jesus College, Cambridge, General Baptists, and Dr Henry Bathurst then at Oxford and later Bishop of Norwich. Reformers like Major John Cartwright and Capel Lofft volunteered their services. Two Members of Parliament, William Smith and Joshua Grigby, voiced their approval. 'Several gentlemen' met to form a local committee in Manchester. The London Committee was quickly reaching beyond Quaker circles to make abolitionism, as Seymour Drescher says, 'a coalition of the whole range of philosophical and religious discourse'.[18]

Joseph Woods, George Harrison and James Phillips helped the Committee connect with abolitionists in other countries. The London Committee soon learned that 'Societies are established at Philadelphia and

New York for the Abolition of Slavery'. Woods, Harrison, and two others were then asked 'to prepare a letter ... and to request they will from Time to Time favour them with such information on the Subject as they may think necessary'.

A few weeks later, James Phillips brought in a letter that he had received from Brissot de Warville in France offering his assistance. Phillips, Woods and another member were directed to reply. They suggested to Brissot that he consider establishing an abolition committee in his country.[19]

The London Committee soon began adding new members. Josiah Wedgwood was among the first. Wedgwood was then establishing himself in the manufacture of classic-style pottery priced to appeal to 'the middling class of people'. Neil McKendrick argues that the pioneering techniques in advertising and retailing developed by Wedgwood made him a key figure in what McKendrick terms the 'consumer revolution' of late eighteenth-century England.[20] Wedgwood was closely associated with Quaker entrepreneur Richard Reynolds, the friend of James Phillips and George Harrison. In 1785, Reynolds and Wedgwood helped found the United Chamber of Manufacturers of Great Britain.[21]

Wedgwood was involved in financial transactions with James Phillips, perhaps through Reynolds or the Chamber of Manufacturers. In 1785, Phillips evidently chastised Wedgwood regarding his handling of some money. McKendrick says Wedgwood's rate of bad debts was 75 per cent during this period. Wedgwood wrote a conciliatory letter to Phillips concerning 'pecuniary considerations'. Referring to himself in the third person, Wedgwood wrote, 'he is willing to make up what he has lent 200£ or 300£ if necessary'. Wedgwood closed by saying 'Mr. Wedgwood begs Mr. Phillips to make his respectful compliments to his Friends ... and leaves his best wishes for the prosperity of the Chamber.'[22]

In autumn 1787, Josiah Wedgwood began producing a medallion for the London Abolition Committee. The medallion was based on a seal designed by an eight-man subcommittee which included Woods, Hoare, Phillips and Harrison. Joseph Woods, reporting on behalf of the subcommittee, described a design with a kneeling and enchained African male 'in a supplicating Posture'. The medallion rendered on Wedgwood's distinctive jasperware background featured a cameo silhouette of a kneeling African, asking, 'Am I Not A Man and A Brother?'[23]

According to Clarkson, the Wedgwood cameo sold well, quickly appearing on snuff boxes, necklaces, rings, cufflinks and hairpins. John Brewer points to Wedgwood as an example of how printers and potters were teaming up with reformers to develop markets for new products. In addition to Wedgwood's cameo, the design was printed on paper and circulated widely.[24] Seymour Drescher observes how the abolitionists 'used commercial techniques ... to rivet public attention'.[25]

The seal designed by Woods, Phillips, Harrison, Hoare and other members of the Committee was thus becoming a public icon for the anti-slave trade movement. But it was an icon symbolizing male experience and showing the African as a kneeling supplicant rather than an equal. As Linda Colley observes in *Britons: Forging the Nation, 1707–1837*, the African man on Wedgwood's medal is portrayed 'from the safe position of his knees'.[26]

Samuel Hoare, meanwhile, was serving as a Committee contact for Clarkson, Wilberforce, and others. In October 1787, Clarkson wrote to Hoare about his travels through the west of England. Two weeks later, Hoare reported 'he has received a letter from William Wilberforce Esquire requesting Information as Speedily as possible relative to the Slave Trade'. Hoare, Sharp, and another Anglican member were designated 'a Committee to confer from time to time' with Wilberforce. In December 1787, Hoare and Joseph Woods were two of a three-member committee of correspondence appointed to answer letters between meetings.[27]

As Treasurer, Hoare handled the Committee's financial accounts, entailing significant amounts of money. In November, he reported receiving more than £400 in subscriptions. By January 1788, the total was more than £1,367. Hoare paid Clarkson, by then at home in Wisbech, for his travels, adding £60 'for sundry articles not included in the account of his Expenses'. At the same time, Hoare paid James Phillips £100 for 2,000 copies of a list of subscribers.[28]

The London Abolition Committee was in close touch with abolitionist activities in Manchester, receiving letters from Thomas Walker and Thomas Cooper on 11 and 18 December 1787 and 1 January 1788. In *The Culture of English Antislavery*, David Turley says that, on 27 December 1787, an anti-slave trade committee was established in Manchester with a Secretary and 31 members, including Thomas Walker and Thomas Cooper. Turley sees Manchester as an example of the 'culture of reform' and describes Walker as 'a latitudinarian Anglican and radical manufacturer' and Thomas Cooper as a political radical who wanted to include women in government.[29]

In his letter to London of early January 1788, Walker reported that 'they had passed a Resolution expressive of their approbation of the views of the London Committee'. Walker also sent 100 guineas from the Committee in Manchester. The London Committee received another 100 guineas from a similar group in Birmingham at about the same time.[30]

On 15 January 1788, the Committee issued its first public report announcing it was 'earnestly requesting ... the assistance of every individual in impressing on the minds of our legislatures the necessity of entering into a serious investigation' of the slave trade. Petitions were to be the means of impressing the minds of the legislators.[31]

Petitioning on behalf of the abolition of the slave trade was a tactic used by the British Quaker organization five years earlier in 1783. On 16 June 1783, the Meeting for Sufferings Parliamentary Committee, which monitored legislation affecting Quakers, discovered that the Commons was considering a Bill forbidding the employees of the African Company from privately engaging in the trade. The London Yearly Meeting was then in session and drew up a petition asking that the proposed restriction be extended to include all persons. The petition was signed by 273 members of the Yearly Meeting and read by Sir Cecil Wray, Member for Westminster. Lord North, speaking for the government, praised Quakers as 'mild and humane' but tabled the petition, saying it would be impossible to abolish the slave trade.[32]

Seymour Drescher questions the importance of this early Quaker petition and argues, instead, that anti-slave trade petitioning originated in Manchester. Yet Drescher acknowledges the Society for Constitutional Information had adopted an abolitionist petition in 1783 'in the wake of the Quaker initiative'. In Manchester, Thomas Walker was an early leader of both the Society for Constitutional Information and a founder of the Manchester Abolition Committee. Since Walker and his ally, Thomas Cooper, were in frequent contact with the London Abolition Committee, which was dominated by Friends, there seems to be a possibility that the Quaker example of 1783 might have had some at least indirect influence on the decision to petition in Manchester.[33]

While the Quaker members of London Abolition Committee were certainly familiar with the petition of 1783 and might have helped influence the Committee's decision in 1788, Thomas Clarkson was also playing a role in organizing petitions from the country in the winter of 1787–88. Clarkson had written to Samuel Hoare from Liverpool in October 1787, reporting that

> In consequence of his personal Application to Gentlemen of Influence in Bridwater, Monmouth, Bristol, Gloucester, Worcester, Shrewsbury, and Chester, there is Reason to expect that Petitions to Parliament may be procured when the Committee gives Information for the Proper Time.

Clarkson himself credited the London Committee with the increasing public support for abolition then beginning to take form in the petitioning campaign. He wrote that the London Committee 'had been both vigilant and industrious' while he was travelling through the country in late 1787. 'They were, in short,' wrote Clarkson, 'the persons, who had been the means of raising the public spirit, which I had observed first at Manchester, and afterwards as I journeyed on.'[34]

The Association Movement had also recently used petitions to press for reform and, in January 1788, Samuel Hoare was directed to write to Christopher Wyvill, the leader of the Association Movement, for help in obtaining a petition from Yorkshire. Other Committee members were 'desired to make application to Glasgow to procure a Petition to Parliament from thence'. Still others were to send letters and reports to the mayors of corporations.[35]

Whatever the origins of the decision to petition Parliament, the London Abolition Committee understood the importance of direct contact with Parliamentary Members. In January 1788 the Committee added two Members of Parliament to their ranks. One was James Martin, Member for Tewkesbury. Martin was independent, conscientious, and reform-minded but, according to Namier and Brook, 'not always well heard'. The other was William Morton Pitt, Member for Poole and cousin of the Prime Minister.[36]

Meanwhile, James Phillips was working with Thomas Clarkson, George Harrison, and other Committee members to prepare and publish more abolition tracts. In late 1787 and early 1788, Phillips was preparing a second edition of Thomas Clarkson's *Essay on the Slavery and Commerce of the Human Species*. In January 1788, Clarkson's brother John promised Phillips, 'You will receive the whole of the alterations by Tuesday's Coach', adding 'My Brother sent you a Turkey by the last coach'.[37] By the spring of 1788, the second edition was printed, and Phillips later sent Clarkson £34 for his share of the sales.[38] At the same time, George Harrison was working with William Dillwyn to correct an edition of a *History and Account of Guinea* by Anthony Benezet so that Phillips could publish 1,500 copies of it.[39]

More publications were needed, because, as Dillwyn said, 'We have so few Tracts to supply the frequent Demand for Information on the Subject'.[40] A correspondent in the country agreed, pointing out the importance of information in raising subscriptions. In February 1788, James Backhouse of York wrote to James Phillips with a list of subscriptions, mostly in guineas, along with orders for new publications. 'People are yet so unacquainted with the subject, hinders the subscription ...', Backhouse noted tersely. 'But many ... highly approve', he continued, 'advocates gain ground fast.'[41]

By then, West Country residents were beginning to write to Phillips with petitions and contributions. 'Room is given to expect there will be [petitions] from Dorchester, Bridport, Lime and Shaftesbury, and I hope from Milbournport', Morris Birkbeck reported. Birkbeck contributed one guinea and estimated he had spent another in travel around the county.[42]

Charles Collins sent a guinea from Swansea, adding, 'Mr. Padley and myself determined at length to have the above Petitions drawn up and sent round the Town to be signed which it has been by most of the principal Inhabitants, and I have by this post sent it up to Sir Herbert Mackworth to be presented.'[43] George C. Fox sent subscriptions from Falmouth to his 'Dear Cousin' James with information that a petition had been signed 'by creditable Tradesmen and Inhabitants', and that their Member of Parliament was supportive.[44]

In the following weeks, 10,000 people signed an anti-slave trade petition in Manchester. Moreover, there was widespread abolition activity throughout the north of England.[45] Abolition activities were certainly organized independently of the London Committee in places throughout Great Britain. Yet, by concentrating on source materials from the north of England, historians like E.M. Hunt, Seymour Drescher, and David Turley underestimate the Quaker example and the centralizing role of the London Abolition Committee.[46]

From London, in January 1788, Joseph Woods wrote to William Matthews that 'Our endeavours respecting the Slave Trade meet hitherto with the Encouragement we wished, and indeed with more than we expected'. Woods credited the success to 'The Humanity of the People of this Country' which he compared 'to Tinder which has immediately caught fire from the spark of Information which has been struck upon it'. He added with caution, 'I hope this Simile will not be ominous as to Duration'. Woods enclosed anti-slave trade tracts in his correspondence, asking Matthews to forward them to others.[47]

At the same time, Richard Reynolds, acting independently of the Committee, wrote to the reformer and educator Sarah Trimmer, suggesting women become involved in the abolition effort, although not by petitioning. 'It was not my idea that a petition to Parliament should even be signed, much less be presented, by women', Reynolds explained in a letter to Trimmer in February 1788.

Reynolds went on to elaborate:

> The most I could desire or expect was, that they would publicly and in print declare their abhorrence of the inhuman traffic, and their wish that the measures pursuing for the abolition of it might be successful, confirmed by a small subscription annexed to their names ....

He also suggested that women might add 'their private and personal influence and interest with those who are most capable of giving effect to the benevolent attempt, whether of the Nobility, Clergy, or Members of Parliament'. Yet, after hearing from Trimmer, Reynolds seemed to retract his suggestions. 'Perhaps even this was more than I should have expected: or, if I had known much of the world should have proposed', he wrote in reply to a letter from her.[48]

A few months after the exchange between Richard Reynolds and Sarah Trimmer, Molly Morris Knowles, the talented widow of Thomas Knowles and friend of James Phillips and Joseph Woods, penned the following 'Inscription for a Tobacco Box':

> Tho' various tints the human face adorn/ To glorious liberty mankind are born;/ O, May the hand which rais'd this fav'rite weed/ Be los'd in mercy and the slave be freed.[49]

Reynolds' suggestions about involving women are in sharp contrast to the attitude to women expressed by Joseph Woods. In his private correspondence with Matthews, Woods mocked some Quaker women ministers. Woods wrote to Matthews, 'I think also that our Female Brethren (as an Irish Friend once called them) to be highly captivated with the musical cadence of their own silver tones.'

Woods also chaffed at the establishment of a separate Yearly Meeting for women Friends in 1784. Woods complained to Matthews about the presence of some American Quakers in the London Yearly Meeting of 1784. 'With the assistance of these wise men and women from the West, Esther Tuke has been enabled to establish her Favourite Point of a Women's Yearly Meeting', Woods wrote.[50]

Women were not involved in the public campaign against the slave trade conducted by the London Abolition Committee although women did participate in Manchester and Newcastle.[51] The minute books of the London Committee record no public correspondence or official action by women. Yet, perhaps other women, like Molly Knowles, did exercise private and personal influence on behalf of abolition as Richard Reynolds had suggested.

As Seymour Drescher recognized, abolition developed rapidly as a national movement in 1787–88 because 'Potential ideological differences were muted'.[52] The variety of letters received by the London Committee indicates that abolition was attracting support from a wide range of men of diverse religious and political backgrounds. The rapid increase of support for abolition suggests a dynamic interaction between the Committee in London and advocates in the country, each building on the other. The Quaker-dominated London Committee was providing organization and focus, while country abolitionists were providing a broad base of religious, socio-economic and geographic support.

In the first week of February 1788, 15 anti-slave trade petitions were presented to Commons. As David Turley says:

> since the 1788 petitions were not part of a movement pursuing significant change in the political system or attacking the *range* of government policy, the application of humanitarian and general interest criteria to a question of trade probably appeared relatively innocuous to those who were not directly involved.[53]

On 11 February a Royal Order in Council was issued, directing the Privy Council to investigate the trade. On 16 February, Samuel Hoare, James Phillips and three other Committee members were assigned to work with Clarkson to begin arranging evidence to be presented to the Privy Council. During March and early April, 88 more petitions were presented to the Commons.[54]

By 8 April, 'There was an anxious expectation' among members of the London Abolition Committee 'that some notice should be taken in the lower house of the numerous petitions which had been presented there'. Joseph Woods and two others were deputed to write to Wilberforce. On 22 April, Samuel Hoare informed the Committee that Wilberforce was gravely ill and could not receive any correspondence about the slave trade.[55]

Not long afterwards, however, Granville Sharp reported he had met William Pitt, the Prime Minister, 'who assured him that his heart was with us, and that he considered himself pledged to Mr. Wilberforce'. On 29 April, William Morton Pitt notified the Committee that the Prime Minister would introduce a resolution committing the House early in the next session to consider the slave trade. A week later, Samuel Hoare told the Committee that 'Mr. William Morton Pitt had been with him this morning' and 'the Right Honorable William Pitt' would bring forward his resolution in three days.[55]

The Committee immediately appointed an eight-person delegation including Thomas Clarkson, Major John Cartwright and, from the Manchester Committee, Thomas Walker and Thomas Cooper to wait on 'leading Members of Parliament'. Only two Quakers were appointed to the Parliamentary subcommittee; none of the four Quaker veterans was included.[57]

As part of his work on the subcommittee, Thomas Clarkson called on Charles James Fox. According to Clarkson, Fox

> paused for a little while, as if in the act of deliberation; then he assured us unequivocally, and in language which could not be misunderstood, that he would support the object of the Committee to its fullest extent.[58]

On 9 May 1788, William Pitt called for the titles of the petitions favouring abolition to be read in the Commons. The slave trade, he observed, was a subject which 'from the great number and variety of petitions presented … had engaged the public interest … and consequently deserved the most serious notice' of the House. Pitt 'studiously avoided' expressing his own opinion. Fox and Edmund Burke, among others, spoke in favour of abolition. The two Members for Liverpool and Sir William Young, the leading advocate of the West Indian Interest, insisted that consideration of the slave trade would be to their advantage. Pitt's resolution was passed unanimously, and the House of Commons stood committed to considering the slave trade early in the next session.[59]

The London Abolition Committee immediately ordered 10,000 copies of the discussion in the Commons to be printed 'by Woodfall with no marks of origin' and 'without stamps or any articles of Intelligence'. Then, each man on the Committee was requested 'to bring ... lists of the names of Members of Parliament whom they believed to be disposed to promote an Abolition of the Slave Trade'.[60]

James Phillips continued to acquire, print, and sell anti-slave trade publications. He contracted with writers such as Alexander Falconbridge for new manuscripts.[61] In April, Phillips sent a complete supply of 12 abolitionist publications, including Joseph Woods' *Thoughts*, to Alexander Alison at the Excise Office in Edinburgh.[62] On 20 May 1788, Phillips was paid £400 for his work and asked to 'treat with' another author about the price of a new manuscript. On 27 May, the Committee ordered Phillips to print 3,000 copies of a new tract by James Ramsay and 2,000 copies of a new essay by Clarkson on the inexpediency of the slave trade, agreeing 'to take the same at 2s. each in Boards'.[63]

The London Abolition Committee, meanwhile, was translating selected anti-slave trade essays into French, Spanish, Portuguese, Dutch and Danish. Phillips sent books to the Marquis de la Fayette. Thomas Walker later asked Phillips to send publications to Dr Benjamin Sigismund Frossard, a Huguenot pastor and abolitionist in Lyons.[64] In March, Phillips sent a Wedgwood cameo along with books to Benjamin Franklin in Philadelphia. In June, the Committee received a letter from Dr Franklin.[65] Meanwhile, other Committee members were arranging to send books to the King of Sweden.[66]

On 10 June 1788, the London Abolition Committee met in a well-attended meeting which included Thomas Walker of Manchester. Thomas Clarkson proposed 'First that some Person or Persons be sent into the different Counties ... whose first object should be to Institute Committees ... upon the plan of that of Nottingham'. The person or persons chosen should urge each committee 'to convince the People of the Evil of the Slave Trade, to procure fresh Subscriptions and Petitions' and to find witnesses knowledgeable about Africa or the West Indies who could testify before the Privy Council. Clarkson then 'offered his services to undertake the business'. The Committee answered they would 'chearfully avail themselves of his offer'.[67]

Clarkson returned with a more detailed plan the following week, and George Harrison, Major John Cartwright and another member were appointed as a subcommittee to advise him. Cartwright, a friend of Granville Sharp, had already 'offered his own services ... for the County of

Nottingham'. Cartwright had been active in the Association Movement, serving as Chairman of the Constituency Committee of Nottingham.[68]

At the same time, James Phillips was directed to send the Committee's publications to booksellers in London and Westminster. Thomas Walker suggested including booksellers in Edinburgh. The next week the Committee sent books to the Sheriffs and Grand Juries of each county.[69]

On 1 July, the Committee began making plans to hold a general meeting of the advocates of abolition. The meeting was scheduled for 7 August at 6:00 p.m. at Paul's Head Tavern in Cateaton Street. Joseph Woods, James Phillips and George Harrison were three of a five-member subcommittee appointed to develop rules for a society and a list of suitable persons to serve as officers.[70]

On 15 July, Wilberforce wrote a letter to Samuel Hoare with 'many forcible arguments' against holding the general meeting. As a result, 'Many doubts respecting the expediency' of the meeting rose in the minds of several members. The Committee 'suspended for the present' preparations for the general meeting. At the same time, the Committee asked Clarkson, who was then preparing to set out on his travels, to 'pay regard to the advice contained in Mr. Wilberforce's letter … to avoid giving any possible occasion of offense to the legislature by forced or unnecessary Associations'. Phillips, Harrison, Hoare and Woods were appointed to a nine-member subcommittee to advise Clarkson 'during his … journey'.[71]

Meanwhile, Sir William Dolben, Member for the University of Oxford, evidently acting on his own, secured a Bill in the Commons to regulate the slave trade while it was being investigated by the Privy Council. Joseph Woods did not support Dolben's bill, 'fearing lest a *regulation* of the Trade might be construed into acknowledgement of the Principle that the Trade was in itself just but had been abused'.[72]

The House of Lords, too, disliked the Bill, but not for the same reason. The Lords considered the Bill an interference with property and amended it almost beyond recognition.[73] One ally in the country saw the Lords' response to Dolben's Bill as a bad omen. In July, Thomas Bland wrote to James Phillips from Norwich requesting anti-slave trade publications but saying

> Some here (I am afraid many) … appear considerably discouraged, if not cooled in their zeal by what has lately passed in the House of Peers and say nothing beyond a *Regulation* is now to be looked for.[74]

Members of the London Abolition Committee expressed no such apprehensions. On 12 August 1788 the Committee issued a second public report, declaring 'The Voice of Humanity calls loudly for the extinction' of the slave trade. Like Woods, the Committee called for abolition, and not merely the regulation, of the slave trade. In almost the exact words used by

Woods, the report feared 'mere regulation by authority of Parliament will … be construed into an approbation of the Principle'.

Yet the report also included the arguments for expediency based on the arguments of Adam Smith – arguments which had been less favoured by Woods. The report trusted that Members of Parliament would see how abolition combined economic benefit and humanitarianism. 'It is no less the interest of this Nation than it is becoming the spirit of Humanity which distinguishes its Character to comply with the Wishes of the People and prohibit the Trade', the report declared. The Committee directed James Phillips to publish 3,000 copies of the report, sending one to each contributor within reach of the Penny Post and to every newspaper publisher in England.[75]

For Joseph Woods, abolition was a moral imperative. He wrote to Matthews that 'On the whole our safest ground is the broad foundation of Justice and Morals … though we meet with great success in proving many points of the Policy'. For Woods the crucial point was to define the acceptable limits of the market economy. Evidently speaking for the Committee, he continued, ' … if it be held as a maxim that nothing of Interest Commercial, Colonial or political, is to be risked, for the prospect of probable advantages, we shall not have made the impression we wish'.[76]

Looking back on the first year of abolition activities, Thomas Clarkson later calculated that 'the Committee held 51 meetings, generally from 6:00 in the evening to about 11:00 at night' and printed and distributed '26,526 reports and accounts of debates, and 51,432 books and pamphlets'. When Woods and Harrison examined the Committee's first year accounts, they found that £2,760 had been received and £2,131 had been spent, including over £1,000 for printing, £618 for collecting evidence, and £100 for postage and carriage.[77]

Thomas Clarkson was especially pleased with the high level of support that the London Abolition Committee had received from the Established Church. 'Even bishops deigned to address an obscure Committee consisting principally of Quakers …', he recorded.[78] The volume of activity and the level of public response in 1787–88 indicates the London Abolition Committee played a key role in what James Walvin described as 'the transformation of abolition from a minority … sentiment into an organized and public debate'.[79]

In August 1788, Joseph Woods wrote to his friend Dr Parke at the Library Company in Philadelphia. 'The voice of the People and the wish of the Minister seem to be for the abolition of the Slave Trade (we do not meddle with the Slavery already established)', he reported. But Woods saw trouble ahead: 'the opposition of Interest … will throw in our way all possible obstacles'.[80]

NOTES

1. Robert I. and Samuel Wilberforce, *Life of William Wilberforce* (Philadelphia, PA: Henry Perkins, 1839), pp. 62–4.
2. Thomas Clarkson, *An Essay on the Slavery and Commerce of the Human Species, Particularly the African, Translated from the Latin Dissertation, which was honoured with the First Prize in the University of Cambridge for the Year 1785, With Additions* (London: Printed By James Phillips, George Yard, Lombard Street, and sold by T. Cadell in the Strand and James Phillips, 1786).
3. Clarkson, *History*, Vol. 1, pp. 212–30, 231–54; Robert and Samuel Wilberforce, *The Life of William Wilberforce*, pp. 62–4.
4. Clarkson, *History*, Vol. 1, pp. 231–2. James Walvin, *England, Slaves and Freedom, 1776–1838*, pp. 102, 105.
5. London, British Library Dept. of MSS, Additional MSS 21,254–21,256, Minute Books of the London Abolition Committee, 3 vols, Vol. 1, 21,254, 22 May 1787, includes a letter from Richard Phillips indicating that the minute books were in Clarkson's possession in 1840. Clarkson made some notations in the minute books and probably used them to write his own *History* (Clarkson, *History*, Vol. 1, pp. 205–30).
6. Brewer, *Consumer Society*, p. 224.
7. Additional MSS 21,254, 22 May–17 July 1787.
8. Thomas Clarkson, *History of the Rise, Progress, and Accomplishment of the Abolition of the British Slave Trade*, Vol. 1, pp. 282–9.
9. Thompson/Clarkson MSS, Vol. I, p. 255, Memorandum of Granville Sharp, 17 April 1797.
10. S. and H. Hoare, *Memoirs*, p. 39.
11. Roger Anstey, *The Atlantic Slave Trade and British Abolition 1769–1810* (Atlantic Highlands, NJ: Humanities Press, 1975), p. 247.
12. Additional MSS 21,254, 4 September 1787, Sharp was named Chair of the Committee. Clarkson, *History*, Vol. 1, pp. 449–50. Matthews MSS, 5 March 1810, gives Woods' assessment of Sharp.
13. Matthews MSS, 27 March 1788.
14. Drescher, *Econocide*. Eltis, *Economic Growth and the Ending of the Transatlantic Slave Trade*.
15. Additional MSS 21,254, 20 July 1784. Clarkson, *History*, Vol. 1, pp. 444–5.
16. Ibid., 12 June 1784.
17. Ibid., 7 August 1787.
18. Additional MSS 21,254. Drescher, *Capitalism and Anti-Slavery*, p. 123.
19. Additional MSS 21,254, 5 July and 27 August 1787.
20. Ibid., 27 August 1787. McKendrick, *Consumer Society*, pp. 126–31. In Judith Jennings, 'Joseph Woods, Merchant and Philosopher, and the Making of the British Anti-Slave Trade Ethic', *Slavery and Abolition* (December 1993), Wedgwood is mistakenly identified as a Quaker. He was not. Thanks to Malcolm Thomas of the Library of the Society of Friends for correcting this error.
21. Rathbone, *Letters*, p. 50.
22. Thompson/Clarkson MSS, Vol. 1, p. 309, Mr Wedgwood to Mr Phillips, 1785. McKendrick, *Consumer Society*, pp. 126–31.
23. Additional MSS 21,254, 16 October 1787. Joseph Woods reported for a subcommittee appointed to design a seal for the Committee. The Committee approved the design and desired the subcommittee to have it well engraved.
24. Clarkson, *History*, Vol. 1, pp. 450–51. Brewer, *Consumer Society*, p. 244. Thompson/Clarkson MSS, Vol. II, p. 34 is an example of the seal printed on paper.
25. Drescher, *Capitalism and Slavery*, p. 73.
26. Linda Colley, *Britons: Forging the Nation, 1707–1837*, p. 355.
27. Additional MSS 21,254, 30 October, 18 December 1787.
28. Ibid., November 1787 – January 1788.
29. Ibid., 11, 18 December 1787 and 1 January 1788, for letters received by the London Committee from Walker and Cooper. D. Turley, *The Culture of English Antislavery*,

pp. 25, 115–39, 160. For Walker, see E.C.P. Thompson, *The Making of the English Working Class* (London: Penguin Books, 1981), p. 57, and Edward Royle and James Walvin, *English Radicals and Reformers*, pp. 36, 45–8, 60.

30. Additional MSS 21,254, 1 January 1788.
31. Ibid., 15, 22 January 1788.
32. Judith Jennings, 'The Campaign for the Abolition of the British Slave Trade: The Quaker Contribution', unpublished dissertation, University of Kentucky, 1975.
33. Drescher, *Capitalism and Slavery*, pp. 67–73, 164.
34. Additional MSS 21,254, 16 October 1787. Clarkson, *History*, Vol. 1, p. 441.
35. Additional MSS 21,254, 22 January 1788.
36. Ibid. James Martin (1738–1810) was Member for Tewkesbury from 1776 to 1807. William Morton Pitt (1754–1836) was Member for Poole from 1780 to 1790 and Member for Dorset from 1790 to 1821. John Brooke and Sir Lewis Namier, *The House of Commons, 1754–1790* (New York: Oxford University Press, 1964).
37. Thompson/Clarkson MSS, Vol. II, p. 157, John Clarkson to James Phillips, 27 January 1788.
38. Thomas Clarkson, *An Essay on the Slavery and Commerce of the Human Species, Particularly the African ... Revised and Considerably Enlarged*, 2nd edn (London: Printed and sold by James Phillips, 1788). Thompson/Clarkson MSS, Vol. III, p. 1, Receipt from Thomas Clarkson to James Phillips, 25 May 1788.
39. Thompson/Clarkson MSS, Vol. II, p. 121, William Dillwyn to James Phillips, 16 January 1788.
40. Ibid.
41. Gibson MSS, Vol. I, p. 12, James Backhouse, York, to James Phillips, 13 February 1788.
42. Thompson/Clarkson MSS, Vol. II, p. 91, Morris Birkbeck to James Phillips, 16 February 1788.
43. Ibid., p. 101, Charles Collins to James Phillips, 21 February 1788.
44. Ibid., p. 165, George C. Fox, Falmouth, to James Phillips, 22 February 1788.
45. E.M. Hunt, 'The North of England Agitation For the Abolition of the Slave Trade', unpublished Master's thesis, University of Manchester, 1959.
46. Drescher, *Capitalism and Slavery*, pp. 67–73. Turley, *The Culture of English Antislavery*, pp. 115–39.
47. Matthews MSS, 28 January 1788.
48. Rathbone, *Letters*, pp. 162–4.
49. Gibson MSS, Vol. I, p. 193, 13 June 1788.
50. Matthews MSS, 25 March 1775. Matthews MSS, 14 June 1784.
51. Clare Midgley, *Women Against Slavery: The British Campaigns, 1780–1870* (London: Routledge, 1992).
52. Drescher, *Capitalism and Anti-Slavery*, p. 123.
53. D. Turley, *Culture of English Antislavery*, pp. 64–5.
54. See Report of the Privy Council Committee, *Journals of the House of Commons*, Vol. 44, (May 1789); Additional MSS, 21,254, 16 February 1788. Cobbett, *Parliamentary History*, Vol. XXVII, p. 506.
55. Additional MSS 21,255, 8, 22 April 1788.
56. Ibid., 8, 22, 29 April 1788. Clarkson, *History*, Vol. I, p. 500.
57. Additional MSS 21,255, 6 May 1788. Only two of the eight subcommittee members were Quakers. The two Quaker members were Robert Barclay and John Vickris Taylor.
58. Clarkson, *History*, Vol. 1, p. 503.
59. Cobbett, *Parliamentary History*, Vol. XXVII, pp. 495–506. *Journals of the House of Commons*, Vol. 44 (May 1789).
60. Additional MSS 21,255, 13 May–3 June 1788.
61. Thompson/Clarkson MSS, Vol II, p. 119. Alexander Falconbridge 'Received of James Phillips 7th Feb 1788 £77 10/- for 3,000 Accounts of Slave Trade'.
62. Thompson/Clarkson MSS, Vol. II, p. 123, Alexander Alison, Edinburgh, to James Phillips, 21 April 1788.
63. Additional MSS 21,255, 20 and 27 May 1788.
64. Additional MSS 21,254, 12 February 1788; 21,255, 5 March and 17, 24 June 1788.

65. Yale University Library, 'Papers of Benjamin Franklin', #11390, James Phillips to Benjamin Franklin, London, 1 March 1788. Additional MSS, 21,255, 24 June 1788, the Committee recorded receiving a letter from Dr Franklin.
66. Additional MSS 21,255, 17, 24 June 1788.
67. Ibid., 10 June 1788.
68. Ibid., 17 June 1788. For Cartwright's earlier offer see Additional MSS 21,254, 30 October 1787. Clarkson, *History*, Vol. I, p. 453. For Cartwright's early reform activities see Caroline Robbins, *Eighteenth Century Commonwealthmen* (Cambridge, MA: Harvard University Press, 1961), pp. 369–70. Ian Christie, *Wilkes, Wyvill and Reform* (London: Macmillan, 1962).
69. Additional MSS 21,255, 17 and 24 June 1788.
70. Ibid., 1 July 1788.
71. Ibid., 15 July 1788.
72. Matthews MSS, 27 March 1788, 6 June 1788.
73. *Journals of the House of Commons*, Vol. 43, 21 May – 4 July 1788.
74. Gibson MSS, Vol. V, p. 45, Thomas Bland of Norwich to James Phillips, July 1788.
75. Additional MSS 21,255, 12 and 26 August 1788.
76. Matthews MSS, 27 March 1788.
77. Clarkson, *History*, Vol. I, pp. 570–72. Additional MSS 21,255, 12 August 1788.
78. Clarkson, *History*, Vol. I, pp. 570–72.
79. Walvin, *England, Slaves and Freedom*, p. 104.
80. Library Company of Philadelphia, Records, 9 August 1788.

4

Investigations, Examinations, Publications, 1788–91

Travelling through the country again in the summer of 1788, Clarkson began to question his plan to visit every county. He wrote to Hoare, Harrison and the other Committee members appointed to advise him about 'the considerable time it would take up to prosecute the business as proposed … added to the consideration of the Expence that must necessarily be incurred'. Clarkson proposed writing letters to potential proponents instead. The Committee agreed and, in August, Clarkson was directed 'to Bristol, Portsmouth, Poole, Exeter, Plymouth, and Falmouth' to gather evidence for the Privy Council investigation.[1]

In London, Joseph Woods and other members of the Committee were cultivating the Committee's international contacts in North America and France. That summer, Woods brought in copies of Acts passed in Massachusetts and Rhode Island prohibiting the slave trade, and the Committee directed him to publish them in the *Morning Chronicle*. A week later, the Philadelphia Society sent a copy of similar legislation passed in Connecticut. At about the same time, the Committee requested a translation of a discourse delivered to the abolition society in Paris and received a progress report from the French organization.[2]

In November 1788, the Privy Council resumed its investigations into the slave trade. The Committee directed Clarkson to return to London, while James Phillips negotiated with anti-slave trade writer Reverend James Ramsay about abolition witnesses and strategies. 'Our Captain Smith by desire of the P. Council attends next Friday to give his Testimony', Ramsay wrote to Phillips on 1 November. 'As he comes up intirely on this business I think the Committee should make good his expenses.'[3]

Phillips was helping Ramsay edit a new anti-slave trade publication. Ramsay wrote to Phillips that 'I have castigated what offended your squeamish stomach and have added a number of new tidbits that I think you will relish'. Like Clarkson, Ramsay saw Phillips as a friend and collaborator. 'You may rub your wise forehead and determine as you please', he told Phillips in discussing whether or not the essay should be printed under a pseudonym, but, at the same time, Ramsay pressed for quick publication. 'I think you should in your Committee next Tuesday determine about the printing of it.' Ramsay went on to advise Phillips and the Committee to appeal publicly for funds. 'I must continue to ring in your ears the necessity of advertising for subscriptions. Whenever I talk of money, the answer is Why do you not advertise?' Public advertisement would be a new step for the Committee. Ramsay insisted: 'You can never get the public to engage but by adopting the universal mode, which is expected and is necessary.'[4]

In November 1788, the business of abolition, along with the rest of the business of the nation, was interrupted by the Regency Crisis provoked by the debilitating illness of the King. When the Privy Council suspended examinations on the slave trade as a result of the crisis, the Committee took Ramsay's advice.

On 11 November, Harrison, Woods and another member were appointed 'a subCommittee to prepare an Advertisement for fresh Subscriptions'. The next week the three reported that 'Expenses ... being ... greatly increased, it is now become expedient to solicit a more publick Assistance'. Accordingly, the Committee resolved 'to publish from time to time the state of their Funds, together with Subscriptions received'. The Secretary was 'directed to advertise once in every London paper and to continue the same once a week in *The Morning Chronicle* and *General Evening Post*'.[5]

By the end of December, the Committee had collected £400 from a wide variety of contributors, bringing the balance in hand to more than £1,000. A Baptist Church at Maze Pond, Southwark, for example, contributed one-half of its Sunday offering, a gift of over £11. These and other funds were used to pay for publications and travel expenses for witnesses testifying before the Privy Council. The Committee also received letters of support from Anglicans, Dissenters, Evangelicals, Methodists, and from strong local committees like the one in Manchester.[6]

With public interest growing, James Phillips had to negotiate quickly and pay premium costs for new anti-slave trade publications. In January 1789, Phillips wrote to the Reverend William Hughes of Ware for 100 copies of his 'Answer to Mr. Harris's Scriptural Researches on the Licitness of the Slave Trade' published the year before by Thomas Cadell. Hughes referred him to Cadell, saying he was sure that the bookseller would expect the usual profit.

Another writer, H. Dannett, Minister of St John's in Liverpool, was 'impatient' with Phillips for not publishing his essay quickly enough. At the same time, Phillips wrote to William Dickson, a former Secretary to the Governor of Barbados, to purchase his *Letter on Negroes* for £56 5s.[7]

Early in 1789, Phillips began printing a broadside developed by the Plymouth abolition committee showing a cross-section of a slave ship. But in so doing he incurred the ire of the local committee chair. William Elford, Chair of the Plymouth Committee and later Member of Parliament, at first did not care for Phillips' 'strictures on the plan of the slave's Deck published by us'. Elford later apologized to Phillips 'from one Gentleman to another'.[8]

Whatever the differences between Phillips and Elford, the cross-section of the slave ship proved to be an effective illustration of the overcrowded condition of slaves during transportation. Years later, Samuel Hoare's daughter remembered 'Horrible engravings of the interior of a slave ship were pinned against the walls of our dining room'.[9]

Phillips worked with Woods and Harrison to maintain strong connections with abolitionists in France. In October 1788, Woods brought in a translation of the discourse delivered to the abolition society in Paris which the Committee had requested earlier. The Committee inserted the translation in the *Morning Chronicle* and directed Woods and Phillips to contact French leaders Necker and Claviere. Not long after, Phillips brought in another French essay on slavery and the slave trade. Harrison, Woods and Phillips reviewed it but thought it was not 'adapted to the present stage of the Business in England'. In January 1789, Brissot de Warville visited the Committee in London.[10]

In February, although the Regency Crisis was still not over, the London Abolition Committee appointed Samuel Hoare and four others to visit Wilberforce to 'represent to him the necessity of bringing on the Business of the Slave Trade in the House of Commons early in the present session'. At the same time, the group suggested calling on 'Peers they may think proper to request their advice'.

On 3 March, 'The Gentlemen appointed to wait upon Mr. Wilberforce report … he perfectly concurred with the Committee'. The group also 'had above an hour's Conference with the Earl of Stanhope'. Stanhope expressed his warmest support and prepared a list of 21 Lords and Bishops whom they should visit.[11]

On 10 March 1789, the day the King's recovery was announced, the Committee directed Phillips, Woods and another member to write

> to the several Committees who are in Correspondence with this Committee and to such Persons as may have Influence with Members of Parliament to inform them that the business of the Slave Trade will soon be brought before the House of Commons and request that an early application may be made to the Members to desire their attention the Subject.

Meanwhile, Hoare, Phillips, Woods and Harrison worked with Clarkson to distribute the plan of the slave ship to all Members.[12]

On 23 March 1789, Wilberforce reminded the House of Commons of their resolution to consider the slave trade and announced that he would present a motion for discussion on 23 April. The next day, Samuel Hoare reported visiting Lord Hawke, the Earl of Derby and Charles James Fox, all of whom promised their support. Later, Hoare visited the Duke of Leeds, while other Committee members called on the remaining Peers on Stanhope's list.[13]

Fixing the date for consideration of abolition in the Commons, according to Clarkson, 'seemed to be the signal for the planters, merchants, and other interested persons to begin a furious opposition'. Hoare, Harrison and Woods helped the Committee keep abreast of new information and counter the charges of opponents. On 31 March, Hoare brought in a copy of a Bill regulating the slave trade in Grenada. On 6 April, Harrison, Woods and another member were directed to edit and publish reports from Jamaica.[14]

On 14 April, Hoare, Harrison and three others were delegated to consider resolutions recently passed by West Indian merchants 'and publish any observations they may think proper'. On 21 April, the subcommittee brought in a statement pointing out 'all considerations of the injustice and inhumanity of the Slave Trade are disregarded' by the West Indians. The statement argued that abolition would not result in the decline of the Sugar Colonies and that the slave trade injured British seamen and prevented legitimate commerce with Africa.[15]

On 25 April 1789, William Pitt laid the completed report based on the Privy Council investigations before the House of Commons. A new date of 12 May was set for consideration of the slave trade to give Members time to read the report. In the interval, the London Abolition Committee continued calling on selected members of the Lords and Commons, distributing the plan of the slave ship to all.[16]

On 12 May 1789, when Wilberforce opened the debate in the Commons, he began by saying, 'A society has been established for the abolition of this trade, in which Dissenters, Quakers, Churchmen – in which the most conscientious of all persuasions have all united ....' He ended by saying, 'Let not Parliament be the only body that is insensible to the principle of natural justice.' Wilberforce then presented, not a Bill to end the slave trade, but 12 propositions favouring abolition. Edmund Burke, William Pitt, and Charles James Fox spoke in favour of the propositions. Further discussion was then continued until 21 May.[17]

Meeting on 14 and 19 May, the London Abolition Committee gave a vote of thanks to Wilberforce and ordered 2,000 copies of the debate of 12 May to be printed by Woodfall. On 21 May, when Wilberforce moved consideration of his 12 propositions, opponents insisted that the Privy Council investigations were insufficient and that the Commons would have to conduct its own inquiry. Wilberforce protested but ended by withdrawing his motion. Hearings in the Commons began the next day but were not completed when the session ended on 23 June.[18]

While the Commons began examining evidence, James Phillips was collecting and publishing abolitionist materials as quickly as he could. According to Committee records, in May and June, he published 'Stanfield's poem entitled "A Guinea Voyage" and C.B. Wadstrom's "Observations on the Slave Trade"'. He paid John Jamieson, Minister to a Congregation of Seceders from the Scottish Church in Edinburgh, £5 for an anti-slavery poem, 'The Sorrows of Slavery'. In mid-June, Phillips received £400 'on his account'.[19]

In addition to acquiring and publishing tracts Phillips served as the London contact for Clarkson and other anti-slave trade writers. Keeping up with Clarkson was no easy task. In July 1789, John Coakley Lettsom, a leading Quaker physician, wrote Phillips an impatient letter concerning two letters that he had requested Clarkson to return. Hearing nothing from Clarkson, Lettsom wrote to Phillips, 'May I trouble thee to inform me, where I can apply, to meet with him. I who am obliged to snatch time, by stealth.'[20] Even while Phillips was on holiday in Dover, he was communicating with abolitionist writers like Henry Hew Dalrymple, who had served in the West Indies.[21]

A manuscript poem attributed to Phillips written about this time shows his good humour and his willingness to mock both fellow Quakers and royal dignity. 'Thy faithful Friends this brief Address/ Do send to thee O King', he wrote, after the recovery of George III. 'It grieves us to the guts to see/ Such Folly in the nation/ For candles stuck in windows are/ To us abomination ...', he continued, referring to Quakers' refusal to participate in the popular custom of illuminating windows. 'With wishes for a lengthened reign/ This address we dare not better./For tho' thou'st been a rare good King/ The next may be a better.'[22]

Phillips, however, took his printing business seriously, and that summer he was involved in a dispute with the Library Company of Philadelphia over his prices. In June, the directors questioned the discount Phillips gave them after a story appeared in Philadelphia newspapers saying he was charging too much for the books he sold them. Phillips answered, 'the allowance of 5% discount ... was I believe the allowance made by those who furnished your books before me. I never heard of a greater.'

Phillips hoped the directors would continue to do business with him but argued they surely did not expect him to operate without a profit. Joseph Woods wrote to the directors on Phillips' behalf, offering to resign as purchasing agent. The directors apologized, protesting they were only inquiring about the price because of the newspaper story. Woods agreed to continue selecting books for the Library Company, and he continued to place his orders with James Phillips.[23]

Meanwhile, Harrison, Woods and others were preparing the Committee's third public report. The report, published in July 1789, praised Wilberforce and Clarkson for their hard work, and lamented the passing of the Reverend James Ramsay. Informing the public of the investigation in the House of Commons, the report called on 'Committees in the Country ... and every subscriber and well wisher, to improve all favourable opportunities of enlarging the quantum of Evidence, and of assisting the influence of Humanity'. The Committee looked for abolition in France, 'that enlightened nation' and referred to the Acts passed in Grenada and Jamaica supporting restrictions on the slave trade. George Harrison later reported that 4,000 copies of the report were printed and distributed.[24]

Hoare and Harrison were again among those appointed 'to Consider Finances and Measures to promote Subscriptions'. Since the last report, the Committee had received £2,237 10s. 8d. and had spent £1,798. Expenditures included £613 for printing and £883 for gathering evidence. With a balance of just over £400 to cover the costs of gathering evidence and locating witnesses for the ongoing investigation by the Commons, the report asked supporters to continue their subscriptions.[25]

'The Exertions of the London Committee respecting their many excellent publications have tended to accelerate the progress of Light and the Operation of Thought', William Peter Lunell reported to Phillips from Bristol in the summer of 1789. Acknowledging that he had received copies of the cross-section of the slave ship and other publications, Lunnell added that 'The Feelings of an honest People are rousing'.[26] About the same time, the London Committee also received a Resolution from the Western Baptist Association in Horsely, Gloucester, thanking them for their efforts and enclosing five guineas.[27]

The Committee kept in touch with developments in France through James Phillips. On 29 April 1789, Phillips reported 'that a translation of the Address of the Society in France to the Balliages of that kingdom had been sent to some of the Publick Papers'. The Committee ordered 2,000 copies of the Address to be printed and distributed to abolitionists in Britain. The Estates General formally opened in France on 5 May 1789. In May and June 1789, the Committee received letters from the Marquis de la Feullade and engaged Dr Frossard to prepare translations of their publications into French.[28]

On 17 June, the Third Estate declared itself the National Assembly and later the Constituent Assembly. Tensions heightened when the King refused his co-operation. On 11 July, the King dismissed Jacques Necker as the Controller General, and three days later the Bastille was destroyed. On

28 July, the London Abolition Committee noted 'Some circumstances having occurred which make it expedient for Mr. Clarkson to go to France ...', and directed the Chairman to give 'Mr. Clarkson a letter of introduction to the Society in France'.[29]

According to Clarkson, 'Mr. Wilberforce was of opinion that, as commotions had taken place ... which then aimed at political reforms, it was possible that the leading persons concerned in them might, if an application were made to them judiciously, be induced to take the Slave Trade into their consideration ....'[30]

On 25 August, the London Abolition Committee received 'A translation of a letter from Mons. Gramagnac, Secretary to the Society at Paris dated 26 June accompanied with two letters wrote by that Society to Mons. Necker with his answer to one of them'. George Harrison and two others were directed to prepare an answer to Gramagnac.[31]

Meanwhile, Clarkson arrived in France, meeting with the Duke de la Rochefoucald, the Marquis de Condorcet, M. De Villeneuve, Brissot, and the Marquis de la Fayette. Clarkson stayed in Paris for six months, writing the London Committee two to five letters per month from September 1789 until February 1790. Woods, Harrison and Hoare were among those directed to answer his letters.[32]

While Clarkson was in Paris, Harrison, Phillips, Woods and other Committee members maintained their correspondence with abolitionist leaders in France and elsewhere. James Phillips and Joseph Woods corresponded with Dr Frossard in Lyons. The Committee also received letters from the Chevalier de Pinto in Lisbon and Anthony Merry at the Escurial.[33]

On 4 January 1790, in Manchester, subscribers to the abolition of the slave trade held a general meeting. The meeting adopted resolutions and sent them to London. On 24 January, the London Committee received resolutions from the Plymouth Committee. Phillips and Harrison, with their strong West Country connections, were directed to write to Plymouth.[34]

On 25 January, Wilberforce convinced the Commons to conduct the slave trade investigations by a Select Committee rather than using the more time-consuming process of the Committee of the Whole. On 26 January, on Joseph Woods' recommendation, the London Abolition Committee agreed to print an Abstract of the Evidence presented to the Privy Council. On 27 January, the investigation in the Commons by the Select Committee began with the examination of witnesses against abolition.[35]

During February and March 1790, while the Commons heard evidence, the London Abolition Committee met weekly. Hoare, Phillips and Woods were appointed to a subcommittee to procure pro-abolition witnesses. Woods and Phillips corresponded with Brissot de Warville concerning the distribution of publications in France. In March, Thomas Clarkson returned to London with a manuscript prepared by Frossard.[36]

Meanwhile, the London Abolition Committee rented a room in a coffee house in Parliament Street. On 23 April, when Wilberforce began examining witnesses in favour of abolition, the Committee scheduled weekly meetings. Yet, after that, the Committee's communication with Wilberforce and the Parliamentary supporters of abolition seemed to break down. Twice in May, not enough Committee members were present for a quorum although Woods, Harrison and Hoare consistently attended. On 11 May, the Committee sent the Secretary to find out when the pro-abolition Members of Parliament usually gathered at the Parliament Street coffee house.[37]

In June 1790, Parliament was prorogued and then dissolved. The slave trade investigations by the Commons were still not complete. With parliamentary elections approaching, the Quaker Yearly Meeting and Meeting for Sufferings notified Friends on 11 June not to vote for any candidate who supported the slave trade nor 'to countenance in any manner, the election of such as are known enemies' of abolition.[38]

On 26 June 1790, Richard Reynolds was writing to Lord Sheffield, Member for Bristol: 'I apprehend thy election will not be opposed'. Even so, Reynolds informed Sheffield that their 'diversity of sentiment' on the subject of the slave trade 'would prevent my giving a vote to the person, who, of all other, I should otherwise deem best qualified and most eligible to represent the commercial city of Bristol'.[39]

The minute books of the London Abolition Committee record no comparable action directed to their supporters. The Committee held a brief meeting on 15 June, and then adjourned for three weeks. When the Committee reconvened on 7 July, the elections were over. The Committee directed the Secretary 'to procure a list of the Members of the present Parliament as soon as possible'.[40]

In July 1790, the London Abolition Committee issued its fourth public report prepared by George Harrison, Joseph Woods and two others. The report reveals a sophisticated understanding of the workings of the market economy and a desire to reconcile trade and conscience. 'The Publick we believe are convinced that there is something both in the principle and conduct of this Trade fundamentally wrong', the report began.

First of all, the report argued, abolition would not hurt the West Indies but, even if ending the slave trade did cause a decline in the supply of slave-produced goods, 'a compensation will probably be found in the higher price of the commodity. The worst that seems possible is that the consumer may pay something more for his rum and sugar ....'

As for merchants engaged in the slave trade, the report pointed to commerce in African produce which 'he may follow with a self-approving conscience'.[41] The concept of the self-approving conscience, as developed by Woods, Harrison and other members of the London Abolition Committee, was an internal, self-regulating mechanism whereby individual merchants and consumers could legitimate some forms of commerce while eliminating others. The London Abolition Committee's self-approving conscience could not condone trade in human beings. At the same time, the self-approving conscience could legitimate the profits of trade in African goods and produce as morally acceptable. As D.B. Davis points out, by isolating and eliminating the slave trade, abolitionists were in effect legitimating other kinds of trade.[42]

The London Abolition Committee still looked to Parliament to end the slave trade. The 'advocates for the Abolition urged no hasty decision nor have they attempted to avoid the fullest investigation', declared the fourth report. The Committee remained convinced that 'such investigation will make the inhumanity and impolicy of the Traffick more evident'.[43]

The lengthy examination by the Commons was, however, straining the finances, if not the patience, of the Committee. Hoare's Treasurer's report showed a deficit of more than £94. The cost of collecting and presenting evidence amounted to more than £1,177, while the Committee had collected only a little more than £219 since the last report. The Committee ordered 4,000 copies of the report printed for distribution and advertised for funds in all London papers.[44]

On 29 July 1790, the Committee sent Thomas Clarkson to northern England and Scotland to 'make inquiry after more evidence relative to the treatment of the Slaves in the Islands'. The Committee needed this information to support its argument that if slaves were better treated, slavery could continue in the West Indies even if the slave trade were ended. At the same time, the Chairman was directed to 'write to the Committees at York, Hull and Edinburgh to assist Mr. Clarkson in his enquiries'.[45]

On 4 August 1790, before Clarkson could reach Scotland, Campbell Haliburton wrote to James Phillips from Edinburgh. 'How stands your Evidence before the House of Commons[?]' Haliburton asked Phillips. '[W]ill so much as has been taken be admitted by the new Parliament, or must the witnesses be examined anew?' Acknowledging the receipt of publications and promising to send £10 1s. 4d. in payment, Haliburton told Phillips, 'Our small Society have had no meetings for many months past'.[46]

The London Abolition Committee met infrequently in the interval between the old and new Parliaments in 1790. The Committee looked to France 'in a reasonable hope that the spirit of humanity will at length abolish the Slave Trade in that Empire'. That summer, Joseph Woods jested in a good-natured way with his long-time correspondent Matthews about developments in France: 'P.S. [probably Philip Sansom] tells me he has a letter from thee full of fun and frolick, and a zeal for french liberty. Huzza!'[47]

By the time the new Parliament met in November 1790, Edmund Burke's *Reflections on the French Revolution* was sounding an alarm not only about what was happening in France but also about *The Proceedings of Certain Societies in London*. As James Walvin writes, domestic politics in Britain must be taken into account in reading Burke's *Reflections*. Burke was particularly concerned that under the guise of celebrating the Glorious Revolution of 1688, the London Revolution Society had 'the manifest design of connecting the affairs of France with those of England'.[48]

In December, the House of Commons met twice as a Committee of the Whole on the Slave Trade, but then adjourned until February 1791. By then, Joseph Woods was expressing some sympathy for Burke's point of view. 'I read Burke not only with "tolerable patience"', Woods wrote to Matthews in February 1791, 'but with Delight not however as approving all his Doctrines or Arguments.'[49]

During Parliament's year-end recess, the Committee met every two weeks. James Phillips distributed tracts by Clarkson to each new Member. In the new year, Phillips began giving the cross-section of the slave ship to newly elected Members. The Commons prepared to resume its investigations in February and March 1791. The London Abolition Committee began meeting weekly, renting rooms in New Palace Yard at a cost of 2 guineas for two-and-a-half weeks.

On 22 March the group engaged column space in two London papers. On 29 March the Committee prompted Wilberforce to move for the muster rolls of slave ships to be presented to the Commons. Wilberforce did, and the Committee then directed Clarkson to ask him about the propriety of calling for an examination of the registers of surgeons of slave ships.[50]

As the Commons moved toward the long-awaited conclusion of its investigation, Harrison, Woods and Phillips scrambled to distribute books and information to Members of Parliament and to the public at reasonable costs. On 5 April, Phillips reported he was 'not able to complete the printing of … the Abstract of the Evidence in time to answer the purpose of the Committee', so another printer was employed. A week later, Harrison and Woods reported

> it advisable to decline engaging the printer of the *Gazetteer* on account of his extravagant demand but that they mean to furnish matter for insertion in *The Morning Chronicle* as often as there is Room.'[51]

In April 1791, the Commons was getting ready to hear the report of the Select Committee on the Slave Trade preparatory to beginning deliberation on abolition. Just then, news began reaching England of a slave insurrection in the French island of St Domingue. According to James Walvin, '... the most cataclysmic repercussion of the Revolution was in the French colony of St. Domingue where the initial political skirmishing' escalated into racial violence, full-scale war, and economic collapse.[52]

Clarkson says the insurrection in St Domingue caused much alarm in Britain. On 7 April, a public meeting of supporters of the slave trade called for an end to the discussion of abolition, saying 'it was the duty of the government, if they regarded the safety of the Islands, to oppose ... abolition'. Suddenly, says Clarkson, '... many looked upon the abolitionists as monsters ... the current was turned against us.'[53]

On 18 April 1791, Wilberforce opened debate in Commons by asking leave to bring in a Bill 'to prevent the farther importation of slaves' into the British West Indies. Yet even as he argued his case, Wilberforce protested that he was 'indifferent to the present decision of the House'. Whatever the Commons might do, Wilberforce believed 'the people of Great Britain would abolish the slave trade'. Opponents in the Commons quickly countered by saying the current unrest among slaves in the Caribbean was a direct result of the agitation for abolition. They predicted that the unrest would spread to Jamaica if discussions continued.[54]

James Martin, Member for Tewkesbury and a member of the London Committee, spoke in favour of abolition. He pointed to the widespread support of all religious sects, especially the Quakers. 'Dissenters of various denominations, but particularly the Quakers (who to their immortal honour had taken the lead in it)' have united with the Established Church in support of abolition, he declared. Discussion of Wilberforce's motion continued late into the night. Pitt then moved to adjourn debate until the next day.[55]

Harrison, Phillips and three other members of the London Abolition Committee met the next day, 19 April. They completed the distribution of the evidence and ordered 3,000 copies of the previous night's debate. That night, Pitt, Fox and Burke spoke eloquently on behalf of abolition. 'The leaders, it was true, were for the abolition', acknowledged an opponent, but, 'the minor orators, the dwarfs, the pygmies, would ... this day carry the question against them'. When the long-awaited vote was taken, Wilberforce's bill was lost by 88 votes to 163.[56]

NOTES

1. Additional MSS 21,255, 26 August 1788.
2. Additional MSS 21,255, 1, 8 July, 12 August 1788.
3. Additional MSS 21,255, 18 November 1788. Thompson/Clarkson MSS, Vol. II, p. 139, James Ramsay (to James Phillips), 1 November 1788.
4. Ibid. Additional MSS 21,255, 18 November 1788.
5. Ibid., 11, 18 November 1788.

6. Ibid., October 1788 – January 1789.
7. Thompson/Clarkson, Vol. II, p. 105, William Hughes, Ware, Herts, to James Phillips, 21 January 1789; p. 127, H. Dannett, Minister of St. John's in Liverpool, to James Phillips, 1788; p. 112, receipt from James Phillips to William Dickson, 30 March 1789.
8. Ibid., p. 93, William Elford to James Phillips, 18 March 1789. Clarkson, *History* Vol. II, p. 93.
9. S. and H. Hoare, *Memoirs of the Hoare Family*, p. 17.
10. Additional MSS 21,255, 21 October, 9 December 1788 and 20 January 1789.
11. Ibid., 24 February, 3 March 1789.
12. Ibid., 10, 17 March, 28 April 1789.
13. Ibid., 31 March, 6, 14 April 1789.
14. Clarkson, *History*, Vol. II, pp. 34–6. Additional MSS 21,255, 31 March 1789, 6 April 1789.
15. Ibid., 14 and 21 April 1789.
16. Ibid., 28 April, 5 May 1789. Cobbett, *Parliamentary History*, Vol. XXVIII, pp. 41–78.
17. Cobbett, *Parliamentary History*, Vol. XXVIII, pp. 78–100.
18. Additional MSS 21,255, 14, 19 May 1789. Cobbett, *Parliamentary History*, Vol XXVIII, pp. 78–100.
19. Additional MSS 21,255, 26 May, 9, 16 June 1789. Thompson/Clarkson, Vol. I, p. 153, Receipt from John Jamieson to James Phillips, June 1789.
20. Thompson/Clarkson MSS, Vol. I, p. 227, John Coakley Lettsom to James Phillips, 27 July 1789.
21. Thompson/Clarkson MSS, Vol. II, p. 89, H. H. Dalrymple to James Phillips, 14 September 1789. Dalrymple declined to write a book on the slave trade but later testified before the House of Commons.
22. Gibson MSS, Vol. II, p. 52, unsigned manuscript poem, with 'James Phillips, George Yard' added in pencil.
23. Library Company of Philadelphia Records, Box II, 1785–89, 5 June 1789, 8 July 1789.
24. Additional MSS 21,255, 28 July, 25 August 1789.
25. Ibid., 26 May, 28 July 1789.
26. Thompson/Clarkson MSS, Vol. II, p. 97. William Peter Lunell, Bristol, to James Phillips, 6 June 1789.
27. Additional MSS 21,255, 6 June 1789.
28. Ibid., 16, 25 June 1789.
29. Ibid., 28 July 1789.
30. Clarkson, *History*, Vol. II, pp. 122–3.
31. Additional MSS 21,255, 25 August 1789.
32. Ibid., 25 August, 22 September, 20 October, 17 November, 15 December 1789.
33. Ibid., 25 August, 22 September 1789–2 February 1790.
34. Additional MSS 21,255, 12, 26 January 1790.
35. Additional MSS 21,255, 26 January 1790. Cobbett, *Parliamentary History*, Vol. XXVIII, pp. 307–15.
36. Additional MSS 21,255, 9, 16 February and 23 March 1790. Frossard had written a two-volume treatise on the slave trade in French in 1789.
37. Ibid., 23 March, 21 April, 18, 25 May 1790. The minutes do not indicate why communications seemed to be breaking down.
38. *Journals of the House of Commons*, Vol. 45, 10 June 1790. Meeting for Sufferings Minute Book, Vol. 38, 11 June 1790. Yearly Meeting Printed Epistles, Vol. 2, pp. 78–9.
39. Rathbone, *Letters*, p. 276.
40. Additional MSS 21,255, 15 June, 7 July 1790.
41. Additional MSS 21,256, 26 July 1790.
42. D.B. Davis, *The Problem of Slavery in the Age of Revolution*, pp. 251–4.
43. Additional MSS 21,256, 20 July 1790.
44. Ibid., 20 July 1790.
45. Ibid., 29 July 1790. Clarkson was sent to Scotland and northern England. On 31 August Clarkson wrote to the Committee from Hull and Scarborough. On 28 September and 26 October 1790 he was in Edinburgh. On 16 November 1790, he was in Durham. On 14

December 1790, he was back in London.

46. Thompson/Clarkson MSS, Vol. II, p. 103, Campbell Haliburton, Edinburgh, to James Phillips, 4 August 1790.
47. Additional MSS 21,256, 20 July 1790. Matthews MSS, 15 July 1790.
48. Edward Royle and James Walvin, *English Radicals and Reformers*, p. 44.
49. *Journals of the House of Commons*, Vol. 46, 10, 16 December 1790, 4 February 1791. Matthews MSS, 15 February 1791.
50. Additional MSS 21,255, 9, 23 February, 8, 15, 22, 29 March 1791.
51. Ibid., 5, 12 April 1791.
52. James Walvin, *England, Slaves and Freedom*, pp. 114–15.
53. Clarkson, *History*, Vol. II, p. 210.
54. Cobbett, *Parliamentary History*, Vol. XXIX, pp. 278–94.
55. Ibid. Clarkson, *History*, Vol. II, pp. 260–7.
56. Cobbett, *Parliamentary History*, Vol. XXIX, pp. 250–359.

5

The Abolitionist Breakthrough, 1791–92

On 26 April 1791, one week after the vote in Commons, Joseph Woods, James Phillips, George Harrison, Samuel Hoare and nine other men gathered for a London Abolition Committee meeting. The meeting was described by Clarkson as 'the most impressive I ever attended. The looks of all bespoke the feelings of their hearts.'

The Committee first 'Resolved, … Thanks … be respectfully given to the Illustrious Minority of the House of Commons', 'particularly' to William Wilberforce 'for his unwearied exertions' and to William Pitt and Charles James Fox 'for their virtuous and dignified cooperation'. The Committee then unanimously elected Wilberforce, Fox, William Smith, William Burgh and John Pennington, Baron Muncaster, to membership.[1]

The Committee 'Resolved', to 'consider the late decision in the House of Commons … as a delay rather than a defeat' and to

> renew their firm protestation, that they will never desist from appealing to their Countrymen till the commercial intercourse with Africa shall cease to be polluted with the blood of its Inhabitants.

Orders were given for copies of this resolution to be sent to the five new Parliamentary members and published 'in all the London Newspapers and once in the Country ones'.

A report to the public, the Committee's fifth, was read and approved. Much of the content and language of the report resembles the arguments and style first expressed by Joseph Woods in his *Thoughts on Slavery*. The report questioned whether 'the luxuries of Rum and Sugar can only be obtained by tearing assunder those ties of affection which unite our species and exalt our nature'. The report equated abolition with 'asserting the claims of Humanity', and called on 'Every Man' in Britain to come to the aid of 'those Unhappy Men' of Africa.

But the report marks the appearance of two new elements in the London Abolition Committee argument. The first was an emphasis on the rights of Africans. Appearing some two months after the publication of Paine's *Rights of Man, Part I*, the report refers to the rights of Africans being violated 'both in the capture and subsequent treatment'. Such violations would not long be tolerated 'in an enlightened Age', the report declares.

As the second new element, the report points with pride to the respectability of the Parliamentary advocates for abolition. Committee members could 'Congratulate each other, that we number amongst our Friends [in] Parliament many of the most distinguished Characters in this Kingdom ….'

After the report was approved, James Phillips was 'desired to print 1,000 Copies thereof, and forward them with a proper Number of the Abridgment of the Evidence to the several Correspondents of this Committee with a Copy of the letter to the [local] Committees'. Thomas Clarkson was directed to prepare an Abstract of the Abridgement of the Evidence presented before the Commons. James Phillips was to print 5,000 copies for 'general distribution'.[2]

Despite the defeat in the Commons, the Committee met weekly through May and fortnightly through June, July and August 1791. On 10 May, the Committee expanded its number to 30, 'Members of Parliament excepted', to accommodate new men like Sir William Dolben. Some new Committee members, like Henry Thornton, Lewis Alexander Grant and Matthew Montague, were friends of Wilberforce and shared his Evangelical views. Others, like Josiah Wedgwood, Jr, and John Clarkson, brother of Thomas, did not.[3]

For the first time, Parliamentary members like William Burgh, Henry Thornton and Wilberforce, began attending meetings regularly with Woods, Phillips, Harrison, Hoare and others. The Committee thus gained greater access to Parliamentary information. On 24 May 1791, for example, Dolben, Wilberforce, Smith, Thornton, Muncaster and Grant were asked to furnish the Committee with the names of Members of Parliament who had voted for abolition.[4]

James Phillips continued to serve as publisher and chief London contact for the Committee. In May, Phillips sent evidence, reports, resolutions and letters to all local committees and correspondents. He was paid £250 'on his account' by Hoare, and £204 six months later.[5] In July, Walter Chandler wrote to Phillips from Bristol, ' … let me know if you have heard of Falconbridge and say is Thomas Clarkson in London'.[6] Even Clarkson's mother, Anne, asked Phillips to forward letters to Thomas 'as I conclude you always know where he is to be found'.[7]

In June 1791, Joseph Woods wrote to Matthews, '… we continue firm and wish all our friends to keep the sacred flame'.[8] That summer, Thomas Walker sent the London Committee resolutions passed at a general meeting in Manchester; Campbell Haliburton sent resolutions from Edinburgh; and William Elford sent the same from Plymouth. In October, Clarkson reported that a 'respectable meeting' of abolitionists in Birmingham had also adopted resolutions. In November, Thomas Walker was in London, attending a London Abolition Committee meeting with Hoare, Harrison, Phillips and other members.[9]

Despite these indications of popular support, the London Abolition Committee continued to face financial problems. On 29 November, Hoare, Woods and two others were appointed 'to consider of an application for an increase of subscriptions and to examine the Finances of the Society'. Two weeks, later the subcommittee reported an £87 deficit. The Committee had received more than £2,100 since July 1790 but had spent nearly £2,200. The subcommittee recommended advertising in newspapers, soliciting the country committees by letter, and directing the Secretary personally to call on previous donors in and around London.[10]

On 13 December, the members of the London Abolition Committee announced that they had

> determined in conjunction with the other Committees of this Society established in various part of Great Britain, to persevere in their Endeavours for the Abolition of the Slave Trade.

The group then agreed to 'solicit the further Assistance of the Friends of this Cause'.[11] Within a week, the London Committee received letters from committees at Plymouth and Exeter. A 15-member abolition committee was formed in Nottingham to collect contributions which were sent to London with a series of resolutions.[12]

The London Committee met on 13, 21, 28, and 30 December 1791, with Hoare, Harrison, Phillips and Woods working alongside Clarkson, Wilberforce, Henry Thornton and other Anglican members. The Committee added two new men: James West, a Member of Parliament and long-time supporter of abolition, and Charles Grant, a friend of Wilberforce recently returned from India. On 28 December, the Committee directed James Phillips to print 3,000 copies of Clarkson's 'Abstracts of the Abridgement of Evidence' and 2,000 of the Abridgement.[13]

On 10 January 1792, at a large meeting attended by Parliamentary members William Wilberforce, William Smith, Charles Grant and James West, the Committee directed James Phillips and Joseph Woods with William Dillwyn and Thomas Clarkson to prepare letters to the country committees. On 17 January, Phillips brought in a rough draft which was approved and 'forwarded without delay'. On 24 January, 'Conceiving it necessary to expedite Petitions to Parliament as much as possible', the Committee appointed James Phillips and three others 'to write a letter to the Committees in the Country to hasten that measure'.[14]

At the meeting on 24 January, Joseph Woods and another member recommended publishing and distributing 5,000 copies of *A Short Sketch of the Evidence Delivered Before a Committee of the House of Commons for the Abolition of the Slave Trade: To Which is Added, A Recommendation of the Subject to the Serious Attention of People in General.*[15] The pamphlet signed W.B.C. was written by William Bell Crafton, a Quaker, from Tewkesbury. The 26-page tract was already being printed and sold for three pence, with money from the sales going to the London Abolition Committee 'after deducting the Expense of Printing'.

Crafton began his tract by saying, 'The people are now called on to behold, to feel, and judge for themselves'. He then went on to summarize succinctly the main points of the case for abolition as presented to the Commons. Crafton appealed first to Members of Parliament, and 'Next to ... all who have any just influence in the election of them, ... particularly ... to consider [the evidence]'.

Crafton went on to say that

> Even those who have no vote, are nevertheless comprehended in our idea of the public mind, nor is any man of sense and virtue, let his situation in a free country be what it may, to be deemed of no account. Upon his judgment, his voice (if not his vote), his example, much may depend.[16]

Clearly, Crafton and the members of the London Abolition Committee were seeking to expand public participation in the discussion of the question of abolition.

By 31 January, William Tuke, a leading Quaker and large-scale retail grocer in York, was writing to James Phillips, requesting additional copies of Crafton's *Short Sketch of the Evidence*. 'Please to send us 100 by waggon', Tuke asked. Calculating the costs, Tuke declared: 'We propose putting them into Bookseller's hands and therefore must have them at Bookseller's prices, for as they don't like to do Business without profit, it is enough for us to lose the carriage.'[17] The London Abolition Committee distributed Crafton's tract in York through Tuke.[18]

Thomas Clarkson, meanwhile, was advocating abstaining from West Indian produce as a means of ending the slave trade. The abstention movement had developed independently of the London Abolition Committee and, according to Clarkson, was spreading rapidly. On 12 January 1792, Clarkson sent a correspondent a printed broadside advertising *An Address to the People of Great Britain on the Propriety of Abstaining from West Indian Sugar and Rum.* 'I wish to suggest it to your consideration, how you would think it an auxiliary to your efforts in bringing about the abolition of the Slave Trade', Clarkson added. If enough people abstained, he continued, 'government could not obtain their revenue unless they gratified the wishes of the people by the Abolition of the Slave Trade'.

Clarkson went on to encourage his correspondent to find a bookseller who would order 1,000 copies of the *Address*. He ended by adding: 'I do not write at the request of the committee … I write merely as an individual.' Respondents were directed to write to Clarkson 'at James Phillips', George Yard, Lombard Street'.[19]

At the same time, Clarkson was linking abolition to support for the French Revolution. On 23 January 1792, Clarkson forwarded a printed notice from the London Committee to an acquaintance in Cumberland. Acting again, evidently, without the sanction of the Committee, Clarkson used James Phillips as his London contact. At the bottom of the notice from the Committee, Clarkson added, 'Have you any Friends to the French Revolution in your town and Neighbourhood and what may be their Names – Direct to me at Mr. James Phillips, George Yard, London'.[20]

Meanwhile, many publications were calling for abstention from West Indian produce. In Birmingham, *An Address to the People of Great Britain, on the Propriety of Abstaining from West Indian Sugar and Rum* was in its tenth edition by 1791. *An Address to the People of Great Britain (Respectfully Offered to the People of Ireland) on the Utility of Refraining from the Use of West Indian Sugar and Rum* went through six editions in London in 1791 and was reprinted in Dublin in 1792. At the same time, *Considerations Addressed to the Professors of Christianity of Every Denomination on the Impropriety of Consuming West Indian Sugar and Rum as Produced by the Oppressive Labour of Slaves* was published in Dublin.[21]

As David Turley and Linda Colley point out, by focusing on the purchase of West Indian products, this unofficial abstention movement gave women an opportunity to take part in the abolition campaign. 'Whether intentionally or not', Colley says, 'this brought the campaign … into the centre of woman's traditional sphere of influence – the home.'[22]

Although Joseph Woods, in his *Thoughts on Slavery* published in 1784, had made the link between abolition of the slave trade and public consumption of slave-produced goods, the London Abolition Committee did not officially endorse abstention at this time. Still, according to Clarkson's estimates, by the winter of 1791–92 as many as 300,000 persons across Great Britain were refusing to buy West Indian sugar and rum.[23]

Meanwhile, the London Abolition Committee was focusing on Scotland. In January 1792, Phillips was working with William Dickson, whom the Committee had engaged to travel to Scotland. The Committee was not acting quickly enough, in Dickson's estimation, to get letters of introduction, information and abolitionist products to him.

On 14 January, Dickson wrote to both Phillips and Samuel Hoare. The cause of abolition was gaining ground in Edinburgh, where the 'Abstract of the Evidence' had been circulated, Dickson told Phillips. Dickson wanted Henry Thornton to give him more information about the Sierra Leone Company, and he asked for more of Wedgwood's cameos. Dickson had posted the cross-section of the slave ship in banks, public houses and coffee houses, but needed letters of introduction to speak to men of influence.

'A Scotchman will not join any cause unless you explain to him the *cur* and the *quare*', said Dickson, 'But *then* he perseveres.' The Committee directed Phillips to send Dickson the letters and information he needed and ordered 5,000 additional copies of Crafton's *Short Sketch of the Evidence* for distribution in Scotland.[24]

The history of the founding of the Sierra Leone Company, mentioned by Dickson, indicates that Quakers had no monopoly on the self-approving conscience when it came to profits from trade. As Clarkson told a country abolitionist later that year, the Sierra Leone Company was 'incorporated under 13 respectable Directors, who have an agent residing there'. The colony was 'expected to yield for exportation cotton, sugar, Tobacco, etc'.

Clarkson explained how the Company had 'raised a Cap'l by Subscription of above Two hund'd Thous'd pounds divided into shares of 50£ each of which ye very respectable William Wilberforce hath Ten ...'. Henry Thornton, cousin of Wilberforce, resident of Clapham, and recently elected member of the London Abolition Committee, was Chair of the Sierra Leone Company. Thomas Clarkson's brother John, another London Abolition Committee member, was governor of the colony.[25]

Meanwhile, diverse supporters from across the country were answering the Committee's call for financial assistance and petitions. On 31 January 1792, two Baptists presented the Committee with a £55 donation. At the same time, the Reverend Joseph Plymley, Archdeacon of Shropshire, wrote to Thomas Clarkson in care of James Phillips with names of potential supporters and information that he was riding his county to gather information and petitions. J. Charlesworth wrote to Phillips from Nottingham to request more abolition publications.[26]

During February 1792, the Committee met weekly, with several Parliamentary members like Dolben, Montague, West, Martin and Wilberforce, working alongside the four Quaker veterans. On 21 February, Joseph Woods, James Phillips and another member were delegated 'to prepare a letter to be circulated among our Friends in the Country to recommend to them the expediting of petitions as early as possible'. In the following week, Harrison and another member were directed to prepare a letter to all correspondents, informing them that the Commons would receive petitions throughout the session and recommending that petitions approved at public meetings be signed by all present.[27]

'Of the enthusiasm of the nation at this time', Clarkson wrote later, 'none can form an opinion but they who witnessed it.'[28] The minute books of the London Abolition Committee record six petitions and 16 letters of support received in February, mostly from local committee chairs.[29] On 16 February, reformer Capel Lofft wrote to James Phillips saying that a petition from Bury is 'approved' and 'will go to Parliament well signed'. Lofft hoped to hear of a 'daily increase of the Petitions', asking 'When does Mr. Wilberforce bring on his Proposition?'[30]

In March, the London Abolition Committee received 52 petitions and 19 letters of support not including sermons, pamphlets, and contributions.[31] On 3 March, Thomas Walker of Manchester sent packages for Clarkson and Sharp via Phillips. 'Our Petition I expect will be very numerously signed, that it is respectable nobody can deny', Walker reported. He was confident of growing support, 'especially among the Methodists'.[32]

On 4 March, Joseph Woods wrote to Matthews saying: 'I expect our friend Wilberforce will give notice of his intended Motion in a few days. His heart is in the business. Petitions are coming up continually from the Country "frequent and full".'[33]

By the end of March 1792, 519 petitions were presented to the House of Commons – 'the largest number ever submitted to the House on a single subject or in a single session'. Seymour Drescher calls this an abolitionist 'break through' or 'take-off'. As Drescher says, the huge number of abolition petitions significantly extended public participation in politics as Parliamentary leaders began to 'accept petitioning as a mode of integrating public opinion into the legislative process'. The petitions also, as Drescher argues, heralded 'the emergence of a new attitude toward slavery and the slave trade', which changed for ever the terms of political discourse on the subject.[34]

On 2 April 1792, Wilberforce opened the debate in the Commons by introducing a motion to abolish the slave trade 'at such time as to the House might seem meet'. Wilberforce paid tribute to the diverse coalition supporting abolition by saying that 'men who differed on many speculative points and most political topics seemed to think alike' on the slave trade.[35]

Opponents declared abolition 'wild, impracticable and visionary' and pointed for proof to the London Abolition Committee and its Quaker membership. One Member charged that abolitionist witnesses had been 'hired by the emmisaries and agents of the Society in the Old Jewry'. Another said pro-abolitionist petitions were 'the manufacture of the sectaries of the Old Jewry'.

Both Pitt and Fox spoke in support of abolition. Fox defended the legitimacy of the petitions and the tactics of the abolitionists. He announced that he was a member of the London Committee and that he had advised the group to distribute evidence and debates as a way of educating the public.

Pitt argued that abolition would be good for the West Indies and said he believed most people wanted to end the trade, the only question was when.

In this highly charged atmosphere, Henry Dundas proposed adding the word '*gradual*' to the motion as 'a moderate and middle way of proceeding'. Those who opposed any form of abolition pressed for a motion to adjourn. The motion to adjourn was defeated by 87 votes to 234. The next vote, on the Dundas amendment, was carried by 193 to 125. The amended motion for gradual abolition was then carried by 230 to 85.[36]

The vote of 1792 seems to justify James Walvin's conclusion that if Wilberforce had been a better Parliamentary manager abolition might have been accomplished as early as 1793.[37] The number of Members of the Commons who voted in favour of abolition in April 1791 was 88. The number who voted for the motion to adjourn in April 1792 was 87; and 85 voted against gradual abolition. These closely matched minorities indicate, as Walvin observes, that 'the balance between the two sides was very fine indeed'. Dundas clearly outmanoeuvred Wilberforce with his amendment by splitting the great mass of undecided voters, something that a more astute parliamentary leader might have foreseen.

The London Abolition Committee met on 3 April 1792, the afternoon of the vote in the Commons. Petitions were still trickling in. Harrison, Woods and Clarkson were appointed 'to consider what measures may be proper to be taken in consequence of the decision of the House of Commons this morning'.[38]

The next day, in the Commons, Wilberforce asked Dundas how he intended to accomplish gradual abolition. Dundas replied that he had not proposed abolition in the first place and that he intended to do nothing now. Charles James Fox 'maintained this was trifling with the public and with the House' and moved for a Committee of the Whole to consider the Slave Trade on 18 April. Wilberforce seconded the motion.[39]

On 5 April, Samuel Hoare, James Phillips, George Harrison, and Joseph Woods met James West, William Burgh and ten other members of the London Abolition Committee. Harrison reported he had attended the debate in the Commons and summarized the votes. The Committee voted thanks to Wilberforce, Pitt and Fox. Resolving 'that a gradual Abolition of the Slave Trade is not an adequate Remedy', the Committee held to its position, articulated by Woods at the beginning of the public campaign, that any attempt to regulate the trade could be construed as implied support for the principle of slavery. The group urged friends 'to use all constitutional means to obtain the *immediate Abolition* of that unjust, inhuman and destructive Traffick'. The four Quaker veterans, Clarkson, Sharp, and another member, were then asked to prepare a circular.[40]

The London Committee met weekly throughout April 1792 but took no part in the parliamentary negotiations concerning gradual abolition, insisting that the slave trade was 'a cruel and piratical system to which the name of Commerce has too long been absurdly applied'. The Committee paid James Phillips £400 on his account and advertised for new subscriptions 'to enable us to prosecute this great Cause to a Conclusion'. Samuel Whitbread answered with £50, and the Committee received resolutions of support from committees at Newcastle, Manchester and Darlington.[41]

On 23 April, Henry Dundas gave notice for a motion naming 1800 as the date for abolition. In the ensuing debate, the role of public opinion supporting abolition became an issue. Charles James Fox, arguing for the earliest date possible, asserted 'the question would not cease to be agitated until it was accomplished'. Fox finished by asking 'would not gentlemen's elections be affected by this question?' A backbencher immediately declared 'he scorned to hold a seat in that House on any other terms than those of freedom'.

Debate continued on 25 and 27 April, with the petitions and the role of the London Abolition Committee again becoming an issue. On 25 April, Lord Sheffield was reported as saying 'As to the petitions ... they were not the voluntary expressions of the people, but far the greater part had been procured by associations'. Sheffield would, he said, 'ever condemn such attempts to control the deliberations of Parliament'.

On 27 April, Lord Carhampton contended that 'numerous ... petitions had been procured from the Islands of Scotland and the mountains of Wales, by the members of that enlightened Society held in the Old Jewry'. Carhampton went on to say that he was not surprised to read the Committee was in need of funds. What was 'the expense of procuring petitions to that House and ... the price of newspaper defamation', Carhampton asked sarcastically.

Wilberforce responded by saying he was proud 'to belong to a Society, of which some persons were members, whose religious opinions had not drawn on them the partiality of the public'. Fox countered by saying it 'behooved the House to concur with the voice of the people' and abolish the slave trade. The House of Commons finally set the date for abolition in 1796 by a vote of 151 for and 132 against after defeating motions for abolition in 1793 by 109 to 158 and 1795 by 121 to 161.[42]

The London Abolition Committee met every few days in late April and early May 1792, but little business is recorded. On 1 May, Phillips reported that he had printed two editions of the debates in the Commons. The Committee directed Phillips, Woods and Hoare to work with Clarkson to distribute 4,500 copies. The Committee received a dozen letters of support, mostly from long-time correspondents, and one gift of £50. Later in May, at a meeting attended by Wilberforce in addition to Hoare, Phillips and Woods, 'it was agreed the list of Petitions should not be added to the end of the Debates' then being publicly distributed.[43]

On 3 May, the resolution to end the slave trade in 1796 was sent from the Commons to the House of Lords. Viscount Stormont immediately claimed that the Lords must conduct their own investigation, while the Duke of Clarence spoke out strongly against abolition. Lord Grenville, Samuel Horsley, Bishop of St David's, and Beilby Porteus, now Bishop of London and a long-time friend of the Abolition Committee, spoke in favour of the resolution. But the Lords were intent on conducting their own investigation. On 8 May, the Lords began the slow process of investigation by the Committee of the Whole.[44]

In spring 1792, Woods and Phillips, but especially Phillips, maintained the Committee's strong links with French abolitionists. On 8 May, the Committee directed Woods, Phillips and Clarkson to write to the Société des Amis des Noirs in Paris. A few weeks later, the group directed Phillips to see about translating the Commons debates into French.

Yet events in France and in Britain were beginning to divide supporters of the abolition of the slave trade. As Edward Royle and James Walvin note, the initial optimism with which some in Great Britain had greeted the French Revolution began to dissipate after the appearance of the second part of Tom Paine's *Rights of Man* in February 1792. Others, however, took up the demand for political rights. The London Corresponding Society issued its first public address on 2 April 1792 claiming for all men 'unalienable Rights of Resistance to Oppression'.[45]

James Phillips continued his friendship with Brissot, who was now a leader in France. On 20 May a young Englishman wrote to Phillips from outside Paris:

> Respected Friend, I can but consider myself much obliged by the trouble thou gavest thyself to introduce me to thy friends at Paris ... Brissot favoured me with a ticket for two places in the gallery of the National Assembly.[46]

On 20 April 1792, the French government declared war on the Hapsburg Empire. In May, a Royal Proclamation against seditious publications was issued in Britain. In mid-June 1792, the Lords postponed their investigation of the slave trade until the next session.

At about this time, George Harrison wrote a strongly worded but anonymous *Address to the Right Reverend the Prelates of England and Wales on the Subject of the Slave Trade*. Harrison reminded the Lords of the widespread public support for abolition, saying 'no apology is necessary for telling you frankly, my Lords, what men of every religious denomination in this country, are expecting from you'. In a straightforward manner, very unlike the careful tone of Joseph Woods, Harrison wrote 'It remains therefore for you, my Lords, to answer the just and reasonable expectation of the public in a business of the utmost moment'. If the Lords refused to answer, Harrison warned, 'Woe to the church-establishment of this country, when its prelacy is fallen into contempt'.

Harrison ended his address by asking the Lords to 'let the voice of Africa be heard at the Bar of your House'. He then closed with a long section in which he assumed a female voice speaking for Africa, appealing for justice to the 'reverend fathers' of the House of Lords. Harrison imagined Africa asking 'those reverend fathers ... whether their researches had enabled them to discover any national distinction in the colour of souls'. Unlike Joseph Woods who, in his *Thoughts on Slavery*, had been willing to accept the argument of the inferiority of Africans, Harrison, here speaking for Africa herself, indicates there is no distinction among souls.

Moreover, Harrison repudiated the Old World/New World double standard which Woods had only questioned in his writings ten years earlier. Woods had tacitly accepted the notion that Englishmen should not engage in the slave trade whatever colonials might do. Harrison, for his part, specifically refuted the idea that any part of the world had a moral superiority over any other. Again speaking in the voice of Africa, Harrison demanded that 'those venerable sages, the learned ministers of the law [in the House of Lords] ... say whether the principles of justice, the distinctions of right and wrong, vary according to the latitude of the countries in which they are recognised'.

Finally, Harrison ended his address not with a supplication but with a delcaration. 'I ask not the instant cessation of my wrongs, as a boon,' he wrote, still speaking as the persona of Africa, 'I demand it as a right ...'. Harrison's pamphlet was not published by James Phillips and distributed by the London Abolition Committee. Instead, it was printed by J. Parson, Paternoster Row and by Ridgway in York Street, near St James's, and sold for three pence.[47]

Despite Harrison's adoption of the literary device of writing as the female voice of Africa, the voice of the London Abolition Committee continued to be male, moderate and conciliatory, although firmly opposed to *gradual* abolition. On 19 June 1792, Joseph Woods brought the Committee a sixth public report which was approved by Hoare, Harrison, Clarkson, Wilberforce and seven other members present. 'The Voice of Humanity and the general abhorrence of the system expressed in the numerous Petitions required an immediate and utter Abolition', the report stated.

Unlike Harrison's pointed remarks, the Committee expressed hope that the 'Noble House' will join 'in extirpating, forever, a System of depredation to which the appellation of Commerce has been too long unworthily applied'. The report ended by requesting all friends 'continue with united efforts, to support our Common Cause'. On 19 June 1792, the Committee ordered 2,000 copies of the report printed and distributed along with 10,000 copies of Pitt's speech in favour of abolition.[48]

NOTES

1. Clarkson, *History*, Vol. II, p. 339. Additional MSS 21,256, 26 April 1791.
2. Additional MSS 21,256, 26 April 1791.
3. Ibid., May–August 1791.
4. Ibid., 24 May 1791.
5. Ibid., 3 May and 29 October 1791.
6. Thompson/Clarkson MSS, Vol. II, p. 69, Walter Chandler, Bristol, to James Phillips, 9 July 1791.
7. Thompson/Clarkson MSS, Vol. III, p. 205, A. Clarkson to James Phillips, 3 October 1791. Ibid., A. Clarkson to James Phillips, 31 October 1791, from Thomas's sister Anne asking Phillips to forward a letter to another brother (perhaps John) via New York.
8. Matthews MSS, 14 June 1791.
9. Additional MSS 21,256, 31 May, 5 July, 25 October, 29 November 1791.
10. Ibid., 29 November, 13 December 1791.
11. Ibid., 13 December 1791.
12. Ibid., 13, 21 December 1791. Clarkson, *History* Vol. II, pp. 348–52.
13. Additional MSS 21,256, 13, 21, 28, 30 December 1791.
14. Ibid., 10, 17, 24 January 1792.
15. Additional MSS 21,256, 24 January 1792.
16. [William Bell Crafton], *A Short Sketch of the Evidence Delivered Before a Committee of the House of Commons for the Abolition of the Slave Trade: To Which is Added, A Recommendation of the Subject to the Serious Attention of People in General* (Tewkesbury: Dyde and Son, no date). James Phillips had printed an earlier tract on Quakerism by Crafton. Gibson MSS, Vol. IV, p. 29.
17. Thompson/Clarkson MSS, Vol. II, 107, William Tuke, York, to James Phillips, 31 January 1792. For Tuke see, Robert Mennell, *Tea: An Historical Sketch'*(London: Effingham Wilson, 1926), and William K. and E. Margaret Sessions, *The Tukes of York in the 17th, 18th and 19th Centuries* (London: Friend's Home Service Committee, 1971).
18. Additional MSS 21,256, 24, 31 January 1792.
19. Thompson/Clarkson MSS, Vol. III, p. 53, 12 January 1792. Printed notice with manuscript note by Clarkson.
20. Thompson/Clarkson MSS, Vol. III, p. 53, Clarkson to Thomas Wilkinson near Penrith, 23 January 1792. Hand-written note on printed notice.
21. *An Address to the People of Great Britain, on the Propriety of Abstaining from West Indian Sugar and Rum*, 10th edn (Birmingham, 1791). *An Address to the People of Great Britain (Respectfully Offered to the People of Ireland) on the Utility of Refraining from the Use of West Indian Sugar and Rum*, 6th edn (London, 1791) and (Dublin, 1792). *Considerations Addressed to the Professors of Christianity of Every Denomination on the Impropriety of Consuming West Indian Sugar and Rum as Produced by the Oppressive Labour of Slaves* (Dublin, 1792).
22. D. Turley, *The Culture of English Antislavery*, pp. 78–81. L. Colley, *Britons*, p. 278.
23. Clarkson, *History*, Vol. II, pp. 347–52.
24. Thompson/Clarkson MSS, Vol. II, p. 113. William Dickson to James Phillips, 14 January 1792. Additional MSS 21,256, 17, 24, 31 January 1792.

25. London, Library of Society of Friends MSS, Elihu Robinson, Diaries and Memoranda, Vol. VI, 13 November 1792. Additional MSS 21,256, 10 May 1791. Henry Thornton was elected to the London Abolition Committee.
26. Additional MSS 21,256, 31 January 1792. Thompson/Clarkson MSS, Vol. III, p. 63. Reverend Joseph Plymley to Thomas Clarkson, 31 January 1792. Thompson/Clarkson MSS, Vol. I, p. 59, J. Charlesworth, Nottingham, to James Phillips, 31 January (1792?).
27. Additional MSS 21,256, 7, 14, 21, 28 February 1792.
28. Clarkson, *History*, Vol. II, p. 352.
29. Additional MSS 21,256, 7, 14, 21, 28 February 1792.
30. Thompson/Clarkson MSS, Vol. I, p. 169, Capel Lofft to James Phillips, 16 February 1792.
31. Additional MSS 21,256, 6, 13 March 1792.
32. Thompson/Clarkson MSS, Vol. I, p. 203, Thomas Walker, Manchester, to James Phillips, 3 March 1792.
33. Matthews MSS, 4 March 1792.
34. *Journals of the House of Commons*, Vol. 47, 9 February–30 March 1792. Drescher, *Capitalism and Slavery*, pp. 80–9.
35. Cobbett, *Parliamentary History*, Vol. XXIX, pp. 1055–158.
36. Ibid.
37. James Walvin, *England, Slaves and Freedom, 1776–1838* (London and Jackson, MS: University Press of Mississippi, 1986), p. 114.
38. Additional MSS 21,256, 3 April 1792.
39. Additional MSS 21,256, 3 April 1792. Cobbett, *Parliamentary History*, Vol. XXIX, pp. 1204–93.
40. Additional MSS 21,256, 5 April 1792.
41. Ibid., 3, 5, 17 April 1792.
42. Cobbett, *Parliamentary History*, Vol. XXIX, pp. 1204–93.
43. Additional MSS 21,256, 24, 26 April, 1, 8, 15, 29 May 1792.
44. Cobbett, *Parliamentary History*, Vol. XXIX, pp. 1349–55.
45. Royle and Walvin, *English Radicals and Reformers*, pp. 50–4, 57. E.C.P. Thompson, *Making of the English Working Class*, pp. 116–18.
46. Additional MSS 21,256, 8, 15, 29 May 1792. Gibson MSS, Vol. IV, p. 95, John Hogkin, Vincennes, to James Phillips, 20 May 1792.
47. [George Harrison], *An Address to the Right Reverend the Prelates of England and Wales* (London: J. Parsons and Ridgway, 1792), pp. 5–7.
48. Additional MSS 21,256, 12, 19 June 1792.

6

The Abolitionist Breakdown, 1792–98

In June 1792, Joseph Woods was hopeful about abolition in Britain but he was becoming doubtful about events in France. In April, France had declared war on the Holy Roman Empire and now the Legislative Assembly was wielding ever greater power. Rumours of revolutionary plots and Royalist counter-plots swept Paris, reverberating in London. 'Being straitened for time', wrote Woods to Matthews, 'I must postpone all reflections upon Revolutions and counter-Revolutions, Plots, Riots and Rebellion, till a more convenient opportunity.'[1] In August, King Louis XVI was deposed. Massacres followed in September, and the National Convention declared France a Republic.

In October, 'Mr. Woods brought in a Draft of some observations upon a Pamphlet addressed to the People at large and annexed to many monthly publications.' A subcommittee, including Woods and Harrison, was assigned to edit Woods' manuscript, and Phillips was to print it. But the Committee met only twice in November and December. Woods, Hoare, Harrison, Phillips, Clarkson, and Wilberforce attended the infrequent meetings but were joined by few others. Committee records indicate only four letters of support received from July to December 1792.[2]

In the autumn of 1792, Clarkson again set out to gather evidence against the slave trade; this time he was in search of witnesses to testify before the Lords. As Clarkson travelled, he talked openly, according to a correspondent of James Phillips, about his support for the French Revolution. On 13 November, Elihu Robinson, a Quaker in Cumberland, wrote to Phillips saying Clarkson had visited and 'entertained us about 5 hours' with his remarks about 'ye abolition of Slavery … ye Revolution and present state of France'. 'With respect to France', Robinson went on, 'He made little doubt but that ye Revolutionists viz. the main body of ye People will stand their ground and that an Excellent Republic will be established.'[3]

In North Shields Clarkson stayed with Henry Taylor, a Quaker seaman and friend of Captain Cook. In November, Taylor wrote to James Phillips with news of Clarkson's visit. Taylor described 'A Riot of Sailors … (but a very peaceable and systematic one) above six weeks', complaining 'any proper Justice of the Peace' could have settled it without 'the five ships of war in our harbour'. Then Taylor added: 'Surely the time is coming that will level the inequalities of Nature, by bringing down the Hills and Exalting the Vallies.'[4] On 20 December, with war looming between Britain and France, Taylor again wrote to Phillips from North Shields saying, I 'lament the sin and folly of our joining in the war against Reason and the Rights of Men'.[5]

Others in Great Britain did not share Taylor's views. As Edward Royle and James Walvin show, 'From November [1792] onwards organized mobs roamed the length and breadth of the country burning effigies of Tom Paine.' In December, King George III called up the militia and warned British subjects against sedition.[6]

In Manchester, a Church and King mob attacked the home of Thomas Walker. Walker, the local abolitionist leader who had worked closely with the London Committee, was also a member of the Manchester Constitutional Society and a friend and supporter of Thomas Paine. According to contemporary accounts, Walker fired in the air, and the mob dispersed. Walker was then arrested for treason.[7]

On 21 January 1793, King Louis XVI of France was executed. Despite this ominous sign, on 29 January Wilberforce called together Harrison, Clarkson, Sharp and six other Committee members and 'informed the Committee he intended making … [a] motion in the House of Commons'. Wilberforce proposed to renew the vote for gradual abolition in the Commons as a way of prompting the Lords to take action. The London Abolition Committee began meeting weekly in preparation for Wilberforce's action. James Phillips, Granville Sharp and Thomas Clarkson were directed to write to friends in the Commons requesting their attendance.[8]

On 1 February, France declared war on Britain and Holland. On 8 February 1793, James Phillips wrote a long letter to Brissot de Warville, who was now an influential leader of the Girondins in the National Convention. Phillips wrote to 'revive our old subject of the Abolition of the Slave Trade', reminding Brissot 'that the Cause of the Africans was the beginning of thy political career'. Phillips went on to ask Brissot to use his influence to spare French attacks on British ships trading to Sierra Leone. Exempting Sierra Leone would be 'perfectly consistent' with the principles of the revolution, wrote Phillips. Phillips made it clear he was still sympathetic 'with the principles of your revolution which (however it may have been stained by the cruelty of some unprincipled villains) manifestly tend to the general improvement of the condition of mankind'. He signed the letter to Brissot, 'sincerely/ Thy Friend'.[9]

On 26 February, only weeks after France had declared war on Great Britain, Wilberforce moved for a Committee of the Whole in the House of Commons to consider the slave trade. Opponents insisted the 'question ought not to be agitated at present'. Pitt and Fox supported Wilberforce, but his motion was defeated by 53 votes to 61.[10]

On 15 March, with Wilberforce's Bill defeated in the Commons and abolition stalled in the Lords, the Committee asked Thomas Clarkson and Samuel Hoare 'to learn what is the state of the Question respecting the slave trade and report the same at the next Committee'. On 19 March

> Mr. Clarkson reported that he, and Mr. Hoare, had separately waited on Mr. Wilberforce ... who had informed them, that he considered the Lords having resolved to examine Evidence, to be a favourable circumstance.

Clarkson, Woods, Harrison and Phillips were appointed 'to write a Letter to our Friends in the Country to inform them of the state of the Business'. Three days later, the letter was approved and 500 copies were sent.[11]

Resuming investigations in the Lords did not, however, turn out to be such a favourable circumstance after all. On 11 April 1793, the Earl of Abingdon, pointing to the correspondence between the London Committee and abolitionists in Paris, asked 'What does the abolition of the slave trade mean more or less in effect than liberty and equality?'. Abingdon then proposed postponing the investigation until 'mankind may be restored to their Senses'.

Abingdon questioned both the public right to petition on the subject of abolition and the concept of humanity as a legitimate basis for government policy. In his view, petitioning was limited to the redress of grievances or for protection against infringement of constitutional rights. 'Humanity', he asserted 'is no ground for petitioning; humanity is a private feeling, and not a public principle to act upon.' Furthermore, the petitions supporting abolition submitted in 1792, Abingdon charged, came from Quakers and other dissenters.

Following Abingdon, the Duke of Clarence attacked Wilberforce by name. '[T]he promoters of the abolition were either fanatics or hypocrites, and in one of those classes he ranked Mr. Wilberforce.' Grenville remonstrated with the Duke, and Clarence apologized, saying he meant Wilberforce 'no personal or political insult'. The Earl of Mansfield and the Bishop of St David's appealed to Abingdon to withdraw his motion for postponement. Abingdon did withdraw, and the hearings were resumed.[12]

As James Phillips had foreseen in his letter to Brissot, the war with France did affect trade with Africa. On 15 April 1793, John Dawson wrote to Phillips from Liverpool requesting an extension on a due Bill. 'Time is such that I can not get any African bill at present discounted but hope it will not be so long', Dawson told Phillips.[13]

But the wartime economy did suggest a new strategy for abolitionists.

On 14 May 1793 Wilberforce asked the Commons for leave to bring in a bill to abolish the slave trade to foreign territories. Speaking in support of the measure, Fox

> warned the House not to trust too much to the good temper of the people, by trifling with their requests, passing resolutions in one session … then abandoning the whole in another session.

Pitt, too, supported the measure, and it passed in a thinly attended House by 41 votes to 34. Wilberforce then moved for leave to bring in a Bill to regulate the importation of slaves to British colonies, but leave was denied by 25 votes to 35.[14]

With Wilberforce's Bill to end the foreign slave trade under consideration, the London Abolition Committee again began meeting each week. With the help of Pitt and Fox, the Bill made its way through its first and second readings. On 12 June, however, the Bill was lost on the third reading.[15] Abolition was now thwarted in both Houses.

On 18 June, Harrison, Hoare, and Phillips met with Clarkson, Sharp, Wilberforce, Henry Thornton, Charles Grant, William Smith, and eight other members of the London Abolition Committee 'to consider the present state of proceedings in Parliament … and what measures should be adopted to promote the success of our cause'. Two days later Harrison, Hoare and Phillips met again with Clarkson, Sharp, Wilberforce, Henry Thornton, Charles Grant, William Smith and seven others. The group 'Resolved, that it appears to this Committee to be expedient to recommend to the Friends of the abolition of the Slave Trade to abstain from the use of West Indian Sugar and Rum.' George Harrison, Thomas Clarkson, Charles Grant and three others were appointed as a subcommittee to

> draw up a Report … stating the different Measures which in their Opinion might be pursued towards carrying into Execution the Plan of abstinence from West Indian Sugar and Rum in the most extensive possible manner.[16]

On 4 July 1793, at a meeting including Harrison, James Phillips, Clarkson, Wilberforce, Sharp, Charles Grant, William Smith and nine others, the Committee

> Resolved that a Letter be written to our Correspondents informing them of the present state of the Question and that in our Opinion it is expedient for the Friends of the abolition to abstain from the use of West Indian sugar and rum.

On 9 July the Committee directed 1,000 copies of a letter written by Harrison's subcommittee be printed and distributed.[17]

Three weeks later, on 30 July, a smaller group, but one still including Harrison, James Phillips, Charles Grant, Sharp and five others, abruptly 'Resolved that the letters prepared by the subcommittee be not sent'. At the next meeting of the Committee, on 5 August, there was no quorum. On 13 August, at a meeting attended only by George Harrison, James Phillips, Charles Grant, Granville Sharp and two others, the London Abolition Committee 'suspended for the present' 'all proceedings respecting the expedience of recommending the disuse of West Indian sugar and rum'.[18]

On 20 August, Harrison, Phillips, Clarkson and Charles Grant presented the draft of the Committee's seventh public report. The Committee had hoped to present 'a plan of proceeding' but could not because, the report stated, 'so difficult is the situation in which we now feel ourselves', offering no further explanation. The Committee now feared the slow investigation in the Lords would mean that 'the Resolution of the Commons to abolish the Slave Trade in 1796 may be totally defeated and the hopes conceived from the numerous Petitions of the People be in great measure disappointed'. The Committee, however, vowed to 'endeavor to reconcile ourselves to the slow proceedings of the Legislature'.

Looking for hopeful signs, the report pointed to two new forms of commerce being developed as alternatives to the slave trade. A ship had just arrived from Sierra Leone, the report stated, filled with produce from Africa 'neither degraded with injustice, nor stained with blood'. As has been noted, Henry Thornton, the Chair of the Sierra Leone Company, joined the London Abolition Committee in May 1791. His home in Clapham was becoming the gathering place for Wilberforce and the other Evangelicals, who were becoming known as the Clapham Sect.

Moreover, members of the London Abolition Committee 'rejoice', continued the seventh report,

> that the increasing importation of East Indian Sugar is likely to enable the Friends of our Cause to supply themselves with that article through a channel unconnected with the horrors of the Slave Trade.

Charles Grant, who had been elected to the London Abolition Committee in December 1791, was one of the four members of the subcommittee who had prepared the report. Grant, another close friend of Wilberforce, was a Scot who had worked in India from 1768 to 1790 for the East India Company. On his return to England in 1790, he became a director of the East India Company. Grant was also a director of the Sierra Leone Company and a close friend of Wilberforce, Henry Thornton and other Evangelicals.[19]

In August 1793, members of the London Committee still believed abolition 'must eventually succeed' but acknowledged 'Circumstances are discouraging'.[20] That summer, the British Quaker organization dismissed its long-standing committee on the slave trade appointed in 1783, 'As it doth not appear ... that any immediate step is likely to be taken respecting that calamitous subject'.[21] In this time of war, as before during the Seven Years War and the American Revolution, the British Quaker organization turned inward and suspended its activities on the slave trade.[22]

Two strong individual leaders of both the Quaker organization and the London Abolition Committee were suffering from serious physical problems that summer. In late August or early September 1793, James Phillips suffered a serious 'fit of gout or palsy', a 'paralytic stroke' from which he never completely recovered.[23] By then, Samuel Hoare was also suffering from 'repeated attacks of nervous illness' that plagued him for the rest of his life. According to family memoirs, Hoare developed a 'nervous' fear of death, resulting in periods of sleeplessness and loss of weight.[24]

Samuel Hoare suffered his first nervous attack in December 1789, a year after his marriage to Hannah Sterry. His doctor prescribed a stay in Bath. Hannah Sterry Hoare, who was 16 when she married 36-year-old Samuel, read to him through the nights when he could not sleep, carefully leaving out references to death or other subjects that might disturb him. In 1790, on his physician's advice, Hoare, Hannah and his children left Stoke Newington and built a fine new home called Heath House in Hampstead.

The move to Hampstead had other consequences for the Hoare family, according to Samuel's daughter Sarah. 'In separating from my grandfather and aunts, we were taken ... from the constant society of Quakers ... and we were thrown upon new acquaintances', she later wrote. 'We had new desires, both parents and children, to become more like our neighbours.' Samuel Hoare's son, Samuel, was sent to a Church of England school, and all the Hoare children were permitted to attend the theatre.[25]

The London Abolition Committee, meanwhile, continued to meet monthly from September until December 1793, but meetings were sparsely attended and little business was recorded. In October, the Committee advertised for subscriptions, but none are recorded.[26] In France, the Girondins fell as Robespierre and the Committee of Public Safety came to power. On 31 October 1793, Brissot de Warville was executed.

By then, one of James Phillips' correspondents was becoming wary of writing openly about politics. Rear Admiral James Bowen of Torbay wrote to Phillips in October: 'I must not say word on Politics ... more of that when I smoke a Pipe with you in George Yard where I hope to carry on the War over a glass of Good Grog.' Bowen, who had become a member of the London Abolition Committee in 1790, added, 'my respects to my good friend Clarkson and all our Friends at the Old Jewry'.[27]

Joseph Woods, for his part, was beginning to have serious doubts about French ideas of equality and reform. That autumn he told his friend

Matthews he was taking up algebra, concluding pointedly 'My Doctrine of Equality is only to equalize A plus B'. By early 1794, Woods considered 'the Times ... wonderfully gloomy'.[28]

Woods' doubts about the French Revolution were beginning to harden into bitter opposition and scorn. 'I suspect', wrote Woods to Matthews in January 1794,

> there may be 'street meetings' in this metropolis between ill-disposed persons of both sexes by which the French Disease is propagated, and practice is combined with principle as it is written in the Apostle or Martyr of Liberty, Thomas Paine.[29]

For Woods, at least, the common ground between radicals and reformers was beginning to disappear.

On 7 February 1794, Wilberforce again asked leave to bring into the Commons a Bill ending the slave trade to foreign territories. Speaking in support, Pitt pointed out that the foreign slave trade had already ceased to exist for all practical purposes because of the war. Wilberforce was granted leave by a vote of 63 to 40.[30]

On 11 February, James Phillips rejoined Hoare and eight other members of the London Abolition Committee for the first time since his stroke. Phillips, Clarkson and two others were appointed as a subcommittee to distribute Pitt's speech, Clarkson's 'Abridgement of the Evidence', and other publications to Members of Parliament. On 25 February, Wilberforce's Bill, again supported by Pitt and Fox, passed its second reading and was sent to the House of Lords.[31]

On 2 May, the House of Lords refused to consider the Bill. Abingdon called it 'a French proposition', and declared 'it has Tom Paine's Rights of Man for its chief and best support'. Even Grenville, who supported abolition, moved to delay the question. Grenville explained that he could not vote for the Bill while the Peers were still investigating the slave trade. He urged the House to hasten their investigation. His amendment to postpone consideration of the foreign slave trade Bill was carried by 45 votes to 4.[32]

By the spring of 1794, the broad-based coalition which had come together to support abolition seemed to be disintegrating. In April, Manchester abolitionist Thomas Walker was acquitted of sedition. By then, Walker's old ally, Thomas Cooper, had left England for Pennsylvania. Walker himself was disillusioned by what he saw as an undue moderation on the part of Dissenters, his former allies. Dissenters, he wrote,

> through fear or some other motive ... have been so strongly the advocates of an overstrained moderation that they have rather been

the enemies than the friends of those who have ventured the most and effected the most for the rights of the people.[33]

On 8 April 1794, the London Abolition Committee suspended regular meetings and adjourned subject to the call of Treasurer Samuel Hoare, Chairman Granville Sharp, or any three members. On 6 May the Committee gave up its headquarters in the Old Jewry and adjourned *sine die*.

In July 1794, Hoare, Wilberforce and six others met and assigned Hoare, Clarkson and another member to write circular letters to committees in the country. The Committee did not meet again for eight months.[34] 'The Committee therefore were reduced to this', Thomas Clarkson wrote later, 'either they must exert themselves without hope, or they must wait till some change should take place in their favour.'[35]

Wilberforce summed up his own assessment of the parliamentary situation on 29 October 1794. It was one day after Thomas Hardy's trial for high treason began at the Old Bailey. Wilberforce seemed oblivious to shifting opinion. '[E]verything continues the same with respect to the Slave-Business', he wrote to a correspondent, probably Member of Parliament and fellow abolitionist, William Smith. 'Parliament I apprehend will meet the 25th of November, but it would hardly be advisable to bring our Subject forward before Xtmas.'

Wilberforce confided to his colleague that he would consider bargaining away emancipation in order to obtain abolition. 'From some Accounts I have received, I am inclined to believe the W. Indians would almost be willing to compound with us for Abolition if they conceived they could thereby preclude Emancipation', he wrote. 'This is a Compromise to which so far as I am concerned I should not be indisposed ....'[36]

In February 1795, Wilberforce moved for leave to bring in a Bill to abolish the slave trade in 1796 in accordance with the resolution for gradual abolition passed by the House of Commons three years before. There was no reason why the Commons should change its opinion about abolition now, Wilberforce argued. He also pointed to the developing trade in African products as a legitimate form of commerce that was replacing the slave trade.

Charles James Fox reminded Members of the petitions of 1792, asking if the House had acted then only to remove public pressure. Pitt tried to distinguish between abolition and radicalism, saying 'a British legislature [should] ... show, by its conduct, the contrast between the wild, spurious, and imaginary tents of the Rights of Man, and the genuine principles of practical justice and rational liberty'. But an amendment by opponents to postpone debate for six months was carried by 78 votes to 61.[37]

On 9 March 1795, 12 members of the London Abolition Committee met for the first time since the previous July to wrestle with the question of what to do next. Thomas Clarkson, unwell and writing from his home in Wisbech, spelled out his position in a letter to James Phillips. 'Dear James', wrote Clarkson, 'It is to me clearly obvious now that the Business will not be done by the Legislature … But if the Legislature will not do it, will the Business be done?'

Clarkson believed 'the slave trade will be abolished by the agency of Events' but only 'in the course of Time'. The question, then, as Clarkson saw it was: should the Committee wait for a change or should they 'endeavour to rouse the people again to apply to the Legislature?' Clarkson believed that such an attempt would probably fail because 'Many of the aristocrats who are our friends, would decline acting in a way which should call up the nation at such a time as this'. And even if it could be done, 'the People have no hold upon the Lords'.

Clarkson saw no other way 'than the old way often mentioned by the Committee of having recourse to the Expedient of prevailing upon People to leave off the W. India produce of [e]very sort'. Clarkson knew 'Some People said at our Committee it would be dangerous to try the expedient, as the Person venturing, would come under the Law'. Clarkson was willing to take the risk but said he would do whatever the Committee wished. He ended by apologizing for not attending the meeting but pointed out he had come twice to London already that year because he thought Wilberforce would be presenting a motion in the Commons only to discover after he arrived that plans had changed.[38]

At the March 1795 meeting, the Committee delegated Samuel Hoare, James Phillips, William Wilberforce and two others to bring in a public report, but the Committee did not meet again for three months. Hunger and starvation were spreading through Great Britain because of a cold winter followed by a hot summer in 1795. Crowds seized food, complaining of unfair prices. In June, the largest crowd ever assembled gathered in St George's Field to hear London Corresponding Society speakers.[39]

On 25 June, Samuel Hoare called the London Abolition Committee together in Old Palace Yard. Hoare brought in a report, the Committee's eighth, stating the 'numerous and pressing declarations of the people of this Country against the Slave Trade' had given cause for hope as had the House of Commons resolution of 1792. But, the report continued, the

> late decision of that House too evidently shews its reluctance to act consistently with its own resolutions, and we are reduced to the sad necessity of informing our friends that all our hopes from that quarter are nearly vanished.

The report went on to observe that 'by rejecting the Petitions of the People',

Parliament 'have taken the whole weight of the trade on themselves'. The Committee did 'not think the present juncture favourable for any further public measure' and left it 'to the serious consideration of every individual, what measures to take'. The report closed by endorsing the use of East Indian sugar and cautiously encouraging abstention from other West Indian products:

> We cannot … well refrain from informing our numerous friends, that the aversion which many in this country have shewn from the use of West Indian produce, has given so much encouragement to the culture and importation of East Indian Sugar, as to produce ample importations of that Article. [W]e are of [the] opinion, during the continuance of the Slave Trade, a decided preference should be given to the East Indian Sugar, as well as to all other substitutes for the produce of the West Indian Islands, the principal of which are Sugar, Rum, Cotton, Coffee, Cocoa, and Chocolate.[40]

George Harrison, meanwhile, had grown even more impatient than before with the House of Lords. In 1795, he wrote, again anonymously, *A Second Address to the Right Reverend the Prelates of England and Wales on the Subject of the Slave Trade*. This was published by J. Johnson of St Paul's Churchyard. As David Turley points out, 'Joseph Johnson of St. Paul's Churchyard published Priestley, Price, Erasmus Darwin, Mrs. Barbauld, Dr. Aiken and others who combined antislavery with a radical political temper'.[41]

Harrison began by saying, 'I addressed your Lordships on the subject of the Abolition of the Slave Trade about three years ago in language void of offense'. Now, 'You will be frankly told the sentiments of a plain man' who does not 'give much heed to the favours or frowns' of others.

'You well know with what degree of attention the question has been investigated during the last three sessions', Harrison told the Lords. '[I]t is my business, in the name of the Friends of Humanity, [to ask] whether you have … discharged your duty … to bring the momentous question of the Abolition of the Slave Trade to speedy, and to a just, decision.'

'Seated in the lap of affluence, and surrounded with plenty,' Harrison acidly observed with even more of an edge than in his earlier address, 'your Lordships are, perhaps, not much acquainted with the distresses that overspread the land.' Harrison then went on to give examples of these distresses. For 'the labouring poor … the present enormous price of provisions has rendered animal food inaccessible … and bread is nearly double its usual price.' The mortality rate was 'at the rate of 40,000 a year, the usual number is about 19,000'. The British army had been defeated in Westphalia. There was unrest in the West Indies.

The Lords should beware 'because an opinion seems to be gaining ground in this island, that the princely incomes which your Lordships possess, are not necessary to the maintenance of virtue and religion amongst its inhabitants'. After a long quote from Necker's *De l'importance des Opinions religieuses*, Harrison concluded with hopes for 'a general reform of conduct, by which may be wiped away the *stain of blood* that is upon us'.[42]

Instead of discussing the slave trade in November and December 1795, Parliament began debating two very different kinds of Acts. A Sedition Bill imposed penalties for inciting hatred of the King or Government by speech or writing. The other prohibited large public meetings.

Some reformers, like William Rathbone, a prominent Quaker merchant in Liverpool, tried to organize petitions against the proposed Acts. Rathbone wrote to James Phillips in early December, but Phillips was, evidently, reluctant to become associated with Rathbone and his efforts. Rathbone considered the Acts 'Treason Against the Constitution' and remarked that Phillips seemed worried about 'simply putting in letters to the Penny Post' concerning the subject.[43]

Despite the efforts of Rathbone and others like him, the Two Acts received the Royal Assent on 18 December 1795. By then, as Edward Royle and James Walvin observe in *English Radicals and Reformers*, with repression at home and war abroad, 'the English radical movement ... lay in pieces'.[44]

On 14 January 1796, Phillips, Hoare, Clarkson and four other Committee members came together for the first time in six months. Their purpose was to consider a letter from Clarkson to local correspondents asking for support for a forthcoming motion by Wilberforce. 'We are extremely desirous that Application should be made by our Friends in the Country to their Respective Representatives to solicit their attendance at the House to support this Motion', the letter began.

The letter was much more cautious than earlier correspondence with abolitionists in the country. 'We leave it to you and our Friends in your Neighborhood (with whom you will probably consult) to adopt that mode of application which you yourselves judge to be most efficacious', Clarkson now advised. The Committee directed James Phillips to print Clarkson's letter. He and Clarkson were to see that it was circulated.[45]

The letter was sent, but Wilberforce's support for the Sedition Bill had cost him the support of some abolitionists. On 19 January 1796, William Matthews wrote to James Phillips, saying that he had received the circular asking friends in Bath to support the forthcoming motion by Wilberforce. 'I am sorry to say that among my Friends here, who were warm and honest supporters of the principles of liberty, patronized, as they supposed by Wilberforce', Matthews wrote, 'there is a general opinion of his insincerity.'[46]

On 18 February 1796, Wilberforce moved for leave to bring in a Bill to end the slave trade 'at a time to be limited', reminding the House of Commons of the resolution passed in 1792. In the debate that followed, William Smith praised the abolition committees, saying they 'had been of great service in informing the minds of the people'. Fox agreed, asking whether the House would now refuse to heed the people 'after the passage of the two bills which have thrown difficulty into the way of expressing the public opinion'.

Supported by both Pitt and Fox, the Bill passed its first reading. On 25 February, the London Abolition Committee gathered in Old Palace Yard, Hoare, Phillips, Wilberforce, Muncaster, Montague, Smith and seven others were present. The purpose of the meeting was presumably related to Wilberforce's motion, but little business is recorded.[47]

On 3 March, when Wilberforce moved for the second reading of his Bill, opponents tried to delay it. 'Gentlemen saw that he had not his friends about him; and hence they wanted to take him by surprise', retorted Wilberforce. This statement raises the question of why Wilberforce moved the second reading at a time when his friends were not present. Still, the Bill passed the second reading by 64 votes to 31.[48]

On 15 March, when Wilberforce's Bill was being reported out of committee, Henry Dundas declared himself 'called upon in discharge of a public duty to come down to the House that evening … to oppose' the measure. William Windham, the Secretary for War, sided with Dundas, declaring 'All the havoc of the rights of man had not blunted him to the rights of Africans, nor had the example of French liberty reconciled him to African slavery'. But Windham believed abolition in any form must wait for peace. Faced with such opposition, Wilberforce's motion was lost by 70 votes to 74.[49]

The minute books of the London Abolition Committee record no meetings from 25 February 1796 until 29 March 1797. Of the four veteran abolitionists, Joseph Woods was by then beginning to withdraw from public life, yearning for 'a state of Repose, a Retreat from the Storms which agitate the world'. His mother died in 1795, and he inherited the family farm at Revel End in Hertfordshire.[50]

In January 1796, Samuel Hoare's father died, leaving his daughter, Margaret Woods, Joseph's wife, £9,000, a portion of the income from his real estate, and one-fourth of the return on a three per cent consolidated fund of £24,000. Joseph and Margaret Woods were now even more comfortably well off, and Joseph seemed more inclined to turn inward. In early 1796 Woods wrote, 'I keep myself as quiet as I can in my own habitation'.[51]

Samuel Hoare and his brother Jonathan benefited even more than Margaret and her sisters from their father's will. Samuel, Jonathan and a male cousin were named Executors, meaning that they received £1,000 each and the right to administer all their kinsman's property in England, Ireland and Pennsylvania. The real estate was divided into 14 shares with each son receiving three shares and each daughter two. In addition, the two sons received outright gifts of £23,000 each.[52]

James Phillips was still active in London politics and business although he continued to be troubled by ill health. 'I see by the public prints a Bill is brought into the H. of Commons for the relief of Friends respecting imprisonment for Tithes', wrote a Quaker from Suffolk to Phillips in April 1796. 'I shall be obliged to thee to procure and send me one by the mail Coach.'[53] Later that year, Phillips corresponded with Major John Cartwright about stationery supplies.[54]

Phillips continued to encourage the purchase of East Indian sugar. 'Dear Cousin', an Irish Friend wrote to a family member in London in 1796, 'From thy description of the East Indian Sugar bought for me and the prices I expect it will answer'. The Friend requested several impressions of a map of Quaker meetings printed by Phillips to be sent 'by the Ship that brings the Sugar'.[55]

But James Phillips was still suffering from the aftermath of the stroke 'which greatly shook his frame, and brought upon unseasonable feebleness and premature decay'. 'My disorder keeps me cold', Phillips told his friend James Jenkins. A correspondent noted that Phillips had 'complainest of being nearly worn out'.[56] James's eldest son William helped with his 'father's affairs ... through his long and painful illness'. A 'strong bond of connection and sympathy' grew between William and 'his beloved and revered father' James.[57]

On 29 March 1797 Granville Sharp and two other members called a meeting of the London Abolition Committee in Old Palace Yard, Westminster. Phillips, Harrison and Woods attended along with William Wilberforce and Matthew Montague. The purpose of the meeting was to refute charges made by Bryan Edwards in *A History of Santo Domingo* and *The Proceedings of the Governor and Assembly of Jamaica*.

Edwards, a member of the still powerful West Indian Interest in the British Parliament, accused the London Abolition Committee of directly encouraging slave insurrections by circulating pro-abolition pamphlets and medals in the West Indies. On 29 March, the Committee 'Resolved That measures be taken to repel these injurious charges by informing the Public ... that the Charges brought against this Committee by Bryan Edwards Esquire have no foundation whatsoever in Truth'.[58]

Before the Committee could act, however, on 6 April 1797 Charles Rose Ellis, another member of the West Indian Interest, secured an Address to the King requesting colonial governors to recommend measures for gradual abolition to their assemblies. On 12 April, Joseph Woods and two other members called a meeting of the London Abolition Committee at White Hart Court, where Woods had his wool shop. All four Quaker veterans attended the meeting, along with Granville Sharp, William Smith and six other members.

The Committee was as firmly opposed to gradual abolition as ever, and even more so now that gradual abolition was to be placed in the hands of the West Indians. 'With whatever confidence this Committee would wish to rely on the Wisdom of the House of Commons', the group resolved, 'They cannot but contemplate with the sincerest regret the address voted by that Honourable House to his Majesty … as a measure … tending to prolong, if not perpetuate the Horrors of the Slave Trade.'

At the same time, the Committee took steps to refute the charges made by Edwards. 'Mr. William Smith produced a draft of a letter to be published in … *The True Briton*, *The Morning Chronicle*, *The Times*, and *The Public Ledger*.' Joseph Woods 'produced the draft of a Pamphlet containing a full refutation of all the Charges … which was read and approved and the mode of Publication left to Mr. Hoare, Mr. Woods' and two others. Finally, the Committee adopted a resolution answering a letter from Edwards printed in the *Morning Chronicle* point by point.[59]

On 17 April 1797, Granville Sharp wrote his agitated memorandum, saying 'I thought (and shall ever think) it my duty to expose the monstrous *impiety* and *cruelty* … not only of the *Slave Trade*, but also of *slavery* itself'. The main purpose of Sharp's memorandum, however, seemed to be to establish his own innocence of fomenting rebellion. He felt the need to explain his actions,

> Having been required by the Committee of the Society in London instituted *'for effecting the Abolition of the Slave Trade'* to sign *officially* and *singly* with my name their late Resolutions in answer to the charges of *Bryan Edwards*, Esq.

Sharp went on to declare that he believed that '*Divine Retribution*' would certainly be visited on any government that tolerated slavery and the slave trade. But, he anxiously added,

> My Declarations on that head, I firmly assert, were always intended *as friendly Warnings against the obvious and ordinary consequences* of that unchristian oppression … but *surely not to excite* those fatal Consequences.[60]

On 15 May 1797, Wilberforce asked the House of Commons for leave to bring in a Bill for abolition of the slave trade 'at a time to be limited'. Bryan Edwards immediately countered by saying, 'The rebellion in St. Domingo, as he could assert from his own knowledge, was owing to the measures that had been agitated in France by those who called themselves "*Les Amis des Noirs*", and this should be a serious lesson to the House'. Sir William Young charged that Wilberforce's motion 'was a bill for enacting a revolution in the West Indies'. The request was denied by a vote of 74 to 82.[61]

By 1797, the economic and political situation in Great Britain was grim. In February, London Abolition Committee member John Lloyd recorded in his diary that 'The Bank of England suspended payments in specie'. A few days later, Lloyd added, 'The Bank issued large quantities of dollars at 4/9 each (stamped with our King's head) in payment of their notes for £5'.[62]

By then, William Phillips, beloved son of James, was thoroughly disillusioned with the leadership of Pitt. In earlier years, Clarkson and other members of the London Abolition Committee had expressed appreciation to Pitt for his support of abolition, but now William Phillips could see no good in Pitt at all. Sharing his father's penchant for epigrams, William Phillips wrote in 1797: 'That Pitt is immaculate loudly they cry/ So glaring a truth surely none will deny/ To prove it is true no one need his brains rack/ He can have no spot who is black and *all* black.'[63]

On 3 April 1798, Wilberforce, acting evidently without the assistance of the London Abolition Committee which had not met for a year, again attempted to introduce an abolition Bill in the House of Commons. This time, Wilberforce particularly addressed 'those gentlemen who had been the most forward in condemning the wild theories of France and her pretended rights of man'. 'Above all others', Wilberforce argued, as Pitt had done before,

> they were bound to show … that their zeal against French principles was not an indiscriminate repugnance alike to every species of innovation, however founded in justice and required by mercy.

Bryan Edwards was quick to retort he 'should not have suspected' Wilberforce 'was any great admirer of French politics or French principles'. Continued discussion of abolition was sure to result in rebellion in the West Indies, Edwards insisted. Slaves will 'murder their masters, and plant the tree of liberty on their graves'. Edwards finished by saying

> That there are fanatics in this kingdom (I do not say in this House) on whom these considerations will have no effect, I do believe; but I think better of the Honourable Gentleman, and trust, that when he finds his motion rejected, he will not again press it on the House.

Henry Thornton and William Pitt spoke in favour of Wilberforce's motion, as did Charles James Fox, but Fox was

> not sanguine of success. I am well convinced that the minds of men,

> some of whom think themselves enlightened, have taken on a very contracted turn, with regard to questions of reform and everything that implicates the principles of public freedom.

Fox was right. The motion was defeated by 83 votes to 87.[64] After the defeat, Wilberforce discontinued his efforts in the Commons, lest, as he said, abolition be reduced to a mere annual motion.[65]

The London Abolition Committee also fell silent. No meetings are recorded in the minute books between 1797 and 1803. During 1798 James Phillips, himself still suffering from ill-health, lost two sons, Edwin aged nine and John aged 27. In April 1798, a friend wrote to him, 'I am truly sorry for the accumulated distress which so much illness in thy family must occasion, and wish that a restoration of health may alleviate your anxiety'.[66]

In the summer of 1799, however, James Phillips, aged 55, died in Dover where he had gone in search of some relief. Phillips maintained his sense of humour and his interest in French affairs until the end. According to James Jenkins, Phillips' last words were, 'I feel as if I were going on a secret expedition', alluding to a British naval expedition then outfitting in Dover against the French.[67] His son William, deeply grieved, wrote 'Stanzas on Leaving Dover' describing 'the spot dear remembrance crave/ where sleeps a fond Father the sleep of the grave'.[68]

James Phillips left behind him mourning friends and messy accounts. 'I am truly sorry for the death of your father', one author wrote to James's son William. 'I have often solicited him, both by letter and when I met him, to settle the account between us; but without effect.'[69] 'I received the account of my lamented Friend your worthy father with true concern', wrote another. 'The account you mention, I thought had been settled.'[70]

James Phillips had few assets apart from his inventory of books and stationery supplies. His will directed his executors to sell his goods including household items 'if need be' at public auction and distribute the money to his wife and children.[71] But the publishing business and bookstore were not dispersed; William took over both. Yet gone was James Phillips, a man 'possessed of uncommon vivacity and good humour',[72] an important hub of Quaker information and activity, and a strong link with Clarkson and reformers of all persuasions.

By then, Joseph Woods was turning 60 and handing his woollen drapery business over to his eldest son, Samuel. Joseph was moving his shop from White Hart Court to George Yard and 'proposing to resign housekeeping in London to Samuel and reside chiefly at Newington', Margaret Woods wrote in her journal. With Samuel's help, Woods was still selecting books twice a year for the Library Company in Philadelphia. Yet in 1798 Woods complained that there was scarcely £100 worth of good books to be had in London.[73]

Woods was now spending more time with his family, journeying with them, for example, to Hastings in 1799 to visit his old friend and fellow-abolitionist the Reverend Thomas Coombe at Sevenoak. Each summer, he and Margaret visited their farm in Hertford, viewing their fruit trees and crops with pride. For her part, Margaret was still struggling for submission. 'Do we watch over our own spirits and keep them in subjection?' she asked herself. 'Do we set a good example in our little circle?'[74]

In 1799, Samuel Hoare and his family went again to Bath. Soon the family began spending two months every winter in Bath and every September at Cromer, their country estate in Norfolk. In Bath, Hoare visited Hannah More, and William Wilberforce became 'His old friend'. Hoare's oldest daughter, Sarah, joined the Church of England. His young wife, Hannah, at first had 'much discomfort in dealing with the children' until about the year 1800, 'when a strong and deep religious influence enabled me to submit'.[75]

George Harrison, at the turn of the century, was a prosperous businessman and a respected Quaker leader. By then Harrison had acquired a home on the Thames where he and his family spent their summers.[76] Harrison was also, by this time, a 'weighty Friend' (as Quakers call respected leaders). In 1800, for example, Harrison was among a dozen Friends chosen personally to present a Quaker address to King George III 'on the occasion of his providential escape from an attempt on his life'.[77]

Within Quaker circles, tensions continued to simmer between quietists, like Woods, and more evangelical Friends, including many Americans. When Samuel Hoare's father died in 1796, for example, he left £100 to the poor of Grace Church Street Meeting, which he attended in London. But, according to James Jenkins, 'that ... Meeting was (by some of our American visitors) persuaded to refuse' the legacy because Hoare paid tithes. Jenkins believed 'his legacy should not have been refused'. The elder Hoare 'died peaceful, and calmly in his bed', continues Jenkins, 'without ever conceiving that "paying Priests' demands" ... would stand as an insuperable bar between him, and the throne of mercy.'[78]

Around the year 1800, these long-simmering tensions erupted in a series of complicated and protracted disputes centring around Hannah Barnard, a ministering Friend from America. According to James Jenkins, Barnard first became an issue in 1799 when she insisted that the London organization reconsider a policy prohibiting the use of Friends' meeting houses by persons of other religions. The London organization refused.

Barnard then went to Ireland where she was influenced, according to Jenkins, by mystical 'New Lights' and the writings of French republicans. In 1800, Barnard applied for a certificate to travel to Europe, but Irish Friends denied her request. Barnard then appealed to a committee of the

London organization in 1801. When the committee refused, she again appealed to the organization as a whole.

The London organization upheld the judgment of the Irish Friends against Barnard, but the dispute deepened divisions among British Quakers. Quaker historian Rufus Jones says the controversy

> differentiated Friends more sharply than before into two groups – those who sympathized with her and who were thus inclined toward a liberal and advanced type of thought, and those ... who felt the Society must draw the lines of its faith more definitely in accord with orthodox standards.[79]

James Jenkins says evangelical Friends attacked Barnard so vehemently because 'she had opposed *reason* to the infallible dogmas of feeling friends'.[80]

Quaker abolitionists were divided by the Barnard dispute. Joseph Woods, certainly no great admirer of women ministers or American Friends, said of Hannah Barnard, 'She appears to be a woman who has both read and thought'. George Harrison was vexed by her persistent appeals but upheld her rights. According to Jenkins, Harrison served as one of her counsellors. But Richard Phillips, a cousin of James Phillips, close friend of Thomas Clarkson, and long-time member of the London Abolition Committee, bitterly opposed Barnard. According to Jenkins, Richard Phillips treated Barnard harshly, despite Harrison's plea for 'tenderness' and 'decency' toward her.[81]

Quaker abolitionists were further divided by the hardening lines separating quietists and evangelicals, even after the Hannah Barnard dispute. William Rathbone, for example, a staunch supporter of abolition in Liverpool, was disowned for speaking out 'against the increasingly rigid sectarianism' he saw among some Friends.[82]

By the turn of the new century, the all-encompassing, multi-denominational coalition that had been so meticulously constructed by the London Abolition Committee was shattered. Aristocratic supporters, as Clarkson said, were no longer willing to trust popular opinion. Charles James Fox had withdrawn from the Commons, leaving political leadership in the hands of the sincere but often inept Wilberforce. Wilberforce, by publicly supporting the Two Acts, had alienated reform-minded abolitionists like William Matthews. Political activity by artisans and wage earners, E.C.P. Thompson contends, had peaked and was on the decline. According to Royle and Walvin, 'popular radical activity entered a secretive, subterranean phase'.[83]

Judging from surviving publications and manuscripts, Joseph Woods, George Harrison, and Samuel Hoare fell silent on the subject of the slave trade. According to the minute books, the London Abolition Committee stopped meeting. In the repressive atmosphere after 1798, the organized effort to end the British slave trade seems to have come to a halt.

NOTES

1. Matthews MSS, 29 June 1792.
2. Additional MSS 21,256, 3 July–18 December 1793.
3. Elihu Robinson, Diaries and Memoranda, Vol. VI, 1792. Elihu Robinson (1734–1809) lived at Eaglesfield in Cumberland. He was a prominent meteorologist and the teacher of John Dalton.
4. 'Henry Taylor' (1737–1823), *Dictionary of Quaker Biography*. Gibson MSS, Vol. II, p. 113, Henry Taylor, North Shields, to James Phillips, 27 November 1792.
5. Spriggs MSS, 156/100, Henry Taylor to James Phillips, 20 December 1792.
6. Edward Royle and James Walvin, *English Radicals and Reformers, 1760–1848*, p. 62.
7. E.C.P. Thompson, *The Making of the English Working Class*, pp. 122, 130, 135.
8. Additional MSS 21,256, 29 January, 7, 12, 13, 19 February 1793.
9. Thompson/Clarkson MSS, Vol. II, p. 35, Letter from James Phillips to Brissot, 8 February 1793.
10. Cobbett, *Parliamentary History*, Vol. XXX, pp. 513, 520.
11. Additional MSS 21,256, 4, 8, 15, 19 March 1793.
12. Cobbett, *Parliamentary History*, Vol. XXX, pp. 513–20, 652–60.
13. Thompson/Clarkson MSS, Vol. II, p. 109, John Dawson, Liverpool, to James Phillips, 15 April 1793.
14. Cobbett, *Parliamentary History*, Vol. XXX, p. 948.
15. Ibid., pp. 948–94. Additional MSS, 14, 28 May, 4, 11 June 1793.
16. Additional MSS 21,256, 18 and 20 June 1793.
17. Ibid., 4 and 9 July 1790.
18. Ibid., 30 July, 5, 13 August 1790.
19. For Henry Thornton, see Howse, *Saints in Politics*. For Thornton's election to the London Abolition Committee, see Additional MSS 21,256, 10 May 1791. Charles Grant is also discussed in Howse, *Saints in Politics*. For Grant's election to the London Abolition Committee, see Additional MSS 21,256, 28 December 1791.
20. Additional MSS 21,256, 20 August 1793.
21. Minute Books of the Meeting For Sufferings, Vol. 39, 26 July 1783.
22. Jennings, 'The Campaign for the Abolition of the British Slave Trade: The Quaker Contribution, 1757–1807'.
23. Additional MSS 21,256, 13, 20, and 27 August 1793. Meeting for Sufferings Minute Book, Vol. 39, 26 July 1793. Spriggs MSS, 156/78, Joseph Gurney Bevan to Richard Phillips, 3 September 1793. Gibson MSS, Vol. IV, p. 63, Samuel Fisher, Philadelphia to James Phillips, 18 December 1793. Gibson MSS, Vol. II, p. 51, Catherine Phillips to Judith Phillips, 28 September 1793.
24. S. and H. Hoare, *Memoirs of Samuel Hoare*, p. 18.
25. London and Middlesex Quarterly Meeting Digest of Marriages, 1788, Samuel Hoare, Junior, and Hannah Sterry, daughter of Henry and Mary Sterry of Bush Hill and Hatton Garden. S. and H. Hoare, *Memoirs of Samuel Hoare*, pp. 22, 49, 51. Heath House, the Hoare home at Hampstead, still stands as a museum.
26. Additional MSS 21,256, 24 September, 15 October, 12 November, 10 December 1793.
27. Thompson/Clarkson MSS, Vol. II, p. 83, Rear Admiral James Bowen, Torbay, to James Phillips, 14 October 1793.
28. Matthews MSS, 22 September 1793, 26 January 1794.
29. Ibid., 26 January 1794.
30. Cobbett, *Parliamentary History*, Vol. XXX, pp. 1439–45.

31. Cobbett, *Parliamentary History*, Vol. XXX, pp. 1448–9. Additional MSS 21,256, 11 February 1794.
32. Cobbett, *Parliamentary History*, Vol. XXXI, pp. 467–70.
33. Thomas Walker, *Review of Some Political Events in Manchester* (1794) as quoted in E. C. P. Thompson, *The Making of the English Working Class*, p. 57. D. Turley, *Culture of English, Antislavery*, pp. 169–70.
34. Additional MSS 21,256, 8 April, 6 May, 8 July 1794.
35. Clarkson, *History*, Vol. II, p. 469.
36. Thompson/Clarkson MSS, Vol. I, p. 319. The letter is signed by William Wilberforce and dated 29 October 1794. Another hand has added 'to William Smith'.
37. Cobbett, *Parliamentary History*, Vol. XXXI, pp. 1321–7, 1341–5.
38. Thompson/Clarkson MSS, Vol. III, p. 203, Thomas Clarkson to James Phillips, 6 March 1795.
39. Royle and Walvin, *English Radicals and Reformers*, pp. 74–5.
40. Additional MSS 21,256, 25 June 1795.
41. D. Turley, *Culture of English Antislavery*, p. 157.
42. [George Harrison], *A Second Address to the Right Reverend the Prelates of England and Wales on the Subject of the Slave Trade* (London: J. Johnson in St Paul's Churchyard, 1795).
43. Dictionary of Quaker Biography, 'William Rathbone' (1757/8–1809). Rathbone married Hannah, daughter of Richard Reynolds and Hannah Darby. His company, Rathbone, Hughes, and Duncan, was the first to begin importing cotton from the US. He opposed the Two Acts and the war against France. Betty Fladeland, *Abolitionists and Working Class Problems in the Age of Industrialization* (Baton Rouge: Louisiana State University Press, 1984). Gibson MSS, Vol. IV, p. 175, William Rathbone, Liverpool, to James Phillips, 5 December 1795. D. Turley, *Culture of English Antislavery*, p. 166, says Rathbone helped organize a petition against the Two Acts.
44. Royle and Walvin, *English Radicals and Reformers*, p. 79.
45. Additional MSS 21,256, 14 January 1796.
46. Gibson MSS, Vol. IV, p. 125, William Matthews to James Phillips, 19 January 1796.
47. Additional MSS 21,256, 25 February 1796.
48. Cobbett, *Parliamentary History*, Vol. XXXII, pp. 862–3.
49. Ibid., pp. 866–902.
50. Matthews MSS, 26 January 1794, undated letter, 23 October 1795.
51. London, Public Records Office, Will of Samuel Hoare, Senior, Prob 11/1279, folio 456. Matthews MSS, 3 January 1796.
52. Public Record Office, Will of Samuel Hoare, Prob. 11/1279 folio 456.
53. Gibson MSS, Vol. I, p. 11, Samuel Alexander (Needham Market, Suffolk) to James Phillips, 30 April 1796.
54. Thompson/Clarkson MSS, Vol. I, p. 55, John Cartwright to James Phillips, 22 September 1796.
55. Gibson MSS, Vol. V, p. 260, Samuel Bewley, Dublin, to [John Pim, Jr, London], 24 November 1796.
56. Jenkins, *Recollections*, p. 316. Spriggs MSS 156/78, Rebecca Jones, Philadelphia, to James Phillips, 28 November 1797.
57. Christiana Phillips, *A Short Memoir of William Phillips*, p. 4.
58. Additional MSS 21,256, 29 March 1797. According to Dale Porter, 'although their economic position was slowly deteriorating, the West Indian planters and merchants remained politically influential all through the latter half of the [18th] century'. *The Abolition of the Slave Trade in England, 1784–1807* (Hamden, CT: Archon Books, 1970), p. 16. Eric Williams identifies Edwards as the holder of 'a small paternal estate in the decayed town of Westbury in Wiltshire' who benefited from having 'two opulent uncles engaged in sugar cultivation in the West Indies'. *Capitalism and Slavery*, 3rd edn (New York: Capricorn Books, 1966), p. 91.
59. Ibid., 12 April 1797. If Woods' pamphlet was published by the Committee, no copy of it has come to light.
60. Thompson/Clarkson MSS, Vol. I, p. 255.

61. Cobbett, *Parliamentary History*, Vol. XXXIII, pp. 569–76.
62. John Lloyd, Diary 1778–1811, February–March 1797.
63. Christiana Phillips, *A Short Memoir of William Phillips*, p. 53.
64. Cobbett, *Parliamentary History*, Vol. XXXIII, pp. 1376–415.
65. Ibid., Vol. XXXIV, pp. 518–65.
66. London and Middlesex Quarterly Meeting Digest of Burials, 1798, Edwin Phillips, John Phillips. Thompson/Clarkson MSS, Vol. II, p. 151, Edward Fox, Bristol, to James Phillips, 30 April 1798.
67. James Jenkins, *Records*, p. 315.
68. Christiana Phillips, *A Short Memoir of William Phillips*, pp. 60–1.
69. Gibson MSS, Vol. II, p. 161, John Whitehead to William Phillips, 1799.
70. Thompson/Clarkson MSS, Vol. II, James Field Stanfield to William Phillips, 26 December 1799.
71. Public Record Office, Will of James Phillips, September 1799, Prob 11/1330, folio 674.
72. James Jenkins, *Records and Recollections*, p. 315.
73. Journals of Margaret Woods, Vol. III, 13 September 1798. Library Company of Philadelphia, Records, 22 February 1798.
74. Journals of Margaret Woods, Vol. III, 5 September 1799 for visit to Coombe; 30 July 1800, 4 July 1801, and Vol. IV, 9 July 1805 for visits to their farm; Vol. III, 20 July 1801.
75. S. and H. Hoare, *Memoirs of Samuel Hoare*, pp. 35, 45, 50.
76. George Harrison's son, George, born in 1790, recalls that from the time he was five his family resided for the summer at Nine Elms on the banks of the Thames ([George Harrison Jr], *Memoirs of Cookworthy*, p. 166).
77. Library of Society of Friends, John Thompson MSS, Vol. 346, folio 199, 'An Address to George III'.
78. James Jenkins, *Records and Recollections*, p. 280.
79. Rufus Jones, *The Later Periods of Quakerism* (London: Macmillan, 1921), p. 306.
80. Jenkins, *Records*, pp. 353–4.
81. Matthews MSS, 24 June 1799. James Jenkins, *Records and Recollections*, pp. 312–71.
82. Fladeland, *Abolitionists and Working Class Problems*, p. 38.
83. Thompson, *Making of the English Working Class*, p. 195. Royle and Walvin, *English Radicals and Reformers*, p. 92.

7

Success, 1803–7

In the early years of the new century, national and international developments began to shift in favour of the abolition of the slave trade. Ireland was now represented in the British Parliament, and the new Irish Members had little interest in the slave trade. The West Indians were still complaining of debt but were taking no steps toward gradual abolition. After long warfare with France, Britain had gained control of the seas. Moreover, as Linda Colley points out in *Britons*, after Napoleon reintroduced slavery into the French Empire in 1802,

> Supporting the cause of slaves became a means to uphold the reputation of the existing order against both radicals at home and the French enemy.[1]

In 1803 after six years of silence on the subject, George Harrison once again began writing about abolition, prompted perhaps by the resumption of war between Britain and France. In October, he was completing *Notices on the Slave Trade in Reference to the Present State of the British Isles*. Harrison, writing anonymously, began by saying 'The following pages were penned with a wish, deeply affecting the heart of the writer' for abolition. He fervently hoped

> this nation and its rulers may, in the present critical situation of public affairs, be impressed with a sense of the miseries … which, for the sordid purpose of gain, we are inflicting on the innocent natives of Africa.

Recalling the 'shocking facts adduced in evidence before the Privy Council', Harrison quoted the speech delivered by Charles James Fox on 2 April 1792 'as reported by Woodfall':

> We … think that these things are not merely *impolitic* but *inhuman* and *unjust*; that they are not in the nature of *trade*, but they are *crimes*, *pollutions* which stain the honour of a country.

Harrison also recalled 'the number of petitions, unprecedented in the annals of parliament' presented in 1792. The petitions prove, Harrison argued, that 'the public mind' understands the injustice and inhumanity of the slave traffic.

Harrison acknowledged that, for some, arguments concerning the impolicy of the trade seem necessary. He quoted Pitt and Fox saying that abolition would lessen threats of slave insurrections in the Caribbean. He quoted Dundas saying that abolition was in the best interests of the planters. For consumers, he added his own observation that 'The plains of Indostan are capable of supplying us and all the rest of Europe with the produce of … the cane … at a price much below' that cultivated by slave labour.

Harrison's pamphlet was published in 1804 and was sold for six pence by Darton & Harvey in Grace Church Street, Hatchard's in Piccadilly, and other booksellers in the City and Westminster. A short quote from Wilberforce appeared on the cover but Harrison did not include any excerpts from speeches by Wilberforce or other Evangelical Members of Parliament throughout his 20-page text. The pages of the pamphlet 'might have been swelled by pertinent quotations from the impressive speeches of those zealous and honourable advocates …', Harrison explained, 'but the reader will perhaps think them sufficiently copious'.[2]

In 1803, Harrison wrote a tract on education. The 24-page pamphlet *Education respectfully Proposed and Recommended As the Surest Means Within the Power of Government to Diminish the Frequency of Crimes* was published under his name and sold by booksellers in the City, in Bond Street, and in Piccadilly. In it, he called on 'all good men, of every rank, and of every religious denomination, to unite in their efforts' to improve public education.[3]

On 13 February 1804, William Wilberforce gave notice to the House of Commons that during the current session he intended to submit a motion respecting the slave trade. On 23 May 1804, the London Abolition Committee recorded its first meeting since 1797. Samuel Hoare and George Harrison met William Wilberforce, Granville Sharp and six other Quaker and Evangelical members in Old Palace Yard, Westminster.

As Seymour Drescher points out, the anti-slave trade campaign 'became the first great reform movement of the 1780s and 1790s to revive in the country at large' after being 'silenced' in the decade after 1795. As Drescher says, unlike other reform efforts, the anti-slave trade movement did not 'need to be reinvented'.[4] The longevity and resilience of the anti-slave trade effort was directly related to the hard work and good faith of Joseph Woods, George Harrison, Samuel Hoare and other continuing members of the London Abolition Committee.

On 23 May 1804, the Committee directed that 'A Concise Statement of the Question Regarding the Abolition of the Slave Trade' be distributed to Members of Commons. The Committee also began nominating new members, electing James Stephen, Zachary Macaulay, Henry Brougham and William Phillips (the son of James). The group then adjourned subject to the call of Wilberforce.[5]

On 30 May 1804, when Wilberforce requested leave to bring in a Bill to end the slave trade, he argued as before that the slave trade was unjust and immoral. But he now pointed out that West Indian profits were down and were as low as four per cent, and he called on the Irish Members for their support. The West Indians protested, but the House agreed to consider the Bill by a vote of 124 to 49. The second reading was scheduled for 7 June.[6]

On 6 June 1804, the London Abolition Committee met again. Granville Sharp resumed his title as Chair. Thomas Clarkson now rejoined his old allies Samuel Hoare and George Harrison, and Parliamentary members Wilberforce, Sir William Dolben, William Morton Pitt and seven others. That night in the Commons, Sir John Anderson, speaking for the West Indian Interest, asked that counsel be heard before any action was taken on the slave trade. Despite Anderson's request, Wilberforce's motion passed its second reading. A date for 1 January 1805 was set for abolition. On 27 June the Bill was given its third reading and sent to the House of Lords.[7]

The abolition Bill was read for the first time in the Lords on 28 June. The second reading was set for 3 July. On 3 July, Samuel Hoare, George Harrison, Joseph Woods, Granville Sharp and seven others attended a London Abolition Committee meeting at Sierra Leone House in Birchin Lane. Henry Brougham reported that he and Wilberforce 'had had a communication' from James Monroe, the American envoy. Monroe told them that he 'had every reason to think the importation [of new slaves] had been prohibited in Louisiana'. Monroe went on to say

> that from the Spirit and Temper of the American government, no doubt whatever could be entertained of the prohibition being rendered absolute and general as soon as the law permits.

No Parliamentary members of the Committee were present at the meeting on 3 July, and no other business was recorded. That night, when the abolition motion was to be read a second time in the House of Lords, Hawkesbury moved to postpone consideration for three months. His motion was carried without a division.[8]

Joseph Woods was among those attending the London Abolition Committee meeting on 3 July. At the age of 66, Woods was becoming gloomy and discouraged. 'I feel no Ardent wish to convert people to my opinions', he wrote to his friend Matthews that summer. 'Now we have a disabled Monarch, a Ministry without the Confidence of Parliament or People, a very formidable Enemy, and a most enormous and increasing

Load of Debt and taxes', he continued, 'as I cannot remedy them, I think and discourse about them as little as possible.'[9]

On 17 July 1804, Wilberforce and Sharp met with nine London Abolition Committee members. None of the three surviving Quaker veterans were there, nor was Clarkson. The Committee decided to seek evidence to be presented to the Lords and to write a letter to friends in the country asking for funds.

The Committee met again on 24 July and 2 August 1804. Wilberforce was present for both meetings. Samuel Hoare participated in one. At the August meeting, the Committee printed 1,000 copies of a circular letter to friends in the country and wrote to the Pennsylvania Abolition Society.[10]

The Committee did not meet again until 22 January 1805. George Harrison attended that meeting in Old Palace Yard with Wilberforce, Sharp, Thomas Clarkson, his brother John and six other members. Preparing for public and parliamentary activities, the Committee revived tactics developed earlier by Joseph Woods, James Phillips, Samuel Hoare, George Harrison and other founding members. The Committee established standing subcommittees to secure evidence, obtain subscriptions, prepare publications, and visit Members of Parliament.

Hoare, Harrison and Woods were named to the contributions subcommittee which decided to begin raising money by subscriptions again. The group started their fund-raising efforts by writing to friends in the country. Harrison was assigned to work with Clarkson and Zachary Macaulay to secure evidence. Harrison was also appointed to work with Clarkson and three others members on publications.

The parliamentary subcommittee was composed entirely of Members of Parliament, many of whom were Evangelicals: Wilberforce, William Morton Pitt, Lord Teignmouth, Dolben, Henry Thornton, William Smith, and Thomas Babington. A separate subcommittee was appointed to call on Charles James Fox 'to request the honour of his advice and co-operation'. Samuel Hoare, along with Sharp, Clarkson and Joseph Woods' old friend Philip Sansom, were appointed to the subcommittee to visit Fox.[11]

Harrison met Dolben, Macaulay and others in London Abolition Committee meetings on 29 January and 19 February 1805. On 15 February, a motion for abolition introduced by Wilberforce passed its first reading but, on 28 February, when Wilberforce moved the second reading, Sir William Young and Banastare Tarleton charged that abolition was 'a remnant of Jacobinism'. Consideration was postponed by a vote of 77 to 70.[12]

On 6 March 1805, the London Abolition Committee directed Harrison, Macaulay and Babington to write a letter to 'the Friends of the Cause' and consider 'further measures' in the present session of Parliament. On 13 March, Harrison, Wilberforce, Babington, Sharp and five other Committee members discussed 'The propriety of calling a public meeting', but on 19 March, Harrison, Wilberforce, William Morton Pitt, Sharp and six others '[r]esolved that ... it will be expedient to postpone for the present the calling of a public meeting'.

Instead, a subcommittee was directed to 'procure support of Members of Parliament and to prepare correct lists of members both friendly and hostile to Abolition'. A list of friends in and about London was drawn up 'with a view to the calling of a public meeting when it shall be judged expedient'. The list of friends was referred to the subcommittee on funds.[13]

On 23 April 1805, the Committee met at Sierra Leone House. Harrison and Hoare attended as did Sharp, Clarkson, Zachary Macaulay, James Stephen and others. The Committee

> Resolved, that in any further discussion in Parliament respecting the Slave Trade ... the Committee will collectively and individually assist in endeavouring to procure a full attendance of Members friendly to those principles.[14]

Six days later, Harrison, Clarkson and five others met again to consider a letter from Wilberforce to Sharp. Wilberforce pressed the need for 'some proper person' to 'procure witnesses to give evidence to Lords'. The person should act 'with great caution and even secrecy'. Wilberforce suggested Clarkson. Clarkson agreed. Two weeks later, the Committee voted Clarkson their gratitude and £50 in bank drafts.[15]

At the meeting on 29 April 1805, the Committee drew up a complete list of members, now numbering 40. The names of Harrison and Hoare appear on the list, but the name of Joseph Woods does not. William Phillips, the son of James Phillips, is listed, although from the minute books it seems William seldom attended meetings. In addition to Harrison and Hoare, five other founding members of the Committee in 1787 are listed: Anglicans Granville Sharp, Thomas Clarkson and Phillip Sansom, and Quakers William Dillwyn and John Lloyd. According to the list, the Committee now included 14 Members of Parliament among its numbers.[16]

Although the abolition campaign had revived by 1805, the London Quaker organization was still seriously divided. That year, Henry Finch, one-time friend of George Harrison and Joseph Woods, brought a public lawsuit against the Quaker organization for disowning him and barring him from meetings. George Harrison was summoned by Finch, who may have been senile or demented, as a witness on his behalf. Harrison was asked by the Judge to explain the difference between Quaker meetings for worship and for business. Harrison's observations on the nature of worship and prayer won public praise from the Judge. The case against the Quaker organization was dismissed, but Woods feared 'Henry Finch has, by his unsuccessful attempt, strengthened the hands of the rigid Disciplinarians amongst us'.[17]

When the London Abolition Committee reconvened, the Quaker organization did not reappoint its Committee on the Slave Trade, but the British Society of Friends did continue to support abolition. In the summer of 1805, the Society of Friends helped distribute a pamphlet, 'The Horrors of Negro Slavery', written by Zachary Macaulay, an Evangelical member of the London Abolition Committee.[18]

Clarkson, Wilberforce, and the members of the London Abolition Committee, meanwhile, were cultivating public support for abolition. William Wilberforce, aged 45, was now taking a more active role in the revived Committee. Several of his Evangelical friends from Clapham – Zachary Macaulay, Henry Thornton, Thomas Babington, Henry Brougham, James Stephen and Robert Grant – were also becoming more active.

George Harrison and Samuel Hoare continued their active participation. They and their Evangelical allies continued to use the same tactics that the Committee had developed earlier. On 1 June 1805, for example, Harrison and eight others met to draft a letter to friends in the country. By 3 June, the letter was drafted and 6,000 copies were ordered to be sent.[19]

On 9 July, Harrison and five others considered a report from Thomas Clarkson. Clarkson, who was evidently not conducting his travels with much secrecy, 'found the ardour of all the former friends of the Abolition with whom he had conversed to remain unabated'. He went on to say, 'wherever he had been all ranks of people were warm in the cause and desirous of lending their aid'. Clarkson reported that local committees were being formed at Bristol, Gloucester, Tewkesbury and Worcester 'who would undertake to instruct the Members of those Places and also to procure instructions from freeholders to their Country Members'.

Clarkson was anxious to maintain the London Abolition Committee's carefully honed focus on the slave trade. He was concerned lest Macaulay's pamphlet, 'The Horrors of Negro Slavery', create 'confusion relative to the object of the Committee'. He called for another 'small publication'. After Clarkson's report, Harrison was appointed to the subcommittee to revise the 'Abridgement of the Evidence' for publication.[20]

Samuel Hoare continued to serve as Treasurer for the Committee. In July, for example, he reported a balance of £700 which the group decided to invest in Exchequer Bills. Yet by 1805 Hoare was undergoing a change in character according to his brother-in-law Joseph Woods. 'His nervous affections has excited a Degree of Impatience which was not in his original character', Woods wrote to Matthews in December 1805. 'Together with the consciousness of superior wealth, have I think, *inter nos*, somewhat altered it.'[21]

Although Woods was growing distant from Samuel Hoare, Woods did maintain contact with George Harrison. 'George Harrison has just dropped in and desires to be kindly remembered', Woods wrote to his friend and life-long correspondent William Matthews in 1804.[22] Yet, according to the minute books, Woods was no longer attending meetings of the London Abolition Committee.

The London Abolition Committee now met less frequently, and its meetings were more directly related to parliamentary action than in the earlier phase of the campaign. William Pitt had returned to office in May 1804 and, according to D.B. Davis, assured Wilberforce that the slave trade to the newly acquired French sugar colonies would be ended by Royal Proclamation. 'Yet it was only when Wilberforce threatened to join opposition leaders in presenting the issue to Parliament that Pitt finally issued an Order-In-Council, on August 15, 1805, cutting off the supply of slaves to captured territories.'[23]

In January 1806, less than six months later, William Pitt died at the age of 47. Pitt had consistently argued, like Adam Smith, that slave labour was uneconomical, yet Pitt had never made abolition a government issue. Wilberforce seemed never to lose faith in Pitt, although abolitionists like William Matthews and William Phillips became disillusioned with Pitt's leadership in the 1790s. It seems as though, for Wilberforce, as D.B. Davis says, while Pitt lived 'always there was the memory of Pitt's great speech in 1792, and the hope that Providence would ultimately permit the Prime Minister to act on his true principles'.[24]

Charles James Fox and Lord Grenville quickly formed a Coalition Ministry. 'We have many more Friends to Abolition in the Cabinet than under the Old Administration', Clarkson confided to his Quaker friend, Charles Lloyd of Birmingham.[25]

Charles James Fox had been unwavering in his support for abolition, but Quaker moderates like Woods and Hoare were not comfortable with his leadership. A few years earlier, Woods had written to Matthews, 'I know not why thou joinest me with Charles Fox and his crew. I do not take [them] to be "sons of quietude"....'[26]

Samuel Hoare's daughter later wrote:

> When Mr. Fox, whom my father never cordially liked, ... came into power, he did not rejoice with the Whigs. To him he was not the delightful companion so deluding to others. He had once dined at our house with some of the gentlemen belonging to the Slave Committee, but said nothing worth remembering.[27]

Regardless of their misgivings about Fox, the London Abolition Committee now moved to take action on the slave trade. On 7 March 1806, Samuel Hoare met with Wilberforce, Clarkson, Macaulay, Teignmouth, Babington and seven others. First, they planned a public strategy, but a cautious one. They

> Resolved … that private applications from Individuals to Members of Parliament earnestly desiring them to attend to the Abolition question this session and support it, will be more advisable at this time than the holding of public Meetings in favour of it.

Then, the Committee further advised that

> applications had better be made by separate letter from several respectable Individuals … than by one only … and by all means … avoid any expressions which may give the appearance of being made at the instigation of others.

Clarkson was directed to ask friends in Ireland to follow the same process.[28]

Clarkson wasted no time, writing to his friend Charles Lloyd in Birmingham the next day. Please 'consult a few select friends and endeavour to procure an address signed by many, or a number of private letters, to your Representatives requesting the favour of their attendance and support', Clarkson wrote.

> You should get this matter accomplished as quietly as you can, first because if the public voice were not general, we should appear to be losing ground; secondly because if our opponents were to hear of what was passing, they might canvass your own Members before you could canvass or instruct them.[29]

On 31 March 1806, the Attorney-General, Sir Arthur Piggot, moved for leave to bring in a Bill extending the Royal Order in Council of 15 August 1805 limiting the British slave trade to foreign colonies. The next day, Clarkson reported to Charles Lloyd that 'The Slave Bill comes on tonight in the House – a little opposition is expected, but it will be of no avail'.[30]

On 2 April 1806, Wilberforce met with London Abolition Committee Parliamentary Members William Smith, Zachary Macaulay, Thomas Babington and Henry Brougham in Old Palace Yard.

> Mr. Wilberforce communicated to the Meeting that several of His Majesty's ministers had expressed to him an earnest wish that he would forbear to take any step for bringing in a Bill for the general Abolition of the Slave Trade until the Bill brought in by the Attorney General for the Abolition of the Foreign Slave Trade had passed through Parliament.

His colleagues considered this new development. Then, they

> Resolved, … it will be advisable for Mr. Wilberforce to pay very great attention to the wish which has been conveyed to him … unless very particular circumstances should make such a step in his opinion advisable.

Based on their previous experience, the members of the Committee added

> that it is highly desirable that Mr. Wilberforce should take such steps as are best calculated to defeat any measures which the slave traders may propose for the purpose of delaying the passage of the Attorney General's Bill.[31]

Supported by the government, the Attorney General's Bill passed its second reading in the House of Commons on 18 April with little discussion and without a division. When the Bill was reported out of committee on 25 April, the West Indians asked for a delay, but Fox would grant no more than two or three days. Bamber Gasgoyne of Liverpool asked Wilberforce if he intended to bring forward an abolition Bill, but Wilberforce ignored his question. The Bill was ordered to be read a third time and passed its third reading on 2 May.[32]

The House of Lords first considered the Bill on 7 May 1806. The Duke of Clarence strongly opposed the Bill. The Earl of Westmorland claimed 'the idea of the abolition first originated, within a few years past, among atheists, enthusiasts, jacobins and such description of persons'. Grenville brushed aside their arguments by saying, 'clearly we should not supply the colonies of the enemies with slaves'. The Bill passed its second reading without a division and was considered for a third time on 16 May. While Clarence and Westmorland again opposed the Bill, the Duke of Gloucester made his maiden speech in support of total abolition. Grenville added that he also hoped for complete abolition. The Foreign Slave Trade Bill was then approved by a vote of 43 to 18.[33]

Roger Anstey and, more recently, Seymour Drescher have made much of the passage of this Bill as a major *coup* on the part of Parliamentary abolitionists, especially James Stephen, in disarming West Indian interests and winning support for abolition by subterfuge. Anstey cites the passage of the Bill to prove that while arguments of humanity and justice failed, 'more could be done behind the cloak of national interest'.[34]

The Bill was undoubtedly crucial, but Wilberforce had proposed a similar Bill in 1793. Pitt, under pressure from Wilberforce, had issued the original Order-In-Council in 1805, so the idea was not unique to James Stephen. Judging from Clarkson's remark that opposition would be of no avail and the fact that the Bill passed most stages without a division, the support of Fox and Grenville seem to be the real key to the success of the Foreign Slave Trade Bill.

From the minutes of the London Abolition Committee and Wilberforce's silence in the Commons, it did seem to be part of the government's strategy to separate the Foreign Slave Trade Bill from Wilberforce's crusade and to neutralize Evangelical arguments. Yet Grenville made no secret of the fact that he supported the total abolition of the slave trade. Who could doubt that Charles James Fox did, too?

On 2 June 1806, Samuel Hoare, George Harrison, Granville Sharp, Thomas Clarkson, James Stephen, Zachary Macaulay, and six others attended a London Abolition Committee meeting in Old Palace Yard. Stephen reported on the passage of the Foreign Slave Trade Bill and summarized its provisions. Harrison, Stephen, and Clarkson were delegated to write to abolitionists in America to inform them of the passage of the Bill, while various members were asked to write to Liverpool, Bristol, and other places.[35]

On the next day, 3 June 1806, Charles James Fox gave notice to the Commons that he intended to bring forward a resolution to consider the final abolition of the slave trade. Clarkson wrote to Charles Lloyd on 9 June saying that

> We expect three motions in this Session. First, The Slave Trade ought to be abolished … Secondly, That no new Vessel be permitted to sail in the Trade. Thirdly, That the King be Addressed to order his Ministers to take Measure and Act in Concert with Foreign Nations for the more complete Abolition of the Trade.[36]

On 10 June, Fox introduced his resolution. Fox said Wilberforce should be presenting the motion, but went on to explain that he was thankful Wilberforce and his friends had asked him to do it instead. 'If during the almost 40 years that I have now had the honour of a seat in Parliament', Fox continued, 'I had been so fortunate to accomplish that [abolition], and that only, I should think I had done enough.'

Then, calling on friends of Pitt to honour his memory by voting for abolition, Fox moved

> That this House, conceiving the African Slave Trade to be contrary to the principles of justice, humanity, and sound policy, will, with all practicable expedition, proceed to take effectual measures for abolishing the said trade.

In presenting his motion, Fox used the language and arguments first developed by the London Abolition Committee, combining Adam Smith's economics and Joseph Woods' humanitarianism. The Irish Members supported his resolution. Few spoke against it. The motion was carried by 114 votes to 15. Two weeks later Grenville saw to it the same resolution was carried in the House of Lords by a vote of 41 to 20.[37]

On 15 July 1806, Hoare, Wilberforce and Clarkson gathered with eight Committee members in Old Palace Yard and appointed a subcommittee to prepare a circular address to the Friends of the Abolition. Acting on two decades of experience, the group directed the subcommittee on publications to counteract anything unfavourable to abolition which might appear in the newspapers. On 30 July, Harrison, Clarkson, Sharp and four others ordered 2,000 copies of the circular letter printed for distribution.[38]

Abolition now appeared certain, but the Quaker organization was coming under attack. In 1806, George Harrison published, anonymously, *Some Remarks on a Letter on Joseph Lancaster's Plan for Education of the Lower Order of the Community in which Quakerism is Described as a disgusting Amalgama of Antichristian Heresies and Blasphemies.* In this, Harrison deplored the unsubstantiated 'portrait of Quakerism at full length as framed and gilt in the cabinet' of an anonymous critic. The critic, Harrison said, had resorted to the rhetoric of the seventeenth century in attacking Quakers. Pointing out that Quakers are 'not deists, not peculiarists but universalists', Harrison defended the organization and called for Christian tolerance and respect for all.[39]

At the same time, Thomas Clarkson was writing and promoting his own two volume *Portraiture of Quakerism.* Throughout the spring and summer of 1806, Clarkson was industriously selling his *Portraiture* to Friends throughout the country. Clarkson wrote to Charles Lloyd in Birmingham with a prospectus for the work, urging Lloyd to help sell the book to Quakers in the North.[40]

'I have as yet only taken a glance at the ingenious "Portraiture"', Woods told Matthews in a letter during the summer of 1806. 'I conceive it to be like others Portraits, … a select assemblage of such parts as may form an agreeable Picture.' Woods added:

> I understand the whole impression (2,500 copies) is taken off the Author's hands, whose profit will amount to a good round sum. I have been told upwards of £1,000.[41]

In the summer of 1806, with Charles James Fox in power, abolition seemed secure. In September, Fox died. Seven members of the London Abolition Committee gathered at Sierra Leone House on 17 October 1806; none of the three Quaker veterans were present. The group directed the subcommittee on publications 'to pursue such measures as may appear to them proper in case of the dissolution of Parliament for promoting the abolition of the Slave Trade'.[42]

Parliament was dissolved, and new elections were set for November 1806. According to Seymour Drescher, 'for the first time in the history of abolition the slave trade became a real election issue'. Drescher makes a close analysis of Wilberforce's Yorkshire election but points out that 'Yorkshire was not alone in giving the slave trade a prominent role in the Election of November 1806'. Abolition was an issue in Durham, Cumberland, and in Liverpool where abolitionist William Roscoe won a seat.[43]

It is unclear what role, if any, the London Abolition Committee played in the Parliamentary elections of November 1806. Opponents and proponents alike later testified that abolition was discussed in many elections throughout the kingdom. When the Commons met, Bamber Gasgoyne complained that

> [t]he attempts to make a popular clamour against this trade were never so conspicuous as in the late Election, when the public newspapers teemed with abuse … and when promises were required from the different candidates that they would oppose its continuance. There never had been any question agitated since that of parliamentary reform in which so much energy had been exerted to raise a popular prejudice … in every manufacturing town and borough.[44]

The friends of Fox and Grenville won the elections of 1806 by a narrow margin. Drescher says 'The results of the November election strengthened the abolitionist forces for the final push'. Grenville established a precarious Ministry. On 26 December, four members of the London Abolition Committee met to consider 'A Letter from Mr. Clarkson … recommending a general application to the Friends of the Abolition'. Harrison, Hoare, and Woods were not among the small group who requested a member 'to prepare a draught of a Letter for that purpose to be laid before the Committee at their next meeting'.[45]

On 2 January 1807, Grenville introduced a Bill in the House of Lords to end the British slave trade, announcing that he would allow two weeks for consideration. Grenville later gave the Peers two additional weeks. On 5 February he called for a vote. Grenville opened the debate by citing the arguments used by Pitt that the West Indies were already overproducing sugar.

Lord Holland added 'a pathetic allusion to the sentiments of Mr. Fox'. The Duke of Clarence was unmoved in his opposition to abolition, but his younger brother, Gloucester, was now just as strongly in favour of it. In the end, Grenville's Bill passed its second reading by 100 votes to 36.[46]

In the Committee stage of the Bill the next day, Grenville set the date for abolition at 1 January 1808. Hawkesbury moved to remove the words 'contrary to justice and humanity' from the preamble of the Bill, saying that the debate should not be conducted about abstract principles. Grenville's motion prevailed with the wording unchanged by a vote of 33 to 10.[47]

Eight members of the London Abolition Committee, including Thomas Clarkson, William Smith and Zachary Macaulay but not Harrison, Woods or Hoare, met on 10 February 1807 at 18 Downing Street. They began drawing up lists of Members who were favourable and unfavourable to abolition. That night the Bill passed its final reading in the House of Lords and was sent to the House of Commons.[48]

Lord Howick moved the first reading in the Commons on the same night, while opponents complained of undue popular pressure. George Hibbert said that the Commons should not be influenced by the decision of the Lords, the resolution adopted last year, or by 'popular sentiment out of doors, however assiduously and enthusiastically excited'. Howick protested that he 'knew of no attempt to raise a popular clamour'. Gasgoyne then delivered his complaints:

> Every Measure that invention or artifice could devise to create a popular clamour was resorted to on this occasion. The Church, the theatre, and the press, had laboured to create a prejudice against the Slave Trade.[49]

George Harrison joined Wilberforce, Clarkson, Sharp and a handful of others at Committee meetings in Downing Street on 11, 13 and 17 February. Members examined and corrected the list of Parliamentary advocates and foes as the time neared for the second reading of the Abolition Bill in the Commons. On 20 February, Samuel Hoare joined the group while Zachary Macaulay was directed to insert a paragraph in several papers on the progress of abolition in the United States.[50]

On 23 February, Howick opened the debate on the second reading of the Abolition Bill. Knowing that 'abolitionists have been branded as theorists and enthusiasts', he appealed to facts and experience. Yet, at the same time, he invoked the memories of Pitt and Fox. William Roscoe, a long-time abolitionist and newly elected Member for Liverpool, spoke in favour of the Bill. Walter Fawkes of York announced he had promised his constituents he would speak against the slave trade.

George Hibbert was almost alone in arguing that abolition was 'a visionary theory' and one of 'those wild projects of reform, to which the spirit of modern philanthropy has given birth'. As Wilberforce later noted, many Members of 'character and talent ... especially younger Members', spoke in favour of abolition. In the end, the House voted by 283 to 16 that the slave trade was 'contrary to the principles of humanity, justice and sound policy' and ought to be abolished.[51]

Harrison, Clarkson and nine others gathered in Downing Street on

24 February, the day after the second reading in the Commons. As members of the London Abolition Committee well knew, the Bill was still not law. Harrison, Clarkson, Sharp and six others met again on 27 February. That night in the Commons, when opponents of abolition protested about the ruin of the West Indian Islands, Henry Arthur of Kerry answered that he was bound to vote for abolition 'in pursuance of the instructions of his constituents'. Harrison, Hoare, Clarkson and Sharp and six more Committee members met again the next day.[52]

On 5 March, Harrison and two other colleagues met in Downing Street. On 6 March, the date of 1 January 1808 was proposed for abolition and was approved by the Commons by 175 votes to 17. The next day Harrison, Wilberforce and six others came together in Downing Street and ordered 1,000 copies of the speeches in favour of abolition to be printed for sale.

On 9 March, the words 'contrary to justice and humanity' were dropped from the preamble of the Bill by Howick with the acquiescence of Wilberforce. The next day, the Bill passed its third reading without a division. George Harrison and six other members of the London Abolition Committee met in Downing Street that day. Harrison and two others were delegated to write to the Philadelphia Society and to insert a paragraph in the newspapers regarding the change in the Bill's preamble.[53]

On 17 March, Harrison, Wilberforce, Muncaster and five other Committee members met in Downing Street. The amended Abolition Bill now had to be sent back to the Lords for final approval. The Lords approved the amended Bill on 23 March. The Bill received the Royal Assent on the morning of 25 March. Grenville and Howick left office that afternoon.[54]

George Harrison, Granville Sharp, Zachary Macaulay, Henry Brougham, and six other members of the London Abolition Committee gathered that day in Old Palace Yard. Two Quaker members, Richard Phillips and Wilson Birkbeck, reported that 'they had this morning heard the Royal Assent given by Commission to the Bill for the Abolition of the Slave Trade'. The Committee then 'Resolved that the warmest thanks … are justly due to William Wilberforce and the other members of the Legislature … for having effected the first great object of its institution'.

The Committee quickly drafted a letter to the 'principal Friends of Abolition in different parts of the United Kingdom' and directed that 500 copies be printed and distributed. The letter announced the passage of the Bill, adding

> We request you to communicate this very satisfactory intelligence to the Friends of the abolition in your neighbourhood and … encourage them to continue their cooperation with this Society in its endeavours to promote the observance of the Act.[55]

Joseph Woods, now 68, had attended only one meeting of the London Committee since 1804, but he was well aware of the success of abolition. He wrote to his friend William Matthews on 18 April 1807 declaring that 'The friends of Humanity have cause to congratulate each other on the Abolition of the Abominable Slave Trade'. Noting that 'The American and Danish governments have passed resolutions of similar import', he concluded 'there appears hopes that this monster with many heads may at length be extirpated from the world'.[56]

NOTES

1. Roger Anstey, *The Atlantic Slave Trade and British Abolition*. Clarkson, *History*. Eltis and Drescher argue that profits from the slave trade were actually on the rise in the early 1800s (Eltis, *Economic Growth and the Ending of the Slave Trade;* Drescher, *Econocide*). Yet it does appear that the political base of the slave trade interest was eroding if not its economic profitability (L. Colley, *Britons*, p. 358).
2. [George Harrison], *Notices on the Slave Trade in Reference to the Present State of the British Isles* (Printed and sold by Darton and Harvey, Grace Church Street; also sold by S. Hatchard, Piccadilly, J. Asperne, Cornhill, and T. Ostell, Ave Maria Lane, 1804). The foreword is dated October 1803.
3. George Harrison, *Education respectfully Proposed and Recommended As the Surest Means Within the Power of Government to Diminish the Frequency of Crimes* (London: Darton & Harvey, John and Arthur Arch, Grace Church Street, R. Faulder, Bond Street, and J. Hatchard, Picadilly, 1803), p. 20. A second edition of the pamphlet was published in 1810 by Longman.
4. Drescher, 'Whose Abolition?', *Past and Present*, p. 166.
5. Additional MSS 21,256, 23 May 1804.
6. Hansard, *Parliamentary Debates*, Vol. I, p. 1080; Vol. II, pp. 474–6.
7. Additional MSS 21,256, 6 June 1804. Hansard, *Parliamentary Debates*, Vol. II, pp. 519–58.
8. Additional MSS 21,256, 3 July 1804. Hansard, *Parliamentary Debates,* Vol. II, pp. 871–926.
9. Additional MSS 21,256, 3 July 1804. Matthews MSS, 7 March and 26 June 1804.
10. Additional MSS 21,256, 17 and 24 July, 2 August 1804.
11. Additional MSS 21,256, 22 January 1805. John Shore, Lord Teignmouth, was elected to the Committee on 17 July 1804. Additional MSS 21,256, 17 July 1804. Thomas Babington was married to the sister of Zachary Macaulay and closely associated with the Clapham Sect. Howse, *Saints in Politics*, pp. 13, 58.
12. Additional MSS 21,256, 29 January, 19 February 1805. Hansard, *Parliamentary Debates*, Vol. III, pp. 521–2, 641–60.
13. Additional MSS 21,256, 6, 13, 19 March 1805.
14. Ibid., 23 April 1805.
15. Ibid., 29 April, 14 May 1805.
16. Ibid., 29 April 1805.
17. London, Library of Society of Friends MSS, Portfolio Series, Vol. 14, folio 74; Portfolio Series, Vol. 32, folio 134. Matthews MSS, 24 June 1805.
18. Additional MSS 21,256, 9 July 1805.
19. Ibid., 1, 3 June 1805.
20. Ibid., 9 July 1805.
21. Ibid., 9 July 1805. Matthews MSS December 1805. Hoare's 'nervous affliction' seems to have been his fear of death described by Hannah Hoare in S. and H. Hoare, *Memoirs of Samuel Hoare*.
22. Matthews MSS, 7 March 1804.
23. D.B. Davis, *Problem of Slavery in Age of Revolution*, p. 443.

24. Ibid., p. 439.
25. London, Library of Society of Friends, Lloyd MSS 2/206, Thomas Clarkson to Charles Lloyd, 25 February 1806.
26. Matthews MSS, 5 January 1796.
27. S. and H. Hoare, *Memoirs*, p. 29.
28. Additional MSS 21,256, 7 March 1806.
29. Lloyd MSS 2/207, Thomas Clarkson to Charles Lloyd, 8 March 1806.
30. Hansard, *Parliamentary Debates*, Vol. VI, p. 805. Lloyd MSS 2/208, Clarkson to Lloyd, 1 April 1806.
31. Additional MSS 21,256, 2 April 1806.
32. Hansard, *Parliamentary Debates*, Vol. VI, pp. 917–19, 1021–7.
33. Ibid., Vol. VI, pp. 917–19, Vol. VII, pp. 227–36.
34. Roger Anstey, *The Atlantic Slave Trade and British Abolition 1760–1810*. Drescher, 'Whose Abolition? Popular Pressure and the Ending of the British Slave trade', *Past and Present*, pp. 141–4.
35. Additional MSS 21,256, 2 June 1806.
36. Hansard, *Parliamentary Debates*, Vol. VII, pp. 508–9. Lloyd MSS 2/209, Clarkson to Lloyd, 9 June 1806.
37. Hansard, *Parliamentary Debates*, Vol. VII, pp. 508–9, 596–603, 801–9.
38. Additional MSS 21,256, 15, 30 July 1806.
39. [George Harrison], *Some Remarks on a Letter on Joseph Lancaster's Plan for Education of the Lower Order of the Community in which Quakerism is Described as a disgusting Amalgama of Antichristian Heresies and Blasphemies* (London: J. and A. Arch, Cornhill, 1806).
40. Lloyd MSS, 2/204-211, 11 October 1806–June 1807.
41. Matthews MSS, 17 June 1806.
42. Additional MSS 21,256, 17 October 1806.
43. Drescher, 'Whose Abolition?', *Past and Present*, pp. 144–8.
44. Hansard, *Parliamentary Debates*, Vol. VIII, pp. 717–22.
45. Additional MSS 21,256, 26 December 1806.
46. Hansard, *Parliamentary Debates*, Vol. VIII, pp. 657–71.
47. Ibid., pp. 701–3.
48. Additional MSS 21,256, 10 February 1807. Hansard, *Parliamentary Debates*, Vol. VIII, pp. 701–3.
49. Hansard, *Parliamentary Debates*, Vol. VIII, pp. 717–22.
50. Additional MSS 21,256, 10, 11, 13, 17, 20 February 1807.
51. Hansard, *Parliamentary Debates*, Vol. VIII, pp. 257–9, 977–95.
52. Additional MSS 21,256, 24, 27, 28 February 1807.
53. Hansard, *Parliamentary Debates*, Vol. VIII, pp. 977–95, 1040–53. Additional MSS 21,256, 5, 7, 10 March 1807.
54. Additional MSS 21,256, 10 and 17 March 1807. Hansard, *Parliamentary Debates*, Vol. XIX, pp. 63-6, 114.
55. Additional MSS 21,256, 25 March 1807.
56. Matthews MSS, 18 April 1807.

8

Three Merchant Philosophers in Retirement, 1807–27

The work of George Harrison, Samuel Hoare and other abolitionist activists did not end in March 1807. As David Eltis observes, the Abolition Act of 1807 was only one in a series of parliamentary regulations relating to the slave trade.[1] Once abolition became law, Harrison, Hoare and other abolitionists took steps to ensure that the public was informed and the Act enforced.

On 30 April 1807, a little more than a month after abolition had received the Royal Assent, Harrison met with Granville Sharp and seven other members of the London Committee at Sierra Leone House. The group approved 500 copies of an advertisement 'for insertion in all the London and Provincial Papers and for distribution among the Friends of the Abolition'.

On 20 May, Samuel Hoare called a meeting to consider 'Information … given to the Committee of an Intention on the part of the Enemies of the Abolition of the Slave Trade to prolong the period of the Abolition'. The Committee debated whether or not 'to take measures to counteract the Effect of such design, which on consideration it was deemed most prudent to defer for the present'.[2]

Evangelical abolitionists, meanwhile, were setting up the African Institute to monitor enforcement of the Abolition Act and to foster education and commercial development among Africans. As David Eltis points out, after 1807 the African Institute served as the watchdog of abolition in the absence of any government agency monitoring the slave trade. Zachary Macaulay was the first Secretary. Eltis calls the African Institute an arm of the Clapham Sect.[3]

Joseph Woods had his doubts about the African Institute from the first. 'A very respectable association is forming for the purpose of civilizing the Africans in their own country by teaching them agriculture and other useful arts', he wrote to his friend Matthews in April 1807. 'But', he added,

> zealots are apt to begin at the wrong end, and instead of teaching them to cultivate the earth, and such productions of the earth as may be useful articles of commerce, they place all the merits of their missions in inculcating certain mysterious dogmas.[4]

By February 1808, both Woods and Matthews were becoming more sceptical of the missionary impulse behind the African Institute and another Evangelical reforming effort. 'I entirely agree with thy Sentiments respecting the African Scheme, which will probably terminate according to thy prediction', wrote Woods to Matthews. 'Nor have I any great opinion for the Bible Society for distributing Bibles among the heathens', Woods continued. 'I fear missionaries must follow to puzzle the poor people with their explanations.'[5]

Meanwhile, Thomas Clarkson was working on the first history of the abolition movement. In August 1807, Clarkson circulated a 'Prospectus of the first volume of a work which is to be comprised in Two thick Octavo volumes, containing the History of the Rise, Progress, and Accomplishment of that Great Event, the Abolition of the Slave Trade'. The price for the first volume was to be one guinea.

Writing to a contact in Bristol, Clarkson suggested that friends of abolition there should print their own prospectus and 'charge it upon the Work'. Clarkson sent a sample prospectus to his friend in Bristol. In the sample, Clarkson struck through several sentences relating to the activities of Quakers in the abolition campaign. He advised his Bristol contact, who was not a Quaker, to omit those sentences. 'I fear the Quakers would appear too prominent for the World', Clarkson explained.

> I fear there are Persons of different religious denominations, who would not like to see others too prominent and this is the reason, why I suggest this amended Copy.[6]

Clarkson began his *History* by tracing all the forerunners, or 'coadjutors' of abolition, including Quakers in England and the US, the association of 1783, and the London Abolition Committee. Clarkson named Joseph Woods as the author of the anonymous *Thoughts on Slavery*, describing the essay as 'highly useful to the cause'. Clarkson recalled how James Phillips had helped him revise and publish his first essay. Phillips 'possessed an acute penetration, a solid judgment, and a literary knowledge', wrote Clarkson. He remembered obtaining a letter of introduction to Samuel Hoare from Sir Charles Middleton, later Lord Barham.

About half-way through the first volume, Clarkson expressed his concern about devoting too much attention 'to considerations relative to himself'. He feared 'that by the frequent introduction of himself to the notice of the reader he may incur the charge of ostentation'. He noted that all members of the abolition effort were important just as are all members of the human body. He then went on to devote the remaining chapters of the first volume and all of the second volume to his own activities. The two-volume history was published in London by Longman, Hurst, Rees and Orme in 1808.[7]

On 28 May 1808, George Harrison, Thomas Clarkson and four other London Abolition Committee members came together at Sierra Leone House for their first recorded meeting since the previous May. Their purpose was to discuss how best to dispose of remaining copies of the Parliamentary debates. The group decided to present a copy to each Member of Parliament who had spoken in favour of abolition. They asked Thomas Clarkson 'to draw up a suitable advertisement and treat with booksellers for the sale of remaining copies'.[8]

On 16 December 1808, George Harrison and Thomas W. Smith wrote 'To the Deputies of the Spanish government in England'. Harrison and Smith were concerned that the recent alliance between the two countries opened the possibility for Spain to resume the slave trade. 'You are implored to represent to your countrymen the ardent wish of many, many thousands of well-wishers in this nation', they wrote, to 'abolish a practice which the great council of this friendly nation has deliberately pronounced *impolitic*, *inhuman*, and *unjust*'.

The Spanish deputy Franco Sangro replied, on 3 January 1809, saying 'the race of Negroes, who are our equals as men, will enjoy liberty, and will be treated by the new Spanish government, in a corresponding manner'. Noting the respectability of the writers, Sangro promised

> I shall exert ... my small influence in the best manner for the accomplishment of your wishes, by immediately transmitting to my government the highly just and reasonable declaration of the rights of nature.[9]

Over the next two years, George Harrison, like Joseph Woods, began to develop doubts about the work of the African Institute. In 1810, Harrison published *Some Remarks on a Communication from William Roscoe to the Duke of Gloucester, Dated March 20, 1809, As stated in the Appendix of the Third report of the African Institute; Respectfully Submitted to the Duke.* He wrote that:

> I have attended the sittings of the Board, under strong impressions of anxiety that the Directors might in the outset adopt a plan of proceeding, not only comfortable to the professed object of the Institute – namely to promote the civilization and happiness of the natives of Africa – but also such as may be wisely adapted to the gradual improvement of a race of savage and uncivilized men.

While William Roscoe had written about encouraging trade with Africa, Harrison stressed the importance of educating Africans first. Education was crucial to establishing the concept of private property, Harrison argued.

Once the security of property was established, Africans could farm and trade on their own. Harrison believed the African Institute should be teaching agriculture, surgery, medicine, mechanics, smithwork, and carpentry so that Africans could become self-sufficient.

Harrison pleaded that

> [d]isposed as we are to promote the interests of trade, let us not, … be dazzled by the splendid display, in this country of wealth accumulated by trade and manufacturing; let not this accumulation be the polar star of our course.

Englishmen, above all, he concluded, should be setting an example of fair treatment of the Africans.[10]

By 1809–10, when Harrison was writing this tract, he was in his early sixties. He had moved out of the City and was living in Wandsworth. His wife Susanna died in 1810, the same year that the youngest of his three surviving children turned 20.[11] Living outside the City, Harrison was beginning to lose contact with his old friend Joseph Woods. In January 1809, Woods remarked to Matthews, 'G.H. is removed to Wandsworth. I see him but seldom.'[12]

Joseph Woods, meanwhile, was continuing to serve as the purchasing agent for the Philadelphia Library Company, although he seemed to be losing his zest for it. 'The Books not sent are not procurable, not published, not translated, not completed, out of print, discontinued, or unknown', Woods had written to the Directors of the Library Company in 1808.

In 1809, Woods told the Library Company Directors that he had completed his selection without consulting William Dillwyn. '[O]pportunities for … [meetings with Dillwyn] are indeed rare, as we both reside in the Country at Distances somewhat remote to each other', he explained. Instead, Woods relied increasingly on the assistance of his eldest son, Samuel.[13]

Woods, now in his seventies, was losing all interest in reform. 'To mend the world's a vast design/ Reforming schemes are none of mine', he wrote in 1809. By 1810, Woods 'had little expectation of Good from any change of Ministry, and not much from a Reform of Parliament'. As usual, he took refuge in family life. He bought a larger house in Paradise Row, Stoke Newington, and began making extensive renovations.[14]

By then, Samuel Hoare and his family had developed many close friends and associates who were not Quakers and were moving in different social circles from those of his old friend and relative Joseph Woods. In Bath, the Hoare family met Mary Ann Schimmelpennick and other members of the literary society who gathered there. Samuel's eldest daughter, Sarah, developed an affectionate relationship with Priscilla Wordsworth, sister-in-law of the poet. Hoare, himself, maintained a close friendship with William Wilberforce.[15]

Samuel Hoare continued to serve as Treasurer of the London Abolition Committee, and George Harrison remained a loyal member. On 5 June 1811, the minute books of the London Abolition Committee record the first meeting since 1808. George Harrison, now 64 years old, met with Thomas Clarkson, Zachary Macaulay and four other Committee members at Sierra Leone House to settle the financial accounts of the anti-slave trade campaign. The group authorized £83 to 'be applied to the discharge of Mr. Wilberforce's share with Mr. Cadell on the loss of his Letter on the Slave Trade'.

Some individuals were now looking to the abolition of slavery, and the group approved the purchase of '100 copies of Dr. Dickson's work entitled "A Plan for the Rational Mitigation of Slavery"'. They also directed 'Richard Phillips to find out from James Stephen when his publication respecting slavery in the West Indies may be expected', but no further meetings were recorded in the minute book for three years.[16]

In June 1812, Joseph Woods, aged 74, died quietly at his new home in Stoke Newington. He had been in the midst of packing his spring shipment of books to the Philadelphia Library Company. His son Samuel completed the selection and sent them on to Philadelphia. The books sent by Joseph and Samuel Woods in the previous few years had contained valuable first editions by Wordsworth, Austin, Lamb and Coleridge. This final shipment contained the first copy of Byron's 'Childe Harold's Pilgrimage' to reach the United States. Along with the books, Samuel sent a letter saying, 'I have the painful task of announcing to you the loss of your long valued correspondent, my late lamented and respected father'.[17]

In a detailed will, Joseph Woods left his wife Margaret the house in Stoke Newington with 'all my household goods and furniture, silver plate, chinaware, wine, books and a pair of Globes and a reflecting telescope'. He also left her a £2,000 bond on the London and Liverpool Canal, £2,000 worth of stock in the London Docks, and a £3,000 trust. The farm at Revel End went to Margaret during her lifetime and afterwards to their children.

Woods provided £400 in cost consolidated bank annuities for his sister Rachel, who was now a widow. Since Rachel had no heirs, Joseph's children would inherit the Woods family property at Winchmore Hill after her death. Woods left £1,000 each to his oldest sons Samuel and Joseph, £1,650 to his daughter Margaret and £600 to his youngest son George who had married a non-Quaker and was experiencing financial difficulties. Woods further directed that the £2,500 bond he had received from his wife's father as her marriage portion would, after her death, be divided among the children. Finally, he left £40 'for the use of the poor' at Grace Church

Street Quaker Meeting, and £20 to 'my old Shopman John Brown'.[18]

In June 1812, not long after his death, an unsigned obituary praising Woods appeared in *The Gentleman's Magazine*. 'He was, from the beginning, a member (and a most efficient one he was by his clear and eloquent pen) of the Committee for the Abolition of the Slave Trade; and by whom his worth and talents were justly appreciated', wrote the eulogist, probably his son Samuel. Samuel later wrote to the Directors of the Philadelphia Library Company, saying Joseph Woods 'left behind him the reputation of a useful and honourable life as an example and consolation to his surviving family'.[19]

In the July issue of *The Gentleman's Magazine*, a letter to the editor concerning Woods appeared, probably written by his old friend, the American Loyalist, Reverend Thomas Coombe. The letter was signed with a 'C' and came from Mayfair where Coombe lived. The writer remarked that Woods' 'mode of faith was different ... but, such as he was, he would have been an honour to any communion of Christians'.

The writer remembered Woods as a man of 'masculine understanding and a benevolent heart'. Calling Woods 'a man of no ordinary excellence', the writer went on to say:

> his opinions, tempered by a liberal way of thinking, and proposed rather than insisted upon, were received by his associates with a consideration ... seldom seen paid to the sentiments of any other person.[20]

After Woods' death, George Harrison continued to monitor the progress of abolition. In June 1814, British Foreign Secretary Castlereagh returned to London after negotiating the Treaty of Paris which included an additional article allowing France to resume the slave trade for five more years. Castlereagh was denounced by Wilberforce in the House of Commons, and petitions were began and meetings were organized to protest against the article.

In June 1814, Harrison presented a petition to the British Parliament voicing his concerns about the recently concluded treaty with France. Harrison prefaced the petition by saying 'The writer of the following Address ... has laboured, during a period of more than 30 years with unabated anxiety, in the cause of Africa'.

Harrison now hoped for 'the complete redemption of Africa from the miseries that have been inflicted on her sons for the sordid purposes of gain'. In closing, he reminded Members of

> the fervent prayers of thousands and tens of thousands of your countrymen ... that Africa ... shall, instead of misery and devastation, receive knowledge and civilization.[21]

In July 1814, the African Institute held a general meeting of the friends of abolition, more than 20 years after the tactic had first been debated by the London Committee. On 2 July 1814 the minute book of the London Abolition Committee records a meeting at the New London Tavern, Cheapside, with Thomas Clarkson in the Chair and three other members attending. The group directed the Treasurer, Samuel Hoare, to pay £240

> to the African Institute, to be applied towards defraying the Expenses incurred by the Committee now sitting at the New London Tavern for the purpose of carrying into effect the Resolutions of the late general meeting of the Friends of the Abolition of the Slave Trade.[22]

Before the year was over, more than 800 petitions protesting against the Treaty, signed by more than 700,000 persons, were presented to Parliament, according to James Walvin. Seymour Drescher argues that the petitions did influence British diplomatic policy in further peace negotiations, but Walvin contends that 'international abolition was merely shunted around the diplomatic circuits of the Congress System'. Whatever the consequences of the petitions, Drescher argues that the widespread petitioning effort of 1814 proves the continuity of anti-slave trade opinion from the 1790s through to the 1820s.[23]

After 1814, George Harrison began turning his attention to questions of religion, especially the religious education of youth. In 1815, he published an abridged edition of Robert Barclay's 'Apology for the True Christian Divinity'. Barclay's work was a cornerstone of Quaker ideas about universal salvation and, according to religious historian Rufus Jones, the bedrock of Quaker quietism. Harrison's abridgment of Barclay's *Apology* was much respected and later reprinted.[24]

The next year, Harrison wrote *A Brief Intimation Respecting the Attributes of the Divine Being*, especially designed to guide young readers in contemplating such moral concerns as justice, truth and goodness. In it, he especially warned young people against any claims of the 'peculiar regard' of the Divine Being by any set of people.[25]

In 1818, Harrison compiled *Adversaria: or Selections and Reflections on Civil, Political, Moral and Religious Subjects; Intended to Instill into the Minds of Youth, who have had a liberal education, A Correct Knowledge of Men and Things*. The work contained 1,130 entries in 382 pages from writers as diverse as Plato, Swedenborg, Patrick Colquhoun and Harrison himself.[26]

Harrison developed his interest in political economy and was still able to give shrewd financial advice. In July 1819, he wrote to David Holt, praising his 'Science of Political Economy'. Harrison had 'long been acquainted with Robert Owen of Lanark', he told Holt. Harrison had 'attended his lectures at the City of London Tavern' presided over by the Duke of Kent. Because of the Duke's 'benevolent Disposition', Harrison went on to say:

> I feel an interest in his Character and Comfort, which induced me a little while ago to make a communication to his Friend Alderman Wood, respecting the Duke's Financial Concerns, for which the Alderman a few days since was commissioned by the Duke to make me his best Thanks.

Harrison told Holt about anonymous articles that he had written concerning political economy. He had 'sent two Strictures of his [Robert Owen's] plan to *The Monthly Magazine*, which the Editor inserted in his number for September 1817 signed Philoponnus', Harrison said. More recently, Harrison had become concerned about the 'demoralizing effects of public houses', where the labouring classes 'swallow a large part of our most burdensome poor rates'. He had, Harrison confided, 'lately sent an anonymous address to *The European Magazine*, the Editor of which tells me it shall appear in his next Number'.

Harrison never forgot his humble origins and maintained a strong commitment to equal economic opportunity. 'My opinion is, that every Man born in a Country, whether England or any other, has as much right to subsistence (I don't mean in Idleness) in *that* Country as any Lord of the Land', Harrison wrote in a letter to Holt. '[I]n other words, that *Every man at Nature's Table has a Right to Elbow Room* and unquestionably it is the first duty of government to provide such subsistence.' At the same time, Harrison strongly believed in individual responsibility, too. Harrison told Holt 'we are all sent into this World to do all the good we can, and every Man is expected to do his duty'.[27]

George Harrison was one of three members present on 9 July 1819 at the last recorded meeting of the London Abolition Committee. Harrison and two colleagues met at 16 George Street, Mansion House. Harrison brought in a statement of funds showing a balance of £129. The three men reported they had been

> individually apprized of the continued and zealous exertions of the Board of Directors of the African Institute to effect the complete abolition of the Trade in Slaves throughout the regions of Africa and elsewhere.

The group 'Resolved unanimously, That the Treasurer Samuel Hoare do pay the sum of £120 to be given to John Thornton, Esq., Treasurer of the African Institute'. The word 'adjourned' is then written with a flourish in the minute book.[28]

Samuel Hoare served as Treasurer throughout the life of the London Abolition Committee. More than his other three Quaker abolitionist colleagues, Hoare developed close social ties with William Wilberforce. Wilberforce called on the Hoare family at Bath and later visited the Hoare country home in Norfolk. A drawing dated November 1822 preserved in the family memoirs depicts Sarah Hoare, Samuel's oldest daughter, walking with the poet Reverend George Crabbe in a field by Cliff House, the Hoare country estate. With them are Mrs Opie, Samuel Hoare and William Wilberforce.[29]

Samuel Hoare died in 1825 at the age of 74. His daughter remembered that 'Earlier than almost anyone in this country he espoused the cause of the distressed Africans'. She recalled:

> My father told me after this [London Abolition] committee was formed, that if he could but see two points carried – the abolition of the slave trade, and the general establishment of Sunday Schools, he should die contented.[30]

He certainly died wealthy. To his wife Hannah, he left £10,000 and five per cent interest on a loan of £2,000 to the Trustees of the parish of Hampstead. He also left her his 'plate, linen, glass, china, book, pictures, horses, coaches, chariots, carts, wagons, wines, and liquors'. Finally, he left her £10,000 in trust 'independent of any future husband she might marry'. In 37 years of marriage, Hannah wrote later, she and Samuel Hoare had spent only two days apart.

To each of his two unmarried daughters, Hoare left £32,000. He left £20,000 to his married daughter, having already given her £12,000 on the occasion of her wedding. His son Samuel received £30,000, the country estate in Norfolk, two houses in Lombard Street, and the 'dwellinghouse, stables, pleasure ground, and garden' in Hampstead.[31]

George Harrison, meanwhile, continued to write about economic matters. He anonymously published several versions of 'Practical Advice to Housekeepers and Others Who May Be in Straitened Circumstances'. In a manner reminiscent of Benjamin Franklin's 'Poor Richard', Harrison advised wage earners to rise early, stay clean, keep everything in its place, and put money in a savings bank. His 12 suggestions were printed in at least three editions including a broadside and were sold in London and Liverpool for three shillings per 100.[32]

Harrison was also instrumental in establishing a loan fund to help enterprising young Quaker men. The purpose of the fund was to assist 'young men of small property but high virtue'. Recipients could obtain loans of up to £100 for two per cent interest per annum for as long as six years. Harrison served as a director of the fund and published two reports of its progress. In 1817, Harrison reported six candidates had received loans. The number of recipients increased steadily over the next few years: 15 in 1818; 20 in 1819; and 24 in 1820. Those receiving loans were 'small farmers and mechanics', Harrison explained, 'not mere Labourers'.[33]

Harrison remained a strong and independent voice within the Quaker organization and had no qualms about speaking out publicly when he felt the organization was in the wrong. In 1818, Harrison was one of three Quaker men asked to investigate the controversial will of a wealthy Friend, Samuel Southall. Their report, which found wrongdoing on the part of some Friends, was not accepted by the organization.

Harrison stood by the report, and in 1820 published *A Plain Statement of Facts relative to the Will of the Late Samuel Southall of Pennsbury*. Harrison's book was then disclaimed by the Quaker organization. The disclaimer was signed by William Phillips, son of James Phillips, Harrison's old friend and fellow abolitionist.[34]

Harrison also continued to work for reform and toleration throughout his life. In 1825, at the age of 78, he published *Letters and Extracts of Letters on the Subject of Universal Toleration from Original Correspondence of the late Christopher Wyvill ... Together with an Appendix, comprising the sentiments of many eminent men and Other Documents on that Subject*.[35]

George Harrison died in March 1827, aged 80, the last of the four Quaker abolition activists. His will was simple. He left £1,000 to a sister in Ireland and an annuity of £50 to a sister in Warrington. The remainder of his property, real and personal, he bequeathed in equal parts to his daughter Lydia and his son George who would serve as joint executor and executrix. A codicil gave lands that he had acquired later in Pennsylvania to his son George.[36] His obituary in a Quaker publication described Harrison simply as the 'friend who edited Barclay and was the editor of several other works'.[37]

NOTES

1. David Eltis, *Economic Growth and the Ending of the Transatlantic Slave Trade*, p. 7. 'British antislave-trade policy comprised a range of legislation and directives, of which the 1807 act is simply the best known.'
2. Additional MSS 21,256, 30 April, 20 May 1807.
3. Eltis, *Economic Growth and the Ending of the Transatlantic Slave Trade*, p. 105.
4. Matthews MSS, 18 April 1807.
5. Ibid., 13 February 1808.
6. Thompson/Clarkson MSS, Vol. III, p. 1, Thomas Clarkson to J. Birtell, Bristol.
7. Thomas Clarkson, *The History of the Rise, Progress, and Accomplishment of the Abolition of the African Slave-Trade By the British Parliament*, 2 vols (London: Longman, Hurst, Rees, and Orme, 1808).
8. Additional MSS 21,256, 28 May 1808.
9. London, Library of Society of Friends, Tracts, Box 38.
10. George Harrison, *Some Remarks on a Communication from William Roscoe to the Duke of Gloucester* (London: George Ellerton, Johnson's Court, Fleet Street, 1810).

11. London and Middlesex Quarterly Meeting Digest of Burials, 1810, Susanna Harrison.
12. Matthews MSS, 28 January 1809.
13. Library Company of Philadelphia, Box VII #7444, folio 37, Joseph Woods to Directors, 25 March 1808; folio 46, Joseph Woods to Directors, 2 April 1809.
14. Matthews MSS, 15 December 1809, 5 March 1810. Journals of Margaret Hoare Woods, Vol. V (1807–12), 27 June 1811.
15. S. and H. Hoare, *Memoirs of Samuel Hoare*.
16. Additional MSS 21,256, 5 June 1811.
17. Library Company of Philadelphia Records, Box VII # 74445 (1805–12), folio 66, Samuel Woods to Robert Waln, 5 August 1812. Invoice, 4 August 1812. Letter about Byron's 'Childe Harold's Pilgrimage', 5 November 1812. Austin Gray, *Benjamin Franklin's Library*, p. 53.
18. London, Public Record Office, Will of Joseph Woods, Prob 111/1535, folio 356.
19. *The Gentleman's Magazine*, Vol. 81 (January–June 1812), p. 669. The obituary was written by someone well acquainted with private details of the life of Joseph Woods. Library Company of Philadelphia, Box VII #7444, f. 66, 5 August 1812.
20. *The Gentleman's Magazine*, Vol. 82 (July – December 1812), p. 99.
21. London, Library of Society of Friends, Tracts, Box 38, 'Petition of George Harrison to Members of Parliament, June 1814' (London: Darton, Harvey, and Co., Grace Church Street, 1814).
22. Additional MSS 21,256, 2 July 1814. The three other members attending were Richard Phillips, Thomas Furley Foster, and his brother Benjamin M. Foster.
23. Drescher, 'Whose Abolition?', *Past and Present*, pp. 159–65. Walvin, *England, Slaves and Freedom*, p. 126.
24. *Barclay's Apology for the True Christian Divinity*, abridged by George Harrison (London: Darton, Harvey and Co., 1815). A second edition was published in London in 1822 by Harvey and Darton. Rufus Jones, introduction to Braithwaite, *Beginnings of Quakerism*, p. xii: '…it is a plain and patent fact that Barclay's formulation is charged and loaded with the essential conditions and tendencies of quietism'.
25. George Harrison, *A Brief Intimation Respecting the Attributes of the Divine Being* (London: Darton, Harvey, and Darton, 1816).
26. George Harrison, *Adversaria* (London: Darton, Harvey, and Darton; William Phillips; J. and A. Arch, 1818).
27. London, Library of Society of Friends MSS, Portfolio 37, folio 48, George Harrison to David Holt, Chorlton Cottage, Manchester, 18 August 1819.
28. Additional MSS 21,256, 9 July 1819. The other two members attending with Harrison were T.F. and B.M. Furley.
29. From T.E. Kebbel's *Life of Crabbe*, quoted in the Preface, S. and H. Hoare, *Memoirs of Samuel Hoare*, p. xi.
30. S. and H. Hoare, *Memoirs of Samuel Hoare*, pp. 17–18.
31. London, Public Record Office, Prob 11/1701, Will of Samuel Hoare. S. and H. Hoare, *Memoirs of Samuel Hoare*, p. 51.
32. [George Harrison], *Practical Advice* (London: T. Bensley, 9 Crane Court, Fleet Street and sold at E. Fry's, 75 Houndsditch, no date). Another version of the broadside was printed by T. Kaye, Liverpool.
33. George Harrison, *Memoirs of the Origin, Nature and Purpose of A Loan Fund Instituted at a General Meeting of Subscribers held at Devonshire House, London* (London: J.and A. Arch, William Phillips, and Harvey Darton, 1821). A second edition was published in 1822.
34. George Harrison, *A Plain Statement of Facts Relative to the Will of the late Samuel Southall* (London: T. Bensley, 1820). A disclaimer signed by William Phillips is pasted in the back of the copy in the Library of the Society of Friends in London. Peter Bedford's manuscript journal in the Library of the Society of Friends contains entries relating to Harrison's role in the continuing controversy in the years 1821–22.
35. *British Library General Catalogue of Printed Books*.
36. London, Public Record Office, Prob 11/1174.
37. *The Annual Monitor*, 3, 16 (1827), p. 18.

9
Significance

What do the lives and actions of these four Quaker anti-slave trade activists collectively reveal about British anti-slavery? The first part of this final chapter shows how the writings and activities of Joseph Woods, James Phillips, George Harrison and Samuel Hoare establish a basis for understanding the origins and development of the anti-slave trade strand of British abolitionism. The second part of the chapter explores how their lives and writings suggest new approaches to understanding the changing politics, economics and society of Britain in the late eighteenth and early nineteenth centuries.

'Any overall assessment', Seymour Drescher writes, 'must acknowledge that antislavery was a durable element of public contention between the late 1780s and the 1840s. The popular mobilizations and innovations of the 1780s and early 1790s had crystallized the modern social movement.' While many historians still 'envision the continuity of abolitionism almost exclusively in terms of the "Saints" and Parliament',[1] this study shows how Joseph Woods, James Phillips, George Harrison and Samuel Hoare helped to create and sustain the anti-slave trade arguments and strategies which became part of the larger culture of anti-slavery.

As Friends, Woods, Phillips, Harrison, Hoare and other Quakers brought skills in collective action and coalition building to the London Abolition Committee. They were committed to working with men of all denominations and used their Quaker experience in collective action to help build an ecumenical abolition coalition. The four were able to work effectively with the radical and impatient Thomas Clarkson, the conservative and cautious Wilberforce, and the quirky Granville Sharp. With the help of these four Quakers, the London Abolition Committee became and remained an effective coalition for change.

At the same time, the four men and their allies on the London Committee worked hard to transform the abolition campaign from the preserve of a few into a national political movement. Beginning with the first informal association in 1783, each of the four placed articles in newspapers, drew up countless circular letters and reports, drafted, edited and published basic information about the slave trade and their reasons for supporting abolition.

By assiduously cultivating public opinion, the four helped make abolition 'a much more broadly-based cause in the 1790s, both in Parliament and in the country, than reform or repeal'.[2]

Through their work on the London Abolition Committee, the four men helped establish petitioning as a respectable political tool. All four had prior experience with petitioning through the Quaker organization. All four, and especially James Phillips with his range of national and international contacts, were actively involved in encouraging and securing petitions. Comments by Members of Parliament concerning the abolition petitions show how the anti-slave trade campaign was expanding the role of public opinion in politics. As James Walvin says, the abolition campaign 'established petitioning ... as *the* central tactic of extra-parliamentary politics'.[3]

The minutes of the London Abolition Committee indicate that William Wilberforce, on the other hand, was much more cautious about involving the public. More than once, he warned the Committee about the dangers of appearing to exert undue pressure on Parliament. Members of the London Abolition Committee often seemed to be mediating between Wilberforce and extra-Parliamentary supporters concerning such issues as whether or not to hold public meetings, whether or not to print lists of petitions, and what the petitions should say.

David Turley shows how the London Abolition Committee helped transform potentially radical tactics such as petitioning into legitimate tools of moderate reform. 'Certainly abolitionists used techniques that had a radical pedigree', writes Turley, 'this was a source of Wilberforce's concern – but most of them [abolitionists] did not tie them to programmes of large-scale reconstruction of the political order.' Thus, says Turley, 'radical techniques became reformist techniques'.[4]

As James Walvin points out, Wilberforce was not a particularly effective Parliamentary leader at this early stage in his political career. Dundas certainly outmanoeuvred him more than once in Parliamentary debates on the slave trade. In his interactions with the London Abolition Committee, Wilberforce often seemed both unaware of public opinion outside Parliament and naïve about political reality inside Parliament.

Wilberforce came to dominate abolition historiography early on partly because, from the beginning, the mostly Quaker London Abolition Committee hailed him as the leader of the campaign while keeping themselves quietly in the background. By repeatedly pointing to the contributions of Wilberforce and other Evangelical Parliamentary leaders in their public reports, the London Abolition Committee underscored the status and respectability of their supporters. By so doing, the Committee also contributed to its own historical marginalization.

In its third public report issued in July 1789, for example, the Committee praised Wilberforce and Clarkson for their leadership. In 1791, the Committee expressed their public gratitude to the illustrious minority in Commons who had voted for abolition, pointing especially to Wilberforce but also mentioning Fox. When abolition was finally accomplished in 1807, the Committee again singled out Wilberforce for thanks.

In the same way, the London Abolition Committee in general and these four men in particular contributed to the historical marginalization of the role of Charles James Fox in the Parliamentary success of abolition. Both Joseph Woods and Samuel Hoare disliked becoming too closely associated with Fox, as has been seen.

It was Fox, however, who called Dundas to account in 1792. It was the Fox Ministry which carried out the abolition of the foreign slave trade, and it was Fox who introduced the resolution for abolition in 1806. Fox himself said that he considered abolition to be a major accomplishment of his political career. His sarcophagus in Westminster Abbey bears statues of African children liberated from the slave trade.

The tendency of Woods, Hoare and the public reports of the London Abolition Committee to play down the role of Fox in favour of the more respectable but less effective Wilberforce is one indication of the social significance of the anti-slave trade campaign. As D.B. Davis says '... for Quakers both in Britain and America, membership in nondenominational societies provided a means of confirming economic success with social acceptability.'[5]

As D.B. Davis recognizes, and contemporary sources confirm, despite the increasing prosperity of many Quakers, social prejudice against them was still strong in the late eighteenth century. In the political debates, some Members of Parliament referred to Quakers as 'sectaries'. William Pitt revealed his biases against both Quakers and Africans by 'jokingly' referring to members of the Quaker-dominated London Abolition Committee as Wilberforce's 'white negroes'.[6]

While most Quakers lacked the status of Wilberforce and others of his Evangelical circle, according to Joseph Woods' wife, Margaret, participation in benevolent efforts like the abolition campaign was raising Quaker social prestige. Near the end of her life, Margaret Woods wrote in her journal:

> We are no longer the poor despised people we used to be. Those of other persuasions, except perhaps a few of high Church principles, feel no repugnance to uniting with us in schemes of public utility.[7]

Quakers won praise from non-Quaker contemporaries for their participation in the anti-slave trade campaign. Lord Holland later wrote of the Friends that '[t]heir zeal for the abolition of the slave trade was one proof, among many, that they practice the tenets they teach'. In 1822, William Peter Lunnell, the Secretary-Treasurer of the Bristol Abolition Committee who was not a Friend, recalled 'Our greatest strength lay with the Quakers – they formed a Band – and never gave ground'.[8]

Participation in the London Abolition Committee brought the four abolitionists studied here into contact with men of wealth and influence in London, across the country and in other nations. In the course of their lifetimes, all four men and their families significantly moved up the social scale, sometimes at the expense of their Quaker connections.

After her death, Margaret Hoare Woods, wife of Joseph Woods, became a public model of female benevolence and family duty. When she died in 1821, she left her manuscript journals numbering seven volumes to her grandchildren. Her grandchildren edited and published them as a good example to other women. The printed volumes went through three editions in England and America.[9]

Samuel Woods, the oldest son of Joseph and Margaret, carried on his father's business and became a leader in the Jennerian Inoculation Society in London. He continued to buy and send books to the Philadelphia Library Company until his own death in 1839.[10] The second son of Margaret and Joseph, also named Joseph, became a respected architect and well-known botanist.[11]

William Phillips, the son of James, continued his father's business as printer to the Quaker organization. William wrote a book on the geology of England and Wales and became a Fellow of the Royal Society. He and Samuel Woods, Joseph's son, remained lifelong friends. Like his father James, William died young with a reputation for good humour.[12]

Samuel Hoare and his family, even during his lifetime, were moving away from their Quaker connections. Jonathan Hoare, the younger brother of Samuel Hoare and Margaret Woods, was known as the 'Handsome Quaker' and drank with the Prince Regent at Brighton.[13] Two of Samuel Hoare's three daughters, Sarah and Grizell, converted to Anglicanism as young women. His son Samuel married Louisa Gurney, sister of Quaker reformer Elizabeth Fry, but Samuel and Louisa Hoare were later disowned by Friends for non-attendance and both became Anglicans.[14]

George Harrison's son became a barrister-at-law. The younger George Harrison, like his father, was not afraid to speak out when he disagreed with the Quaker organization. In 1856, he was disowned by Quakers for writing *A Few Thoughts on the Present State of the Society of Friends*. A contemporary described Harrison's disownment as being 'lynched ecclesiastically'. Like his father, the younger Harrison was interested in the ideas of Swedenborg and wrote a memoir of his grandfather William Cookworthy.[15]

This study of Joseph Woods, James Phillips, George Harrison and

Samuel Hoare seeks to show how their participation in the anti-slave trade campaign both influenced and was influenced by the dynamics of change in the late eighteenth- and early nineteenth-century world. By distinguishing more carefully between the anti-slave trade strand and later abolitionism it is possible to see how these four men helped shape the developing anti-slavery culture.

In *Britons: Forging the Nation 1707–1837*, Linda Colley argues that abolition reveals 'as much if not more about how the British thought about themselves, as it did about how they saw black people on the other side of the world'. Colley shows how the origins of the anti-slave trade campaign were bound up with British defeat in the American Revolution and the belief that Divine Retribution would result if the slave trade continued.[16]

This was a consistent theme in the public reports and writings of these four Quakers and other members of the London Abolition Committee. George Harrison's *Second Address to the House of Lords*, for example, describes the near-apocalyptic conditions of war, famine, and disease in Britain and directly connects them to the continuation of the slave trade.

On the other hand, as Colley shows, support for abolition became 'an emblem of national virtue'. Again, this was a theme in the writings of these four men and other members of the London Abolition Committee. The second report issued by the London Abolition Committee in August 1788 proclaimed that the abolition of the slave trade was becoming to the spirit of humanity, distinguishing the character of the nation. After 1802, as Colley points out, when Napoleon reintroduced slavery into the French Empire, the campaign against the slave trade became not only safe but patriotic.[17]

In *The Culture of English Antislavery*, David Turley carefully delineates the elements he considers to be central to the development of an abolition culture. Some of the key elements include: 'a dense personal texture underlying cooperative activity', a distinctive literature and language of abolition, political styles and strategies, and visual symbols.[18] Again, this study shows how many of the elements identified by Turley were being created by these four men and the London Abolition Committee.

The personal and business ties between these four men were certainly dense, as this study shows. These strong links helped the men work together effectively. The men also helped to create the moderate mix of extra-Parliamentary activities and Parliamentary lobbying that characterized the political strategy of the campaign against the slave trade. For example, Joseph Woods and George Harrison helped to design the Wedgwood cameo of the kneeling African which, according to Clarkson, became such an effective visual symbol for the anti-slave trade campaign.

Woods, Harrison, and Phillips all helped to create the language and literature of the anti-slave trade campaign through their writings and publications. Many of the public reports and much of the debate concerning abolition was conducted in the language of humanity developed by Woods as well as the language of self-interest put forth by Adam Smith. The fact that the final request of the defeated West Indian Interest in March 1807 was to drop the words 'contrary to justice and humanity' from the preamble of the Abolition Bill is a tribute to the power of those words, first used by the London Abolition Committee.

While Colley and Turley explore specific links between abolition and the development of British nationalism and the culture of antislavery, two earlier historians have suggested other links which have not yet been fully explored. In his now classic study, *The Problem of Slavery in the Age of Revolution*, D.B. Davis argues that 'the anti-slavery movement reflected the needs and values of the emerging capitalist order'.[19] In his equally well-regarded *Capitalism and Antislavery*, Seymour Drescher suggests '[i]t was the capitalists' intensive involvement with the market *per se* which produced the conditions for their withdrawal' from the slave trade at a time when profits from the trade were increasing.[20]

This study suggests some links between these four men and the capitalist values emerging from their involvement in the market economy. From the earliest days of the association of 1783, these four Quaker tradesmen and bankers conducted their anti-slave trade activities much like their business transactions. Woods, Harrison, Hoare and their associates kept careful minutes, noting the duties and responsibilities of each member of the group. They also paid for the publication of Woods' *Thoughts* and worked with James Phillips, a professional printer.

Almost as soon as the London Abolition Committee was formed in 1787, the group rented a permanent meeting place and hired a clerk. They held regular meetings at fixed times announced in advance. The clerk kept careful minutes of the actions taken, although not the discussions, and assisted with correspondence. Each letter the Committee received was numbered and entered into a letter book, which has, unfortunately, been lost. The Committee also kept careful financial accounts, periodically directing members to review the Treasurer's accounts.

As a businessman, Joseph Woods, unlike his colleague Granville Sharp, supported the decision made by the London Abolition Committee to focus on the slave trade and not on the larger issue of slavery. That decision defined the anti-slave trade strand of British anti-slavery. The focus of this first effort would be on the business of buying and selling slaves not on the larger issues of human rights and freedom.

Abolition literally meant business for banker Samuel Hoare and printer James Phillips. As treasurer, Hoare received and deposited money and paid the accounts of the London Abolition Committee. As the principal publisher of the Committee's anti-slave trade tracts and pamphlets, Phillips received regular payments for his work.

At least two of the four men frequently referred to their anti-slave trade activities as the 'business' of abolition. Joseph Woods, for example, assured William Matthews in 1792 that Wilberforce's 'heart is in the Business' of abolition. George Harrison declared 'It is my business, in the names of the Friends of Humanity' to address the Right Reverend Prelates of England and Wales.[21]

These four Quakers were not alone in blending business and benevolence. Thomas Clarkson carefully considered the economic consequences of the decision to devote his life to ending the slave trade. Clarkson literally made his living from the profits of his anti-slave trade publications and his work for the Committee. London publisher Thomas Cadell refused to give the London Abolition Committee a discount for purchases of anti-slave trade tracts in 1789. Booksellers in York expected the usual profit on William Bell Crafton's *Short Sketch of the Evidence*, as William Tuke reminded James Phillips in 1792.

All the members of the London Abolition Committee participated in adapting popular economic tactics to the business of abolition. Members of the Committee collected subscriptions and advertised for funds. As the letter from James Ramsay to James Phillips in 1788 indicates, these tactics were not new, but the Committee did successfully incorporate economic practices which not only raised money but engaged consumers and contributors in the abolition campaign at a time when the market economy was expanding rapidly.

John Brewer offers another avenue of inquiry into the links between abolition and the expanding market economy that has been little explored by historians of abolition. In *The Birth of a Consumer Society*, Brewer hypothesizes that as England was becoming rapidly commercialized, 'men of moveable property, members of professions and shopkeepers' were seeking to distinguish themselves politically and socially from aristocrats and workers. In the process, they were inventing the English middle class just as the working class was being invented about the same time.[22]

A study of four men cannot prove or disprove Brewer's hypothesis, but the study does substantiate some of Brewer's points as far as these four are concerned. First, all four fit Brewer's definition of men of moveable property, professionals, and tradesmen seeking to distinguish themselves politically and socially from aristocrats and workers.

The Monthly Ledger, edited by Thomas Letchworth in the 1770s with anonymous contributions from Woods, Harrison, and Phillips, is an early indication of how these men were trying to distinguish themselves from aristocrats and labourers. Many of the essays published in *The Ledger* are specifically aimed at 'the middling sorts' or 'intermediate class', who were presented as models of civic virtue distinct from workers or aristocrats. For example, essays appeared 'On the Dangers of Poverty and Riches' and 'On the Actions of the Different Classes of Mankind'. The latter stated, 'it is from the intermediate class that the most extensive usefulness and public advantages are reasonably expected'.[23]

In his essays and advice written in the 1790s and early 1800s, George Harrison clearly positioned himself between the aristocratic Lords, whom he scorned and the mere labourers whom he declared ineligible for his loan fund. Harrison praised David Holt in 1819 for his concern for the labouring poor. By this very concern, Harrison reinforced the distinction between himself as a self-made businessman and mere labourers. These kinds of distinction were necessary to draw class lines in the absence of such characteristics as inherited land and noble heritage.

Brewer sees the penetration and mixing of social and moral values and the language of commerce as another characteristic of the emerging middle class in late eighteenth-century Britain.[24] This is clearly seen in the writings of Joseph Woods. For Woods, good humour, good cheer and wisdom were 'commodities', and 'astonishment' was a 'fund'. Double-entry bookkeeping became a metaphor for life: '[E]njoy the fleeting hour', Woods wrote, 'and enter it on the Credit side of the account as a *Good* received'.[25]

Brewer further observes how pleasing manners were becoming an important part of good business practices and middle-class life. Joseph Woods, keenly aware of his place in society, carefully – if grudgingly – cultivated the manners of a tradesman. In 1776, Joseph Woods wrote from his shop, then located at White Hart Court in the City, of the 'habitudes which at a certain period of life become fixed and settled into the pliant obsequious Civility (read Servility if you wish) of a Tradesman'.[26]

Participation in the anti-slave trade campaign can itself be seen as one way in which these four men and others like them were distinguishing themselves politically and socially from aristocrats and workers. By attacking the slave trade as a tainted form of commerce, these four merchants and bankers were identifying abolition with the duties and privileges of middle class tradesmen. By using petitions and publications, they targeted literate citizens and voters. By focusing on the purchase of slave products, they appealed to consumers. By identifying themselves and their cause with Wilberforce, Clarkson, Sharp and other Anglicans, they increased the social respectability of their cause and of themselves.

Joyce Appleby points the way to yet another new path in the quest to understand more fully the links between the anti-slave trade campaign and larger cultural dynamics. In *Liberalism and Republicanism in the Historical Imagination*, Appleby digs deeply into certain 'core liberal affirmations' that were 'expressed explicitly for the first time' in the last quarter of the eighteenth century. While Appleby's primary focus is on American liberalism, she probes its Anglo-American origins.

The first of the core liberal affirmations identified by Appleby is the belief that 'human nature manifests itself universally in the quest for freedom'.[27] Writing to William Matthews in 1776, Joseph Woods specifically addressed the issue of the free will of human beings. 'The prejudice of my education ran altogether in favour of Liberty', Woods wrote, as he and Matthews discussed Joseph Priestley's doctrine of necessity. After a close reading of Locke, Woods said: 'I cannot attain any satisfactory idea of liberty'. But, he continued, 'does it follow that because I have no adequate idea of liberty ... that liberty therefore does not exist? I think not.'[28]

Another of Appleby's core liberal affirmations is the idea that 'nature has endowed human beings with the capacity to think for themselves and act on their own behalf'.[29] It can be argued that this was the implicit assumption underlying all the activities of the association of six after 1783 and the London Abolition Committee after 1787. By acting on their own behalf, the abolitionists were able to change long-standing attitudes and policies toward the slave trade. In his letters to William Matthews, Joseph Woods repeatedly indicated his belief that others, too, would take action on their own behalf when confronted with the facts of the slave trade.

Appleby's final liberal affirmation is that 'the human personality' is presumed to be male.[30] There were no female members of the association of six or of the London Abolition Committee, as has been seen, although women were later prominently involved in the anti-slavery campaign. Two contemporaries used male terminology in characterizing the writings of Joseph Woods. Thomas Clarkson described Woods' *Thoughts* as manly. The anonymous eulogist writing to *The Gentlemen's Magazine* praised Woods for his masculine understanding.

Joseph Woods himself often used the word *liberal* or the phrase *liberality of sentiment* to describe his friends. In 1779, he described William Matthews as possessing 'liberality of sentiment'. In 1780, he told Matthews that the American Loyalist Thomas Coombe was a man 'of good sense and good nature, liberal and friendly'.[31]

In 1788, Joseph's wife Margaret wrote that 'liberality of sentiment is so often commended in conversation, that it has sometimes led me to query what liberality was?' Margaret looked up *liberality* in the dictionary and found that it meant bountiful, generous, and possessing 'freedom of spirit'. She concluded, 'When we hear one man speak of another as being a liberal man, we form our idea of the person spoken of, from what we know of the character of him who speaks.'[32]

This study indicates that in helping to construct the anti-slave trade campaign, these four men were also helping to fashion a new way of thinking that can be called bourgeois benevolence. Developed by men like Joseph Woods, James Phillips, George Harrison and Samuel Hoare, bourgeois benevolence can be seen as growing out of the interests and aspirations of the emerging middle class. Like the old aristocratic notion of *noblesse oblige*, bourgeois benevolence carried with it class status as well as duties.

A sense of humanitarian duty, as articulated first by Joseph Woods and later by the reports and statements of the London Abolition Committee, was an important component of the new idea of bourgeois benevolence. Opponents of abolition were not wrong when they insisted that humanitarianism was a new principle of action in the British political scene. As George Hibbert pointed out in the House of Commons debate on the final approval of abolition, a new spirit of modern philanthropy was at work drawing its energy from the rising middle class and fuelling the anti-slave trade campaign.

Born in the anti-slave trade campaign and developing as part of British national consciousness, bourgeois benevolence can be characterized by national pride and patriotism. At the same time, it is marked by the paternalistic sense of superiority evident in Woods' *Thoughts on Slavery*. Finally, bourgeois benevolence, as evinced in the campaign against the British slave trade, can be described as liberal and male.

It is, perhaps, too bold to speculate on such a broad-ranging development based on the study of four men. Yet, as this book makes clear, the anti-slave trade activities of these men were linked to much larger global dynamics, some of which must still be explored by historians of abolition.

NOTES

1. Drescher, 'Whose Abolition?', *Past and Present*, pp. 143, 166.
2. G.M. Ditchfield in Christine Bolt and Seymour Drescher (eds), *Antislavery, Religion, and Reform: Essays in Memory of Roger Anstey* (Hamden, CT: Archon Books, 1980), p. 114.
3. James Walvin, 'The Public Campaign in England against Slavery, 1787–1834', in David Eltis and James Walvin (eds), *The Abolition of the Atlantic Slave Trade: Origins and Effects in Europe, Africa and the Americas* (Madison: University of Wisconsin Press, 1981), p. 63.
4. D. Turley, *Culture of English Antislavery*, p. 81.
5. D.B. Davis, *Problem of Slavery in Age of Revolution*, p. 247.
6. As quoted by Roger Anstey in *The Atlantic Slave Trade and British Abolition 1760–1810* p. 272.
7. Journals of Margaret Hoare Woods, Vol. VII, 31 October 1818.
8. London, Library of Society of Friends, J T MSS, 214, copy of undated letter signed by Holland, probably written to Thomas Clarkson in 1807 or 1808. Thompson/Clarkson MSS, Vol. III, p. 211, Letter from William Peter Lunnell, 25 December 1822.
9. *Extracts from the Journal etc. of the late Margaret Woods* (London: John and Arthur Arch, 1829); 2nd ed. (1830); 3rd ed. (Philadelphia, PA: Henry Longstreath, 1850).

10. Journals of Margaret Hoare Woods. Library Company of Philadelphia Records.
11. Dictionary of Quaker Biography, 'Joseph Woods' (1776–1864). Journals of Margaret Hoare Woods, 26 November 1805. Matthews MSS, 12 December 1805. A descendant of Joseph Woods, the Reverend Frank Theodore Woods, became Bishop of Peterborough in 1916. London, Library of Society of Friends, Records of Woods' family, Box 237.
12. Thompson/Clarkson MSS, Vol. I, p. 203. Margaret Woods Journal, Vol. VII (1817–21), 17 September 1819. Christiana Phillips, *A Short Memoir of William Phillips*.
13. Green, 'Historical and Biographical Notices of Jonathan Gurnell'.
14. S. and H. Hoare, *Memoirs*. Dictionary of Quaker Biography, 'Samuel Hoare' (1783–1847), 'Louisa Gurney Hoare' (1784–1836).
15. *The Friend*, 3, 76 (1 April 1867), pp. 91–2. [George Harrison, Jr], *Memoir of William Cookworthy*.
16. L. Colley, *Britons: Forging the Nation 1707–1837*, pp. 353–4.
17. Ibid., p. 354.
18. D. Turley, *The Culture of English Antislavery*.
19. D.B. Davis, *The Problem of Slavery in the Age of Revolution*, pp. 348–50.
20. Drescher, *Capitalism and Antislavery*, pp. 19–21.
21. [Harrison], *Second Address to the Right Reverend Prelates of England and Wales*, p. 6.
22. John Brewer, Neil McKendrick, and J.H. Plumb, *The Birth of a Consumer Society*, pp. 197, 215. E.C.P. Thompson, *The Making of the English Working Class*.
23. *The Monthly Ledger*, 1 (August 1774), 'On the Dangers of Poverty and Riches'; 2 (April 1775), 'On the Actions of the Different Classes of Mankind', p. 414; 3 (November 1775) contains an essay on the parable of the rich man and Lazarus showing the danger of riches and the misery of the poor.
24. Brewer, *The Birth of a Consumer Society*.
25. Matthews MSS, 6 December 1774, 24 June 1805, 5 March 1810, 27 March 1788, undated letter late 1794 or early 1795, 3 January 1796.
26. Matthews MSS, 9 January 1776.
27. J. Appleby, *Liberalism and Republicanism in the Historical Imagination* (Cambridge, MA: Harvard University Press, 1994), p. 1.
28. Matthews MSS, 15 June 1776.
29. J. Appleby, *Liberalism and Republicanism in the Historical Imagination*, p. 1.
30. Ibid.
31. Matthews MSS, 10 August 1779, 9 February 1780.
32. Journals of Margaret Hoare Woods, Vol. III, 30 October 1788.

Appendix: Family Histories of Joseph Woods, Samuel Hoare, James Phillips, and George Harrison

Joseph Woods' father, Edward, was the son of William Woods of Malden in Essex, a yeoman, and his wife Elinor. At the time of his first marriage in 1718, Edward Woods was described as a pastry cook in Little Eastcheap in the City as well as a freeman and member of the company of vintners. Edward and his first wife, Mary Quelch, had five children. Two of the five, both sons, lived to be adults. Mary Quelch Woods died in 1729 aged 32.[1]

In 1732, Edwards Woods married Sarah Neale, daughter of Edmond and Rachel Neale of Hammonds End in Hertford. They had two children, Joseph and Rachael. In 1765, Rachael Woods married Nicholas Marshall, a druggist and chemist in St Andrew's parish, Holborn. A newspaper account announced their wedding at Tottenham High Cross. The newspaper identified Rachael as 'the sister of Mr. Joseph Woods', a woollen draper in Blackfriars.[2]

The paternal grandmother of Margaret Hoare Woods and Samuel Hoare was Margaret Satterwaithe Hoare, a travelling minister in Ireland.[3] Their maternal grandmother was Grizell Wilmer, daughter of John Wilmer, a silk merchant in Friday Street, London. The Wilmer family supported Cromwell and was granted land in Ireland.

Grizell Wilmer married Jonathan Gurnell of London. Jonathan Gurnell was described in London newspapers as 'a very eminent Merchant of this City', and a man of 'ample fortune'. William Penn attended the wedding of Grizell and Jonathan Gurnell.[4]

Grizell Gurnell, daughter of Grizell and Jonathan, married Samuel Hoare's father, Samuel. When Grizell's father Jonathan died in 1753, Samuel Hoare, Senior, inherited an interest in a family silk mill, £20,000 in a joint trust, and a partnership in the Gurnell family firm. Jonathan Gurnell also left Grizell £4,500.[5]

Jonathan Hoare, the younger brother of Samuel Hoare and Margaret Hoare Woods, built Clissold House which still stands in Stoke Newington. Jonathan Hoare's unwise investment in a pile of industrial waste was later satirized by Charles Dickens as 'Harman's Heap' in *Our Mutual Friend.*

Margaret Woods, the daughter of Joseph and Margaret Hoare Woods, was an invalid who never married. Her youngest brother, George Woods, married a non-Quaker and was disowned by the Friends.[6]

James Phillips' mother Frances died in childbirth in 1745. William Phillips married Catherine Payton when she was 46 and, as a contemporary observed, past the child-bearing age. According to James Jenkins, William Phillips 'waited in a kind of negative bondage until she had arrived at that period of life when she was no longer capable of becoming a mother'.[7]

James Phillips' older brother, Richard, took over the family mining business, married, and settled at The Woodlands, near Swansea. James also had a cousin named Richard Phillips who was a member of the London Abolition Committee. His cousin Richard's father was John, the younger brother of James' father, William. John Phillips married Mary Jones, a non-Quaker, and left the Society of Friends. Their son Richard read law at Lincoln's Inn and became a close friend of Thomas Clarkson. This Richard Phillips became a Friend in 1789.[8]

Little can be found about George Harrison's family, but the life of his father-in-law, William Cookworthy, is well documented. William was born the son of Edith and William Cookworthy of Kingsbridge in Devon. He was apprenticed as an apothecary to Silvanus Bevan in London. Cookworthy returned to Devon and became a wholesale druggist. He married Sarah Berry, who was also a Quaker minister, and they had five daughters.[9]

Cookworthy discovered 'China-earth' on the estate of Thomas Pitt, Lord Camelford. Cookworthy and Camelford started a china factory in Plymouth, financed by 14 stockholders and employing 50 to 60 skilled workers. Cookworthy later turned the patent over to Richard Champion for an annual fee.[10]

NOTES

1. London, Library of Society of Friends MSS, Devonshire House Monthly Meeting, 3 July 1718, Certificate of Marriage for Edward Woods and Mary Quelch. London and Middlesex Quarterly Meeting Digest of Marriages, 1718, Edward Woods and Mary Quelch. London and Middlesex Quarterly Meeting Digest of Births, 1720, Susanna Woods; 1722, Edward Woods; 1723, William Woods; 1725, Joseph Woods; 1727, George Woods. London and Middlesex Quarterly Meeting Digest of Burials, 1723, Susanna Woods, aged 3; 1726, Joseph Woods, aged 1; 1738, George Woods, aged 11; 1732, Mary Quelch Woods. The two surviving sons of this marriage predeceased their father. London and Middlesex Quarterly Meeting Digest of Burials, 1743, William Woods, aged 20; 1753, Edward Woods, aged 31.
2. London and Middlesex Quarterly Meeting Digest of Marriages, 1732, Marriage of Edward Woods and Sarah Neale. London and Middlesex Quarterly Meeting Digest of Births, 1733, Joseph Woods; 1742, Rachael Woods. London, Library of Society of Friends MSS, Enfield Monthly Meeting, December 1764, Certificate of Marriage for Rachael Woods and Nicholas Marshall. The newspaper account is in Library of Friends Society Tracts, Vol. 00/174.
3. S. and H. Hoare, *Memoirs*, p. 3.
4. J.J. Green, 'Biographical and Historical Notices of Jonathan Gurnell', pp. 30–6.
5. Dictionary of Quaker Biography, 'Samuel Hoare' (1716–96). S. and H. Hoare, *Memoirs of*

Samuel Hoare, pp. 2, 45. Joseph Joshua Green, 'Biographical and Historical Notices of Jonathan Gurnell', pp. 30–6.

6. J.J. Green, 'Biographical and Historical Notices of Jonathan Gurnell', describes Jonathan Hoare's home and his unwise purchase with his cousin Harman. Journals of Margaret Woods, Vols VI–VII, tell about George and Margaret Woods.
7. Cornwall Quarterly Meeting Digest of Deaths, Frances Phillips, 1745. For Catherine Phillips, see *Memoirs of the Life of Catherine Payton Phillips*. Frost (ed.), *Records and Recollections of James Jenkins*, p. 261,
8. Dictionary of Quaker Biography, 'William Phillips'. [Mary Phillips], *Memoirs of the Life of Richard Phillips* (London: Seeley and Burnside, 1841).
9. J. Penderill-Church, *Cookworthy*. William Tallack, 'William Cookworthy', *Friends Quarterly Examiner*, 27 (1893), pp. 219–30. London and Middlesex Quarterly Meeting Digest of Births, 1736, Lydia; 1738, Sarah; 1740, Mary; 1743, Elizabeth and Susanna.
10. Dictionary of Quaker Biography, 'William Cookworthy' (1705–80). [George Harrison, Jr], *Memoir of William Cookworthy* (London: William and Frederick Cash, 1854), pp. 22–3. John Penderill-Church, *William Cookworthy 1705–1780*, p. 69. William Tallack, 'William Cookworthy', *Friends Quarterly Examiner*, pp. 219–30. A. Douglas Selleck, *Cookworthy, 1705–80, and His Circle* (Plymouth: Baron Jay, 1978). Theodore Compton, *William Cookworthy* (London: Edward Hicks, 1895).

Bibliography

MANUSCRIPT SOURCES

London, British Library, Department of Manuscripts
Additional MSS, 21,254-21,256 Minute Books of the London Abolition Committee

London, Library of Society of Friends
Diaries of William Dillwyn, 9 vols (microfilm)
Dictionary of Quaker Biography
Digests of Births
Digests of Burials
Digests of Marriages
Gibson MSS, 6 Vols, Autograph Collection
Letters Between London and Philadelphia Meetings for Sufferings
Lloyd MSS, Letters to Charles Lloyd
John Lloyd, Diary (1778–1811)
Matthews MSS, Letters from Joseph Woods to William Matthews
Minute Books of the Meeting for Sufferings
Minute Book of the Meeting for Sufferings Committee on the Slave Trade
Minute Books of the Morning Meeting
Minute Books of the Six Weeks Meeting
Minute Books of the Two Weeks Meeting
Minute Books of the Yearly Meeting
Monthly Meeting Minute Books, Enfield and Devonshire
Norman Penney Notebooks
Portfolio Series MSS
Elihu Robinson, Diaries and Memoranda, 9 Vols (1762–1806)
Spriggs MSS
Temporary MSS
John Thompson MSS
Thompson/Clarkson MSS, 3 Vols and index

Wandsworth MSS
Journals of Margaret Hoare Woods, 7 Vols, 1771–1821

London, Public Record Office
Wills

Philadelphia, Library Company of Philadelphia
Records of the Library Company, Boxes 1–7 (1732–1812)

PRINTED PRIMARY SOURCES

An Address to the People of Great Britain, on the Propriety of Abstaining from West Indian Sugar and Rum, 10th edition (Birmingham, 1791).

An Address to the People of Great Britain (Respectfully Offered to the People of Ireland) on the Utility of Refraining from the Use of West Indian Sugar and Rum, 6th edition (London, 1791 and Dublin, 1792).

Considerations Addressed to the Professors of Christianity of Every Denomination on the Impropriety of Consuming West Indian Sugar and Rum as Produced by the Oppressive Labour of Slaves (Dublin, 1792).

Clarkson, Thomas. *History of the Rise, Progress and Accomplishment of the Abolition of the African Slave-Trade By the British Parliament*. 2 vols, new impression (London: Frank Cass, 1968).

Cobbett, William. *A Parliamentary History of England*. Vols XXVIII–XXXVI.

Compton, Theodore. *Recollections of Tottenham Friends and the Forster Family* (London: Edward Hicks, 1893).

C[rafton], W[illiam] B[ell]. *A Short Sketch of the Evidence Delivered Before a Committee of the House of Commons for the Abolition of the Slave Trade: To Which is Added, A Recommendation of the Subject to the Serious Attention of People in General* (Tewkesbury: Dyde and Son, no date).

[Dillwyn, William and John Lloyd]. *The Case of Our Fellow Creatures, the Oppressed Africans* (London: James Phillips, 1784).

Gregg, Mrs Eustace, editor. *Reynolds and Rathbone Diaries and Letters, 1753–1839* (privately printed, 1905).

Hansard, T. C. *Parliamentary Debates*. Vols I–IX.

Frost, J. William, editor. *The Records and Recollections of James Jenkins Respecting Himself and Others from 1761 to 1821* (New York: Edwin Mellen Press, 1984).

[Harrison, George]. *An Address to the Right Reverend the Prelates of England and Wales* (London: J. Parsons and Ridgway, 1792).

Harrison, George. *Adversaria* (London: Sold by Dalton, Harvey, and Dalton; William Phillips, J. and A. Arch, 1818).

Harrison, George, editor. *Barclay's Apology for the True Christian Divinity* (London: Darton, Harvey & Co., 1815).

Harrison, George. *A Brief Intimation Respecting the Attributes of the Divine Being* (London: Darton, Harvey, and Darton, 1816).

Harrison, George. *Education respectfully Proposed and Recommended As the Surest Means Within the Power of Government to Diminish the Frequency of Crimes* (London: Darton and Harvey, John & Arthur Arch, Grace Church Street, R. Faulder, Bond Street, and J. Hatchard, Piccadilly, 1803).

Harrison, George. *Memoirs of the Origin, Nature and Purpose of A Loan Fund Instituted at a General Meeting of Subscribers held at Devonshire House, London* (London: J. & A. Arch, William Phillips, and Harvey Darton, 1821. 2nd edition, 1822).

[Harrison, George]. *Notices on the Slave Trade in Reference to the Present State of the British Isles* (Printed and sold by Darton and Harvey, Grace Church Street, also sold by S. Hatchard, Piccadilly, J. Asperne, Cornhill, and T. Ostell, Ave Maria Lane, 1804).

[Harrison, George and Thomas Smith]. 'Petition to the Members of Parliament, June 1814' (London: Darton and Harvey, 1814).

Harrison, George. *A Plain Statement of Facts Relative to the Will of the late Samuel Southall* (London: T. Bensley, 1820).

[Harrison, George]. *Practical Advice* (London: T. Bensley, 9 Crane Court, Fleet Street and sold at E. Fry's, 75 Houndsditch).

[Harrison, George]. *A Second Address to the Right Reverend the Prelates of England and Wales on the Subject of the Slave Trade* (London: J. Johnson in St Paul's Churchyard, 1795).

Harrison, George. *Some Remarks on a Communication from William Roscoe to the Duke of Gloucester* (London: George Ellerton, Johnson's Court, Fleet Street, 1810).

[Harrison, George]. *Some Remarks on a Letter on Joseph Lancaster's Plan for Education of the Lower Order of the Community in which Quakerism is Described as a disgusting Amalgama of Antichristian Heresies and Blasphemies* (London: J. and A. Arch, Cornhill, 1806).

[Harrison, George, Jr]. *Memoir of William Cookworthy. By his Grandson* (London: William & Frederick Cash, 1854).

Memoirs of the Life of Catherine Payton Phillips (London, James Phillips, 1795).

Phillips, Christiana. *A Short Memoir of William Phillips* (London: James Wade, 1891).

Pettigrew, Thomas Joseph. *Memoirs of the Life and Writing of the late John Coakley Lettsom*, 3 vols (London: Nichols, Son, & Betley, 1817).

Smith, Adam. *An Inquiry into the Nature and Causes of the Wealth of Nations.* Edited by R.H. Campbell, A.S. Skinnner and W.B. Todd (Oxford: Clarendon Press, 1976).

Rathbone, Hannah Mary. *Letters of Richard Reynolds, With A Memoir of His Life* (London: Charles Gilpin, 1852).

Wilberforce, Robert I. and Samuel. *Life of William Wilberforce* (Philadelphia, PA: Henry Perkins, 1839).

[Woods, Joseph], *Thoughts on the Slavery of Negroes* (London: James Phillips, 1784, 2nd edition, London: James Phillips, 1785).

Extracts from the Journal etc. of the late Margaret Woods (London: John & Arthur Arch, 1829; 2nd edition 1830; 3rd edition, Philadelphia, PA: Henry Longstreath, 1850).

SECONDARY SOURCES

Anstey, Roger. *The Atlantic Slave Trade and British Abolition, 1769–1810* (Atlantic Highlands, NJ: Humanities Press, 1975).

Appleby, Joyce. *Liberalism and Republicanism in the Historical Imagination* (Cambridge, MA: Harvard University Press, 1994).

Bolt, Christine and Seymour Drescher, editors. *Antislavery, Religion, and Reform: Essays in Memory of Roger Anstey* (Hamden, CT: Archon Books, 1980).

Braithwaite, William. *The Beginnings of Quakerism* (Cambridge: University Press, 1955).

Braithwaite, William. *Second Period of Quakerism*, 2nd edition (Cambridge: Cambridge University Press, 1961).

Brewer, John, Neil McKendrick, and J.H. Plumb. *The Birth of a Consumer Society: The Commercialization of Eighteenth-Century England* (Bloomington, IN: Indiana University Press, 1982).

Brewer, John and Roy Porter, editors. *Consumption and the World of Goods* (London: Routledge, 1993).

Brooke, John and Sir Lewis Namier. *The House of Commons, 1754–1790*, 3 vols (New York: Oxford University Press, 1964).

Brookes, George. *Friend Anthony Benezet* (Philadelphia, PA: University of Pennsylvania Press, 1937).

Colley, Linda. *Britons: Forging the Nation, 1707–1837* (New Haven, CT: Yale University Press, 1992).

Compton, Theodore. *William Cookworthy* (London: Edward Hicks, 1895).

Coupland, Reginald. *Wilberforce* (Oxford: Clarendon Press, 1926).

Croner, Betsy and Christopher Booth. *Chain of Friendship: Selected Letters of Dr. John Fothergill of London, 1735–1780* (Cambridge, MA: Belknap Press, 1971).

Davis, David Brion. *The Problem of Slavery in Western Culture* (Ithaca, NY: Cornell University Press, 1966).

Davis, David Brion. *The Problem of Slavery in the Age of Revolution 1770–1823* (Ithaca, NY: Cornell University Press, 1975).

Drescher, Seymour. *Capitalism and Anti-Slavery: British Abolition in Comparative Perspective* (Oxford: Oxford University Press, 1987).

Drescher, Seymour. *Econocide: British Slavery in the Era of Abolition* (Pittsburgh, PA: University of Pittsburgh Press, 1977).

Drescher, Seymour. 'British Way, French Way: Opinion Building and Revolution in the Second French Slave Emancipation', *American Historical Review*, Vol. 96, No. 3, June 1991.

Drescher, Seymour. 'Review Essay of *The Antislavery Debate*', *History and Theory*, October 1993.

Drescher, Seymour. 'The Long Goodbye: Dutch Capitalism and Antislavery in Comparative Perspective', *American Historical Review*, Vol. 99, No. 1, February 1994.

Drescher, Seymour. 'Whose Abolition? Popular Pressure and the Ending of the British Slave Trade', *Past and Present*, 1994.

Eltis, David. *Economic Growth and the Ending of the Transatlantic Slave Trade* (Oxford: Oxford University Press, 1987).

Eltis, David and James Walvin, editors. *The Abolition of the Atlantic Slave Trade: Origins and Effects in Europe, Africa, and the Americas* (Madison, WI: University of Wisconsin Press, 1981).

Fladeland, Betty. *Abolitionists and Working Class Problems in the Age of Industrialization* (Baton Rouge, LA: Louisiana State University Press, 1984).

Gray, Austin. *Benjamin Franklin's Library* (New York: Macmillan, 1936).

Howse, E.M. *Saints in Politics* (Toronto: University of Toronto Press, 1952).

Hunt, N.C. *Two Early Political Associations: The Quakers and the Dissenting Deputies in the Age of Sir Robert Walpole* (Oxford: Clarendon Press, 1961).

Jennings, Judith. 'The American Revolution and the Testimony of British Quakers Against the Slave Trade', *Quaker History*, 70, 2, Fall 1981, pp. 99–103.

Klingberg, Frank. *The Anti-Slavery Movement in England* (New Haven, CT: Yale University Press, 1926).

Landes, David S. *The Unbound Prometheus: Technological Change and Industrial Development in Western Europe from 1750 to the Present* (Cambridge: Cambridge University Press, 1969).

Lipscomb, Patrick and Edward Milligan, 'A Note on the Authorship of *The Case of Our Fellow-Creatures*', *Quaker History*, Vol. 55, Spring 1966.

Midgley, Clare. *Women Against Slavery: The British Campaigns, 1780–1870* (London: Routledge, 1992).

Mortimer, Russell. 'Quaker Printers 1750–1850', *Journal of the Friends Historical Society*, Vol. 50, No. 3, 1962–64, pp. 100–14.

Penderill-Church, John. *William Cookworthy 1705–1780* (Truro: Bradford and Barton, 1972).

Porter, Roy. *London: A Social History* (Cambridge, MA: Harvard University Press, 1995).

Royle, Edward and James Walvin. *English Radicals and Reformers* (Lexington, KY: University Press of Kentucky, 1982).

Selleck, A. Douglas. *Cookworthy, 1705–80, and His Circle* (Plymouth: Baron Jay, Ltd., 1978).

Soderlund, Jean. *Quakers and Slavery: A Divided Society* (Princeton, NJ: Princeton University Press, 1985).

Tallack, William. 'William Cookworthy', *Friends Quarterly Examiner*, Vol. 27, 1893, pp. 219–30.

Thompson, E.C.P. *The Making of the English Working Class* (London: Penguin Books, 1981).

Turley, David. *The Culture of English Antislavery, 1780–1860* (New York: Routledge, 1991).

Turner, A.J. *Science and Music in Eighteenth-Century Bath* (Bath: University of Bath Press, 1977).

Vann, Richard T. *The Social Development of English Quakerism, 1655–1755* (Cambridge, MA: Harvard University Press, 1969).

Walvin, James, editor. *Slavery and British Society, 1776–1846* (Baton Rouge, LA: Louisiana State University Press, 1982).

Walvin, James. *England, Slaves and Freedom, 1776–1838* (Jackson, MS: University Press of Mississippi, 1986).

Williams, Eric. *Capitalism and Slavery* (Chapel Hill, NC: University of North Carolina Press, 1994).

INDEX